The Sociology of Childhood

Sociology for a New Century

A PINE FORGE PRESS SERIES

Edited by Charles Ragin, Wendy Griswold, and Larry Griffin

Sociology for a New Century brings the best current scholarship to today's students in a series of short texts authored by leaders of a new generation of social scientists. Each book addresses its subject from a comparative, historical, and global perspective and, in doing so, connects social science to the wider concerns of students seeking to make sense of our dramatically changing world.

- *Global Inequalities*   York W. Bradshaw and Michael Wallace
- *Schools and Societies*   Steven Brint
- *How Societies Change*   Daniel Chirot
- *Constructing Identities: Race and Ethnicity in the Modern World* Stephen Cornell and Douglas Hartmann
- *The Sociology of Childhood*   William A. Corsaro
- *Cultures and Societies in a Changing World*   Wendy Griswold
- *Crime and Disrepute*   John Hagan
- *Gods in the Global Village: The World's Religions in Sociological Perspective*   Lester R. Kurtz
- *Waves of Democracy: Social Movements and Political Change* John Markoff
- *Development and Social Change: A Global Perspective*   Philip McMichael
- *Constructing Social Research*   Charles C. Ragin
- *Women and Men at Work*   Barbara Reskin and Irene Padavic
- *Cities in a World Economy*   Saskia Sassen

Forthcoming:

- *Sociology of the Environment*   Michael M. Bell
- *People and Populations: Demography and the Human Experience* Dennis P. Hogan
- *Deviance and Social Problems*   Gary F. Jensen
- *Family Change and Public Policy*   Diane Lye
- *Gender and the Welfare State*   Ann Orloff
- *Aging, Inequality, and Public Policy*   Fred Pampel
- *Health and Societies*   Bernice Pescosolido
- *Gender, Family, and Social Movements*   Suzanne Staggenborg
- *Sociology of Law*   Robin Stryker

The Sociology of Childhood

William A. Corsaro

Indiana University

PINE FORGE PRESS
Thousand Oaks, California ◆ London ◆ New Delhi

For information, address:

 Pine Forge Press
A Sage Publications Company
2455 Teller Road
Thousand Oaks, California 91320
(805) 499-4224
E-mail: sales@pfp.sagepub.com

Sage Publications Ltd.
6 Bonhill Street
London EC2A 4PU
United Kingdom

Sage Publications India Pvt. Ltd.
M-32 Market
Greater Kailash I
New Delhi 110 048 India

Production: Dusty Davidson, The Book Company
Copy Editor: Jane Townsend
Interior Designer: Lisa Mirski Devenish
Compositor: The Cowans
Cover Designer: Lisa Mirski Devenish
Print Buyer: Anna Chin

Printed in the United States of America

01 10 9 8 7 6 5 4 3

Library of Congress Cataloging-in-Publication Data

Corsaro, William A.
    The sociology of childhood / William A. Corsaro.
      p. cm. — (Sociology for a new century)
    Includes bibliographical references and index.
    ISBN 0-8039-9011-1 (alk. paper)
    1. Children. I. Title. II. Series.
HQ767.9.C675   1997
305.23—dc21
                                         96-45388
                                            CIP

 This book is printed on acid-free paper that meets Environmental Protection Agency standards for recycled paper

To Veronica,
il mio tesoro

ABOUT THE AUTHOR

William A. Corsaro is Professor of Sociology at Indiana University, where he won the President's Award for Distinguished Teaching in 1988. He teaches courses on social psychology, childhood socialization, the social problems of children, the sociology of childhood, and ethnographic research methods. His primary research interests are the sociology of childhood, children's peer cultures, the sociology of education, ethnographic research methods, and discourse analysis. Corsaro is the author of *Friendship and Peer Culture in the Early Years* (1985) and was a Fulbright Senior Research Fellow in Bologna, Italy, in 1983–1984.

ABOUT THE PUBLISHER

Pine Forge Press is a new educational publisher, dedicated to publishing innovative books and software throughout the social sciences. On this and any other of our publications, we welcome your comments. Please call or write us at:

Pine Forge Press
A Sage Publications Company
2455 Teller Road
Thousand Oaks, CA 91320
(805)499-4224
E-mail: sales@pfp.sagepub.com

Visit our new World Wide Web site, your direct link to a multitude of on-line resources:

http://www.sagepub.com/pineforge

Contents

Foreword

Sociology for a New Century offers the best of current sociological thinking to today's students. The goal of the series is to prepare students, and—in the long run—the informed public, for a world that has changed dramatically in the last three decades and one that continues to astonish.

These goals reflect important changes that have taken place in sociology. The discipline has become broader in orientation, with an ever-growing interest in research that is comparative, historical, or transnational in orientation. Sociologists are less focused on "American" society as the pinnacle of human achievement and more sensitive to global processes and trends. They also have become less insulated from surrounding social forces. In the 1970s and 1980s sociologists were so obsessed with constructing a science of society that they saw impenetrability as a sign of success. Today, there is a greater effort to connect sociology to the ongoing concerns and experiences of the informed public.

Each book in this series offers a comparative, historical, transnational, or global perspective to help broaden students' vision. Students need to comprehend the diversity in today's world and to understand the sources of diversity. This knowledge can challenge the limitations of conventional ways of thinking about social life. At the same time, students need to understand that issues that may seem specifically "American" (for example, the women's movement, an aging population bringing a strained Social Security and health care system, racial conflict, national chauvinism, and so on) are shared by many other countries. Awareness of commonalities undercuts the tendency to view social issues and questions in narrowly American terms and encourages students to seek out the experiences of others for the lessons they offer. Finally, students need to grasp phenomena that transcend national boundaries—trends and processes that are supranational (for example, environmental degradation). Recognition of global processes stimulates student awareness of causal forces that transcend national boundaries, economies, and politics.

In what is perhaps the first sociology of childhood text, William A. Corsaro's *The Sociology of Childhood* synthesizes an extraordinary range of theoretical ideas and empirical research on children. He shows how children contribute to both social stability and social change through a process of interpretive reproduction and breaks entirely new ground by stressing the conceptual autonomy of children. By understanding children as social agents who collectively participate in and produce a series of peer cultures, rather than viewing them in terms of their futures as adults, Corsaro has written much more than a text. *The Sociology of Childhood* sparkles with illuminating vignettes, novel insights, and an all-too-rare and profound humanness.

Larry Griffin

Preface

This book is about children and childhood from a sociological perspective. It brings together my ideas and experiences from research and teaching in this area over the past twenty years. Sociology has no tradition for studying children and childhood; until recently those areas have been relegated to the margins of the field. Those of us who consider childhood worthy of study in its own right have had to tie our work to other theoretical traditions such as socialization, or link it to other accepted conceptual categories such as families and education. There are no basic texts in sociology on children or childhood, and until recently few courses on the sociology of childhood were offered at colleges and universities.

Things are changing, however. New and important theoretical and empirical work has been done by a number of scholars who advocate the *conceptual autonomy* of children and childhood (Thorne, 1987). Their work focuses on children as the basic units and categories of study. Children and childhood become the *center* of analysis; they are no longer linked to other categories, such as families or schools, upon which they are supposedly dependent (Qvortrup, 1994a). In addition, we have seen the development of the research section of "Sociology of Children" in the American Sociological Association and a thematic group on "Sociology of Childhood" in the International Sociological Association. Finally, more and more courses are being taught on children and childhood in sociology. I hope that this book can contribute to these efforts.

Having said that children and childhood have been neglected in sociology, I must point out that it would be extremely difficult to cover what is now becoming a vast quantity of theory and research highly relevant to a new sociology of childhood. Therefore, my coverage of the topic is by no means all-encompassing. I focus much more on children's relations with peers than with adults, and my coverage of children's peer cultures ends with the transition to adolescence. Furthermore, I offer an interpretive perspective to the sociology of childhood, which I contrast with more traditional socialization or outcome approaches to children and child development. In the process, I slight much of the good work in the socialization tradition, but this does not mean I feel there is no place for socialization studies in the sociology of childhood.

Another challenge in writing about children concerns doing justice to both micro (social psychological) and macro (structural) approaches to the sociology of childhood. My main theoretical orientation of interpretive reproduction is clearly social psychological; however, at times I felt I needed to write two books, just as many of us who teach courses on childhood feel we need two courses or at least two semesters to cover both micro and macro issues. Nevertheless, I do give much attention to historical, demographic, and socioeconomic aspects of childhood.

Part One of the book reviews traditional approaches to socialization and child development and contrasts them with my perspective of interpretive reproduction. I present an orb web model of children's developing memberships in their cultures and integrate this model, along with the concept of interpretive reproduction, with structural approaches to childhood.

Part Two places the new sociology of childhood in historical and cultural perspective. I present what I feel is a much-needed detailed review and evaluation of classic work on the history of childhood, and I introduce the new history of childhood and present some representative examples of it. I then go on to consider children and childhood cross-culturally by examining children, families, and social change in industrialized and developing societies.

Part Three defines and discusses the importance of children's peer cultures for a new sociology of childhood. In the first chapter in this section (Chapter 5) I discuss children's introduction to symbolic and material aspects of peer culture in their families and from the media. In the next two chapters I consider the basic themes of control and communal sharing in children's initial peer cultures. In Chapter 8, I explore these same themes and consider the importance of autonomy, self, and identity in preadolescent peer cultures.

Part Four brings us back to more macro issues. Here I consider children as social problems and also the social problems of children. I first examine growing levels of anxiety about children's potential victimization in rapidly changing industrialized societies in which adults feel they have less control over their children's lives. I then explore the reverse of this phenomenon, the tendency in modern societies to blame some children, most especially poor children and youth, for their own vulnerability. The last two chapters provide a detailed discussion of the nature and extent of social problems of children (including disturbing global trends in poverty, family instability, and violence) and present some proposals (both major and more modest) to begin to address them. In this last part of the book my appreciation and celebration of children's lives and child-hoods develop into clear political advocacy. This more public active advocacy of children, especially America's poor and disadvantaged children, is long overdue in my case. I am aware that many readers may disagree with some of the specifics of my positions. Others (I hope a minority) will see them as misguided. In either case, I challenge all of you to join the debate.

This book was long in the making, and I am indebted to a number of people who inspired me to write it and several others who have had to put up with my fitful writing of it. Several scholars were influential in my first developing a theoretical interest in children, and others have inspired me to expand and refine my theoretical approach. The first group includes Aaron Cicourel, whose work on socialization started me on the quest. The late Leonard (Slats) Cottrell was very important in providing me with support in my graduate student days. Slats convinced me that I should do the research I believed in and wanted to do even if it was out of the mainstream. He encouraged me to swim against the tide, and I have not drowned yet. A central intellectual role model for me has been Shirley Brice Heath, whose ethnographic work with children and families shines through with rigor, compassion, and integrity. Most recently I have been inspired and challenged by the theoretical views and writings on children and childhood of Candy Goodwin, Jens Qvortrup, Barrie Thorne, and James Wertsch.

I was pretty much a loner in my early work, but lately a number of collaborators have helped me clarify, refine, and sharpen my thinking. Many of these collaborators have also assisted me in the field and all are good friends. They include Sigurd Berentzen, Jenny Cook-Gumperz, Donna Eder, Franca Emiliani, Ann-Carita Evaldsson, Dave Heise, Doug Maynard, Peggy Miller, Luisa Molinari, Tom Rizzo, Katy Rosier, Jürgen Streeck, and the late Graham Tomlinson. I also want to thank my colleagues in the Department of Sociology at Indiana University, Bloomington, who have always strongly supported and encouraged my work with young children. Finally, I wish to thank the three reviewers of the manuscript who provided a number of helpful and insightful comments: Barrie Thorne, University of California, Berkeley; Gerald Rosen, California State University, Fullerton; and Elizabeth Grauerholz, Purdue University. They are, of course, in no way responsible for how I have interpreted and incorporated their suggestions.

A second, patient group of people put up with me in what seemed the never-ending process of finishing this book. I wish to thank several people who have worked with me through Pine Forge Press. Anne Draus (at Scratchgravel Publishing Services) and Dusty Davidson (at The Book

Company) were a pleasure to work with as the book moved from manuscript form through copy editing and then through typesetting, proofreading, and indexing. They were always patient, cheerful, and highly professional in their efforts to get things just right. Becky Smith's editorial suggestions provided needed organization and sharpening of the initial chapters, and Jane Townsend made important editorial contributions to the entire book. Both Becky and Jane helped me formulate my ideas to reach a wide audience of readers. Larry Griffin, the series editor who worked with me, was a strong supporter of this project from the beginning. He remains a great friend. I wish to thank Steve Rutter for his prudent prodding of me during the years that I have worked on this book. Steve certainly had the right to have some doubts about my ever completing the project, but he always knew how to move me along without pushing too hard.

The two people who have put up with me the most throughout this project are my wife, Vickie Renfrow, and my daughter, Veronica. Vickie understandably grew very tired of my laments about lack of time, conflicting deadlines, and writer's block. She had her own work to do and did not need to hear my constant complaining. Yet, she more than once held her peace, and has provided daily help and support in the final stages of the book. Veronica has always had a lot of attention from her dad, but she, too, has tired of hearing about the book and has yearned for a more calm and relaxed father. She will now have one, at least for a while.

Finally, I wish to thank all the teachers and children who have allowed me to enter and be a part of their worlds in my research over the past twenty years. Their friendships have enriched my life and given me strong optimism concerning the present and future of childhood.

At the time of the final editing of this preface, I was informed of the tragic death of my colleague, Sigurd Berentzen, who died in an accident near his vacation home on a small island near Bergen, Norway. Sigurd was a pioneer in ethnographic research on children and youth, carrying out perhaps the first ethnography of preschool children in 1968. In this work Berentzen drew attention to the need for studying children from their own perspectives and in natural settings. Although Sigurd was a quiet and unassuming person, his research on and deep love of children shine brightly as a model for all of us who wish to capture the spirit, vision, and promise of children and childhood in our work. His death is a tragic loss for us all, but his work will always inspire us to pursue the study of children in their own right and on their own terms.

William A. Corsaro

The Sociological Study
of Childhood

Bologna, Italy—May 1985

It was a bright, sunny day and I was sitting with a group of boys who were digging in the outside play area of an Italian preschool. This was my second time doing research at the school. I had spent nine months with the children and their teachers in the previous year, and now I was back for a two-month follow-up. The boys were talking about military matters—the navy, warships, and the boss or *il capo* on such ships—as they dug holes and buried rocks in the dirt.

At some distance I saw three children marching around the yard carrying a large, red milk carton. The teachers used the carton to carry play materials to the yard, and I had seen the children playing with it before. What I didn't know was that the carton was now a forbidden object. As I was to find out later, earlier in the year, before my arrival, a child had placed the carton on her head and chased after several other children. She eventually fell and suffered a minor injury. After this incident, the children were prohibited from playing with the carton.

But they were playing with it today. In fact, they were now marching in my direction and I could begin to make out their chant. It sounded like *"Arriva la barca! Arriva la barca!"* ("Here comes the boat! Here comes the boat!"). I was not sure about the last word, though; it could be *"barca"* or *"banca"* (bank). They were right up close to me now; Antonio was leading the way and Luisa and Mario were helping him carry the carton. There was a bucket inside the carton, and it was filled with rocks.

"La barca?" I asked Antonio.

"No, la banca con soldi!" ("The bank with money!") he said as he cupped his hand in a familiar Italian gesture.

I was intrigued. These kids had created a whole new dimension in banking, a bank that makes house calls! "Give me some money," I asked Antonio.

The children now put the carton down, and Mario took out the small bucket with rocks and said, "I'll give the money to him." "How much do you want?" he asked. "There are thousands. . . ."

"Forty thousand," I quickly responded. (This sounds like a lot, but forty thousand lire is only about twenty-five dollars.)

Mario began counting out the rocks, doing exactly as they do in Italian banks by announcing the final sum as he counted out each ten thousand lira note: "Forty thousand, forty thousand, here's forty thousand."

But he counted only three rocks. "No, no, three—thirty thousand. I said forty!"

Arriva La Banca

"Four," said Luisa. "Four!"

Mario then reached in the bucket to get more rocks and counted, "Thirty, forty, here," and handed me three more rocks and then a fourth.

"Sixty now," I said laughing. "Seventy. I said forty!"

"How many?" Mario asked.

Luisa was now getting impatient with Mario and seemed to think she could be a better bank teller. "Four, he said four!" she exclaimed as she reached to take the bucket from Mario.

The three children now began to struggle over the bucket, and Antonio scooped the rocks from my hand and dropped them back into the bucket. "Let's go," he commanded. And the children marched off again, chanting: *"Arriva la banca! Arriva la banca!"* I waved, and called out, *"Ciao la banca!"*

Oklahoma City, Oklahoma—April 1995

At 9:02 A.M. on April 19, 1995, a major explosion destroyed the Alfred P. Murrah Federal Building in Oklahoma City. In the blast 168 lives were lost, including 19 children and a nurse who was killed during the rescue attempt. More than 600 people were injured. The explosion was caused by a car bomb containing an estimated forty-eight hundred pounds of explosives. The children ranged in age from six months to five years old and attended the America's Kids Day Care Center in the federal office building. Two teachers and the administrator of the day care center were also killed.

A suspect was arrested and his trial began in June 1996. The reason for the bombing has not yet been determined. It appears, however, that all of the victims, including the children, died because they happened to be in a United States Government office building that was targeted for destruction.

I purposely selected these two incidents because of their stark contrast. (I should point out that events like the first [children's joyful and creative reproduction and embellishment of the adult world within their peer cultures] and the second [the vicious and cowardly taking of children's lives by adults] can occur anywhere in the world.) My reason for presenting them is to illustrate two central concepts of a new sociology of children.

First, children are active, creative social agents who produce their own unique children's cultures while simultaneously contributing to the production of adult societies. Take the Italian preschoolers. They weren't supposed to play with the milk carton. But they didn't like the adult rule, so they played with it anyway. They created a highly unique "traveling bank"—an idea taken from the adult world but extended and given new meaning. (After this incident one of the teachers told me that she saw the children playing with the carton but overlooked the rule violation because, like me, she was so impressed by the children's ingenuity.)

Second, **childhood**—that socially constructed period in which children live their lives—is a structural form. When we refer to **childhood as a structural form,** we mean it is a category or a part of society, like social class and age groups. In this sense children are members or incumbents of their childhoods. For the children themselves childhood is a temporary period. For society, on the other hand, childhood is a permanent structural form or category that never disappears even though its members change continuously and its nature and conception vary historically. It is somewhat difficult to recognize childhood as a structural form because we tend to think of childhood solely as a period when children are prepared for entry into society. But children are already a part of society from their births, as childhood is part and parcel of society.

As a structural form, childhood is interrelated with other structural categories like social class, gender, and age groups (Qvortrup, 1994a). Thus, the structural arrangements of these categories and changes in these arrangements will affect the nature of childhood. In modern societies, for example, changes in social structural arrangements of categories like gender, occupation or work, family, and social class have resulted in many mothers working outside the home and their young children spending much of their time in institutional settings like day care centers and early childhood education programs, which didn't exist in the past. The young Oklahoma victims and the kids in the Italian preschool inhabited such settings; their experiences remind us that children both affect and are affected by society.

The first part of this book further develops these two basic tenets of a new sociology of childhood: Children are active agents who construct their own cultures and contribute to the production of the adult world; and childhood is a structural form or part of society. Chapter 1 contrasts the first tenet—that children are active social agents—with traditional views of socialization in sociology and psychology. Here, the notion **of interpretive reproduction**—the idea that *children* actively contribute to societal preservation (or reproduction) as well as societal change—is offered as an extension of the heretofore almost exclusive focus on the *individual child's* development and adaptation to society. Chapter 2 integrates the notion of interpretive reproduction with the general assumptions of the second tenet, which holds that childhood is a structural form or part of society. The importance of children's contributions to their own childhoods (and to childhood as a more abstract structural form) through their negotiations with adults, and through their creative production of a series of peer cultures with other children is examined.

1

Social Theories of Childhood

This chapter examines the reasons for the resurgent interest in children in society and, especially, in sociology. Traditional theories of socialization and child development are considered, and basic assumptions that have now been called into question are examined. Finally, an alternative theoretical approach to childhood, one that reconceptualizes the place of children in the social structure and stresses the contributions they make, is presented.

Sociology's Rediscovery of Childhood

As recently as ten years ago there was a near absence of studies on children in mainstream sociology (Ambert, 1986). Today the situation is very different. A large and growing number of monographs, edited volumes, and journal articles address theoretical issues and report empirical findings related to the sociological study of children and childhood. Childhood socialization has been given expanded coverage in basic introductory texts in sociology and social psychology, and new journals and sections of national and international associations devoted to the sociology of childhood have been established.

These developments are long overdue and very encouraging. But why have children been so long ignored in sociology? Jens Qvortrup (1993a) aptly notes that children have not so much been ignored as they have been *marginalized*. Children are marginalized in sociology because of their subordinate position in societies and in theoretical conceptualizations of childhood and socialization. As I will discuss more fully below, adults most often view children in a forward-looking way, that is, with an eye to what they will become—future adults with a place in the social order and contributions to make to it. Rarely are they viewed in a way that appreciates what they *are*—children with ongoing lives, needs, and desires. In fact, the current lives, needs, and desires of children are often seen as causes for alarm by adults, as social problems that are threatening, that need to be resolved. As a result, children are pushed to the margins of the social structure by more powerful adults (including social theorists), who focus instead on the potential and the threat of children to present and future societies.

Another question prompted by the resurgence of interest in childhood is why ideas are now being put forth that reconsider, challenge, refine and even transform traditional lay and theoretical approaches to children and childhood. One reason is that consideration of other subordinate groups by sociologists (for example, minorities and women) has drawn attention to the lives of children. Unlike other subordinate groups, children have no representatives among sociologists; however, the work of feminists and minority scholars has, at least indirectly, drawn attention to the neglect of children. Barrie Thorne (1987) notes that in some ideological constructions, *"women are closely and unreflectively tied* with children; womanhood has been equated with motherhood in a mixing of identities that simply does not occur for men and fatherhood."* Indeed, feminists who find themselves labeled (most especially by political conservatives) as selfishly negligent of children have responded that children should be the responsibility of women *and* men. In their call for recognition of more diverse and equitable roles for women and men, feminists have been slow to note the marginalization of children in sociology. However, feminist analyses of gender ideologies have provided a lens for what Thorne (1987) has called the "re-visioning of children," resulting in a number of important recent studies of children, gender and identity (Eder, 1995; Heath & McLaughlin, 1993; Thorne, 1993).

New ways of conceptualizing children in sociology also stem from the rise of **constructivist and interpretive theoretical perspectives in sociology** (Connell, 1987; James & Prout, 1990). From these perspectives, assumptions about the genesis of everything from friendship to scientific knowledge are carefully examined as social constructions rather than simply accepted as biological givens or obvious social facts. What this means is that childhood and all social objects (including things like class, gender, race, and ethnicity) are seen as being interpreted, debated, and defined in processes of social action. In short, they are viewed as social products or constructions. When applied to the sociology of childhood, constructivist and interpretive perspectives argue that children and adults alike are active participants in the social construction of childhood and in the interpretive reproduction of their shared culture. In contrast, traditional theories viewed children as "consumers" of the culture established by adults.

Traditional Theories: Socialization

Much of sociology's thinking about children and childhood derives from theoretical work on **socialization,** the processes by which children adapt to and internalize society. Most have focused on early socialization in the family, which views the child as internalizing society. In other words, the child is seen as something apart from society that must be shaped and guided by external forces in order to become a fully functioning member.

Two different models of the socialization process have been proposed. The first is a **deterministic model,** in which the child plays a basically passive role. In this view the child is simultaneously a "novice" with potential to contribute to the maintenance of society and an "untamed threat" who must be controlled through careful training. In the second, a **constructivist model,** the child is seen as an active agent and eager learner. In this view, the child actively constructs her social world and her place in it. Let's look first at the deterministic model.

The Deterministic Model: Society Appropriates the Child

Early theorists of socialization had a problem. In their day, the philosophy of individualism held sway; it was popular to focus on how individuals relate to society. And yet society was also recognized as a powerful determinant of individual behavior. How were these theorists to resolve the contradiction (Wentworth, 1980, pp. 38–39)? The solution to this problem was a theoretical view describing appropriation of the child by society. *Appropriation* means the child is taken over by society; she is trained to become eventually a competent and contributing member. This model of socialization is seen as deterministic, because the child plays a primarily passive role. Within the deterministic model, two subsidiary approaches arose that differed primarily in their views of society. The functionalist models saw order and balance in society and stressed the importance of training and preparing children to fit into and contribute to that order. The reproductive models, on the other hand, focused on conflicts and inequalities in society and argued that some children have differential access to certain types of training and other societal resources.

Functionalist models. **Functionalist models,** which were popular in the 1950s and 1960s, focused on describing rather superficial aspects of socialization: what the child needed to internalize and which parental child-rearing or training strategies were used to ensure such internalization. Functionalists had little concern for why and how children become integrated into society. Alex Inkeles, for example, maintained that the study of socialization must be inherently "forward looking," specifying what the child must become to meet requisites for the continued functioning of society (1968, pp. 76–77).

The major spokesperson of the functionalist perspective, Talcott Parsons, set the tone for Inkeles' forward-looking view of socialization. In Parsons' view the child is a threat to society; he must be appropriated and shaped to fit in. Parsons envisioned a society as an "intricate network of interdependent and interpenetrating" roles and consensual values (Parsons & Bales, 1955, p. 36). The entry of the child into this system is problematic because although she has the potential to be useful to the continued functioning of the system, she is also a threat until she is socialized. In fact, Parsons likened the child to a "pebble 'thrown' by the fact of birth into the social 'pond'" (Parsons & Bales, 1955, pp. 36–37). The initial point of entry— the family—feels the first effects of this "pebble," and as the child grows older the effects are seen as a succession of widening waves that radiate to other parts of the system. In a cyclical process of dealing with problems and through formal training to accept and follow social norms, the child eventually internalizes the social system (Parsons & Bales, 1955, p. 202).

Reproductive models. As sociological theory developed, the functionalist view of socialization lost favor. Some social theorists argued that the internalization of the functional requisites of society could be seen as a mechanism of social control leading to the social reproduction or maintenance of class inequalities (Bernstein, 1981; Bourdieu & Passeron, 1977). These **reproductive models,** as they are known, focus on the advantages enjoyed by those with greater access to cultural resources. For example, parents from higher social class groups can ensure that their children receive quality education in prestigious academic institutions. Reproductive theorists also point to differential treatment of individuals in social institutions (especially the educational system) which reflects and supports the prevailing class system.

Weaknesses of the deterministic model. Reproductive theorists provide a needed acknowledgment of the effect of social conflict and inequality on the socialization of children. However, both functionalist and reproductive theories can be criticized for their overconcentration on the outcomes of socialization, their underestimation of the active and innovative capacities of all members of society, and their neglect of the historical and contingent nature of social action and reproduction. In short, these abstract models simplify highly complex processes and, in the process, overlook the importance of children and childhood in society.

   A key question is: Where do children and childhood fit into these abstract theories of social structure? Not surprisingly, some of these social theorists downplayed the importance of children's activities, which they considered to be inconsequential or nonfunctional. Other determinists looked to theories of child development and learning that fit their views for explanations about the mechanisms of socialization. Parsons, for example, linked his views on socialization to Freud's theory of psychosexual development. In his model, socialization takes place as the child learns to act in accordance with social norms and values rather than according to innate sexual and aggressive drives. Inkeles opts for another type of determinism, behaviorism, and points to the importance of explicit training in the skills needed for living in society, supported by a system of rewards and punishments (1968, pp. 97–103).

Both functionalist and reproductive models overlook the point that children do not just internalize the society they are born into. As we saw in the earlier example of the Italian preschoolers' traveling bank, children act on and can bring about changes in society. Reproductive theorists are, however, more inventive than functionalists in their views of socialization. Bourdieu (1977), for example, offers the complex and intriguing notion of the *habitus* to capture how members of society (or *social actors*), through their continual and routine involvement in their social worlds, acquire a set of predispositions to act and to see things in a certain way. This set of predispositions, this *habitus*, is inculcated in early socialization, and plays itself out reproductively through the tendency of the child and all social actors to maintain their sense of self and place in the world (Bourdieu, 1993).

Bourdieu is on a track that usefully leads us away from determinism and provides a more active role for the child. However, this conceptualization of socialization limits children's involvement to cultural participation and reproduction while ignoring children's contributions to cultural refinement and change. For a model that truly incorporates an active child, we must consider the rise of constructivism.

The Constructivist Model: The Child Appropriates Society

Much of the early sociological study of childhood socialization was influenced by the dominant theories in developmental psychology at the time. The theories that sociologists most often turned to, most especially varieties of behaviorism, relegate the child to a passive role. In these theories development is basically unilateral, with the child being shaped and molded by adult reinforcements and punishments. Many developmental psychologists, however, have come to see the child as active rather than passive, involved in appropriating information from her environment to use in organizing and constructing her own interpretations of the world.

Piaget's theory of intellectual development. Perhaps the best representative of the constructivist approach is the Swiss psychologist Jean Piaget. He studied the evolution of knowledge in children, which was a way of integrating two of his enduring interests: biology and epistemology (the study of knowledge) (Ginsburg & Opper, 1988). Piaget's many empirical studies of children and their development had a major impact on the image of the child in developmental psychology. Piaget believed that children from the first days of infancy interpret, organize, and use information from the environment, and that they come to construct conceptions (known as **mental structures**) of their physical and social worlds.

Piaget is perhaps best known for his view that intellectual development is not simply an accumulation of facts or skills, but is rather a progression through a series of qualitatively distinct stages of intellectual ability. Piaget's notion of stages is important for the sociology of children because it reminds us that children perceive and organize their worlds in ways qualitatively different from adults. Consider, for example, the following incident, which occurred in my very first ethnographic study of young children. A three-year-old boy drew a squiggly line on a chalkboard. I asked him what it was and he responded, "A snake." "A snake!" I replied and then asked, "Have you ever seen a snake?" "Sure," he said, pointing to his squiggly line, "right there!" I then realized that my perspective of the "squiggly line" as a *representation* of a snake was different than his perspective of his creation, which was that the line was exactly what he said it was—a snake!

As a result of many similar experiences, I have gotten much better at adopting children's perspectives in my fieldwork. I have also come to appreciate, in line with Piaget's theory, that any sociological theory of children and childhood that attempts to explain children's understanding and use of information from the adult world, as well as children's participation in and organization of their own peer worlds, must consider the child's level of cognitive development.

Although Piaget's conception of stages of development is the most known element of his theory, the most important element of his theory is his conception of equilibrium. **Equilibrium** is the central force that propels the child through the stages of cognitive development. Unfortunately, this concept is not only often overlooked, it is also frequently misunderstood. Many sociological and psychological theorists (such as Parsons) use the idea of equilibrium to explain societal, behavioral, or attitudinal change as a return to a state of balance (in other words, an occurrence that creates disequilibrium will be followed by attempts on the part of a society or an individual to regain balance). Piaget, however, is concerned with the process of equilibration, or the actual activities the child undertakes to deal with problems in the external world. Piaget conceives equilibrium as the "compensation resulting from the activities of the subject in response to external intrusions" (Piaget, 1968, p. 101). Intrusions are compensated for only by activities, and the maximum equilibrium involves not a state of rest but rather a maximum of activity on the part of the child.

Piaget believes that the tendency to compensate for disequilibriums is innate. This biological or nativist assumption does not mean, however, that Piaget is a biological determinist. Biological determinists hold that things like innate tendencies, processes, or knowledge are the causes or determiners of children's development. For Piaget the innate tendency to compensate for disequilibriums is just one part of his complex model of intellectual development. Although Piaget believed children have an innate tendency to compensate for environmental intrusions, the nature of the compensations is dependent on the *activities of children in their social-ecological worlds.*

We can get a more concrete understanding of Piaget's concept of equilibrium as well as his developmental stages by considering the following case study of a Piagetian experiment of children's understanding of the conservation of mass.

Children's Understanding of Conservation of Mass

In a classic experiment, Piaget would present a child between the ages of four and nine with two identical balls of clay. The child would be asked if each ball contained the same amount of clay. If the child did not think so, he or she would be asked to take away or add some clay to make the balls identical. Then, Piaget would change one of the balls into a sausage shape as the child watched. The child would then be asked if the ball and sausage now contained the same amount of clay. This experiment can be seen as illustrating the process of equilibration, with the child attempting to compensate through a series of strategies. We can capture the nature of the series each child will go through by examining how children of different ages deal with the problem:

1. The very young child, age four or five, concentrates on one characteristic or dimension of the objects, usually length, and is apt to say with a great deal of conviction, "This one, cause it is longer!" The child is unaware of the notion of conservation of mass and refers only to one dimension. Again the child shows a great deal of certainty, and there is limited mental activity or thinking. In fact, the child may even claim that the problem is too easy, silly, or possibly a trick.

2. The slightly older child, age six or seven, tends to reverse her original claim because she notices a second dimension (width or thinness). At this point a new strategy becomes probable because the uncertainty of the child leads to *more activity* in dealing with

the intrusion. In thinking about the intrusion the child oscillates back and forth in her thinking and may become vaguely aware of the interdependence of the sausage's elongation and its thinness. Here a child might start out with confidence: "This one cause it's longer. No, no wait this one cause it's fatter. Oh, I don't know!"

3. The seven-to-nine-year-old child acts on the insight of interdependence. She places a mental emphasis on the transformation rather than the static configuration with dimensions. She will make them both the same and now claim that they are equal. Here the child will often be very careful rolling the ball into a second sausage and holding the two next to each other to see if they match. If not she will go back to work, shortening one or lengthening the other until she convinces herself that they are the same. Here there is a maximum of activity in the equilibration process as the child approaches the mental insight of conservation of mass.

4. For the nine-to-eleven-year-old the strategy begins with the discovery of the compensations of the transformation (that is, as clay lengthens it becomes thinner, as it broadens it becomes shorter). Here the child may scoff at the question, saying, "They are obviously the same!" or, "See, it makes no difference. I can make this ball a sausage or the sausage a ball," doing so as she talks. At this point conservation is accepted and the child understands reversibility. Certainty now returns and related problems in the future will seem simple.

Adapted from Piaget (1968: 112) and Ginsburg & Opper (1988:150–51)

Vygotsky's socio-cultural view of human development. Another important constructivist theorist is the Russian psychologist, Lev Vygotsky. Like Piaget, Vygotsky stressed children's active role in human development. Vygotsky, however, believed that children's social development is always the result of their collective actions and that these actions take place and are located in society. Therefore, for Vygotsky, changes in society, especially changes in societal demands on the individual, require changes in strategies for dealing with those demands. For Vygotsky, strategies for dealing with changes in societal demands are always collective; that is, they always involve interaction with others. These collective strategies are seen as practical actions that lead to both social and psychological development. In this sense, the child's interactions and practical activities with others lead to her acquisition of new skills and knowledge, which are seen as the transformation of previous skills and knowledge.

A key principle in Vygotsky's view is the individual's internalization or appropriation of culture. Especially important to this process is language, which both encodes culture and is a tool for participating in culture. Vygotsky argues that language and other sign systems (for example, writing, film, and so on), like tool systems (for example, material objects like machines) are created by societies over the course of history and change with cultural development. Thus, argued Vygotsky, children, through their acquisition and use of language, come to reproduce a culture that contains the knowledge of generations.

Vygotsky offered a quite different constructivist approach to human development than that of Piaget. Although both theorists viewed development as resulting from the child's activities, Vygotsky made no nativistic assumption similar to Piaget's notion of equilibrium to account for the motivating factor that generates the child's activities. Vygotsky saw practical activities developing from the child's attempts to deal with everyday problems. Furthermore, in dealing with these problems, the child always develops strategies collectively—that is, in interaction with others. Thus, for Piaget, human development is primarily individualistic, while for Vygotsky it is primarily collective.

Other differences exist between the two theorists. Piaget concentrated more on the nature and characteristics of cognitive processes and structures, while Vygotsky emphasized their developmental contexts and history. As a result, rather than identifying abstract stages of cognitive development, Vygotsky sought to specify the cultural events and practical activities that lead to the appropriation, internalization, and reproduction of culture and society.

How, specifically, do these processes of internalization, appropriation, and reproduction occur? Two of Vygotsky's concepts are crucial. First is the notion of **internalization.** According to Vygotsky, "every function in the child's development appears twice: first on the social level, and later on the individual level; first, *between* people (*interpsychological*) and then *inside* the child (*intrapsychological*)" (1978, p. 57). By this Vygotsky means that all our psychological and social skills (cognitive, communicative, and emotional) are always acquired from our interactions with others. We first develop and use such skills at the interpersonal level before internalizing them at the individual level.

Consider Vygotsky's conceptions of self-directed and inner speech. By self-directed speech, Vygotsky is referring to the tendency of young children to speak out loud to themselves, especially in problematic situations. Piaget saw such speech as egocentric or emotional and serving no social function. Vygotsky, on the other hand, saw self-directed speech as a form of interpersonal communication, except that in this case the child is addressing himself as another. In a sense, the child is directing and advising himself on how to deal with a problem. In experimental work, Vygotsky found that such speech increased when children were given a task like building a car with tinker toys or were told to draw a picture. Vygotsky believed that over time, self-directed speech was transformed or internalized from the interpersonal to the intrapersonal, becoming inner speech or a form of thought. We can grasp his ideas when we think about how we first learn to read. Most of our early reading as young children is done out loud as we read to ourselves and others. Over time we begin to mumble and then to mouth the words as we read, and eventually we read entirely at a mental level. In short, the intrapsychological function or skill of reading has its origins in social or collective activity—reading out loud for others and oneself. For Vygotsky internalization occurs gradually over an extended period of time.

In a second important concept, Vygotsky builds on his view of language as a cultural tool. According to Vygotsky, human activity is inherently mediational in that it is carried out through language and other cultural tools. A significant proportion of children's everyday activities take place in what Vygotsky calls the **zone of proximal development**: *"the distance between the actual developmental level as determined by independent problem solving and the level of potential development as determined through problem solving under adult guidance or in collaboration with more capable peers"* (Vygotsky, 1978, p. 86). Let's go back to our example of learning to read. A child's *actual* level of reading ability would be measured by her ability to read, summarize, and talk about a story like Cinderella or Snow White. A child's *potential* level of development would be estimated by her ability to read, summarize, and discuss the story with help from teachers, parents, and more developed peers. The first indicates the child's full mastery of a particular ability or skill, while the latter indicates her potential level of mastery. The distance between the two levels is the zone of proximal development, as depicted in Exhibit 1.1.

As we can see in Exhibit 1.1, the child, in interactions with others, is always a step ahead in development of where she is alone. In this sense interactions in the zone of proximal development "are the crucible of development *and* culture, in that they allow children to participate in activities that would be impossible for them alone, using cultural tools that themselves must be adapted to the specific activity at hand, and thus both passed along to and transformed by new generations" (Rogoff et al., 1989, p. 211). Thus, the model of development is one in which children gradually appropriate the adult world through the communal processes of sharing and creating culture (Bruner, 1986).

EXHIBIT 1.1

Vygotsky's Zone of Proximal Development

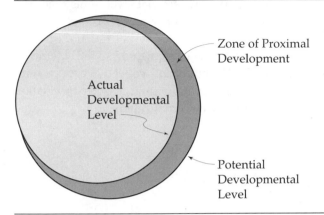

Zone of Proximal
Development

Actual
Developmental
Level

Potential
Developmental
Level

Weaknesses of the constructivist model. Although the general acceptance of constructivism moved theory and research in developmental psychology in the right direction, its main focus still remains squarely on individual development. We can see this in repeated references to the *child's* activity, the *child's* development, the *child's* becoming an adult. In Piaget's theory the focus is on the individual child's mastery of the world on her own terms. Constructivism offers an active but very lonely view of children. Even when others (parents, peers, and teachers) are taken into account, the focus remains on the effects of various interpersonal experiences on individual development. There is little, if any, consideration of how interpersonal relations reflect cultural systems, or how *children*, through their participation in communicative events, become part of these interpersonal relations and cultural patterns and reproduce them collectively.

Another limitation of constructivist developmental psychology is the overwhelming concern with the endpoint of development, or the child's movement from immaturity to adult competence. Take, for example, research on friendship. The focus of nearly all of the research is on identifying stages in the child's abstract conceptions of friendship. These conceptions are elicited through clinical interviews, and their underdeveloped conceptions are compared to those of the competent adult (Damon, 1977; Selman, 1980). Yet few psychologists study what it is like to be or to have a friend in children's social worlds, or how developing conceptions of friendships are embedded in children's interactions in peer culture.

This emphasis on the endpoint of development is also apparent in contemporary developmental psychologists' interest in Vygotsky's notion of internalization. As we saw previously, Vygotsky stressed both children's collective interactions with others at the interpersonal level and their internalization of these interactions at the intrapersonal level in his theory of children's appropriation of culture. Yet, current research by con-structivists places so much emphasis on the second phase of internalization that many now view the appropriation of culture as the movement from the external to the internal. This misconception pushes children's collective actions with others to the background and implies that an individual actor's participation in society occurs only after such individual internalization.

Interpretive Reproduction: Children Collectively Participate in Society

Sociological theories of childhood must break free from the individualistic doctrine that regards children's social development solely as the child's private internalization of adult skills and knowledge. From a sociological perspective, socialization is not only a matter of adaptation and internalization but also a process of appropriation, reinvention, and reproduction. Central to this view of socialization is the appreciation of the importance of collective, communal activity—how children negotiate, share, and create culture with adults and each other.

However, to say that a sociological perspective of socialization stresses the importance of collective and communal processes is not enough in constructing a new sociology of childhood. The problem is the term *socialization* itself. It has an individualistic and forward-looking connotation that is inescapable. One hears the term and the idea of training and preparing the individual child for the future keeps coming right back to mind (Thorne, 1993, pp. 3–6). Instead, I offer the notion of **interpretive reproduction.** The term *interpretive* captures the *innovative* and *creative* aspects of children's participation in society. In fact, as we shall see throughout this book, children create and participate in their own unique peer cultures by creatively taking or appropriating information from the adult world to address their own peer concerns. The term *reproduction* captures the idea that children are not simply internalizing society and culture, but are actively *contributing to cultural production and change.* The term also implies that children are, by their very participation in society, *constrained by the existing social structure and by societal reproduction.* That is, children and their childhoods are affected by the societies and cultures of which they are members. These, societies and cultures have, in turn, been shaped and affected by processes of historical change.

Let's pursue this notion of interpretive reproduction further by looking at two of its key elements: the importance of language and cultural routines and the reproductive nature of children's evolving membership in their culture.

Language and cultural routines. Interpretive reproduction places special emphasis on language and on children's participation in cultural routines. Language is central to children's participation in their culture both as a "symbolic system that encodes local, social, and cultural structure" and as a "tool for establishing (that is, maintaining, creating) social and psychological realities" (Ochs, 1988, p. 210). These interrelated features of language and language use are "deeply embedded and instrumental in the accomplishment of the concrete routines of social life" (Schieffelin, 1990, p. 19).

Children's participation in **cultural routines** is a key element of interpretive reproduction. The habitual, taken-for-granted character of routines provides children and all social actors with the security and shared understanding of belonging to a social group. On the other hand, this very predictability empowers routines, providing a framework within which a wide range of sociocultural knowledge can be produced, displayed, and interpreted. In this way, cultural routines serve as anchors that enable social actors to deal with ambiguities, the unexpected, and the problematic while remaining comfortably within the friendly confines of everyday life (Corsaro, 1992).

Participation in cultural routines begins very early, almost from the minute children are born. Early in infancy, at least in Western societies, when children's language and communicative abilities are limited, social interaction proceeds in line with an **"as-if" assumption.** That is, infants are treated as socially competent ("as if" they are capable of social exchanges). Over time, because of this "as if" attitude, children move from limited to full participation in cultural routines.

Consider, for example, the well-known parent-infant game of "peek-aboo." In their study of six mother-infant dyads, Bruner and Sherwood (1976) identified four basic phases in peekaboo: (1) initial contact or shared attention (usually established by the mother through vocalization and/or gaze); (2) disappearance (usually the mother hiding her or her child's face with her hands or a cloth, accompanied by vocalizations such as "Where's baby?"); (3) reappearance (removal of hands or cloth, usually by the mother); and (4) the reestablishment of contact (usually with vocalizations such as "boo," "there's the baby," and so on by the mother, marking a response such as a smile or laugh from the child). Bruner and Sherwood note that what the child appears to be learning "is not only the basic rules of the game, but the range of variation that is possible with the rule set" (1976, p. 283). Thus, by participating in the routine, the children are learning a set of predictable rules that provide security, and they also are learning that a range of embellishments of the rules is possible and even desirable. In this way children gain insight into the generative or productive nature of cultural participation in a play routine from which they derive great pleasure. Furthermore, we know from later work (Ratner and Bruner, 1977) that there is a movement from the "as if" function of these games in the first months of life, where children's participation is often limited to a responsive role, to a point where the same children at one year old are initiating and directing the games and even creating and participating in other types of disappearance-reappearance games alone and with others (see Corsaro, 1985, p. 196).

Now to say that adults always strive for shared understanding with children and the adoption of an "as-if" attitude in parent-child games is crucial in attaining joint activity, does not mean that shared understanding is always achieved and maintained in adult-child interaction. What is important is not that shared understanding is always achieved, but rather that attempts by both the adult and child to reach such understanding are always made. Often, especially in adult-child interaction, children are exposed to social knowledge and communicative demands they do not fully grasp. Interaction normally continues in an orderly fashion, and any persisting ambiguities must be pursued over the course of the children's experiences with adults and peers.

Do Chips Have Blood on Them?

To illustrate the power and importance of cultural routines, let's consider a real life example: an everyday interactive routine between a two-and-a-half-year-old boy, Buddy, and his mother, which I video recorded in their home as part of my dissertation research a number of years ago. Buddy and his mother talked every weekday at this time as she prepared lunch. In this conversation, Buddy is still curious about "blood" from his cut finger the day before:

Mother: What?

Buddy: Chips [potato chips] have blood on them? Do they have blood on 'em?

Mother: No, I don't believe so.

Buddy: Kids and people do.

Mother: Um-hum.

Buddy: And monsters.

Mother: Yeah.

Buddy: Like Grover has blood on him.

Mother:	Well, Grover's a pretend monster. He's really a puppet, you know?
Buddy:	Yeah.
Mother:	So he wouldn't have any blood on him.
Buddy:	But Harry does.
Mother:	Well, they're just like your puppets. Your Big Bird and your Cookie Monster.
Buddy:	Yeah.
Mother:	They're made out of cloth and furry things.
Buddy:	Yeah, like—
Mother:	Somebody made them—
Buddy:	Harry has blood.
Mother:	I don't think so. Pretend blood maybe.
Buddy:	Yeah, maybe—maybe Grover and Cookie Monster and Harry have pretend blood. Maybe they do—maybe they have real blood.
Buddy:	Mommy, someday I wanna go to Sesame Street and we can see if those monsters have blood.
Mother:	You do?
Buddy:	Yeah.
Mother:	I don't know. We'll have to see about that. But you know what? Sesame Street is really a make-believe land.
Buddy:	Oh, I didn't notice that.
Mother:	You can pretend a lot of things about Sesame Street.

A number of issues are raised in this short episode that are relevant to interpretive reproduction:

1. *Why Is This a Routine?*

   Everyday talk of this type and at this time of day is recurrent and predictable in this family. In fact, this recurrence and typicality provides an opportunity to pursue issues that are problematic and confusing in the everyday activity of "having lunch." Through their very participation in this everyday routine the mother and child reaffirm their relation to one another and address problems and confusions about the world.

2. *How is Buddy Using the Routine?*

   First, Buddy uses the opportunity to address his curiosity about blood and who does and does not have it. At a surface level his confusion about blood concerns a distinction between animate and inanimate objects. But soon the discussion moves beyond that distinction, to a discussion of "real" and "pretend" animate objects. Second, the routine allows Buddy an opportunity to display his knowledge and to discuss his interests with a receptive and supportive adult caretaker. In this sense, the repetitive enactment of such routines reaffirms these bonds and Buddy's status as active member of the family.

3. *How Does Buddy's Mother Use the Routine?*

First, on one level the routine provides her with information about a confusing concept that Buddy is trying to deal with (the distinction between animate and inanimate objects). However, on another level, Buddy's mother gains insight into the tie-in (for Buddy) between this distinction and a more general and complex distinction between real and pretend in modern culture. Consider the complexity: animate versus inanimate, pretend animate objects (dolls, puppets, and so on) versus inanimate objects (potato chips, apples, a flower pot), and the dramatic characters from a familiar television show. Second, the mother sees that the issue has a larger cultural significance when Buddy proposes to go to Sesame Street. She sees that her knowledge of the Sesame Street culture is different from her child's: She knows it is a fabricated television culture; he doesn't. She must now decide how far to push in addressing these distinctions given our culture's beliefs and values (and her interpretation of and commitment to such beliefs and values) regarding the existence of certain pretend figures (such as Santa Claus, the Tooth Fairy, and Big Bird). Third, the mother uses the routine to reaffirm the close relationship and bonding she has with her son. She takes the opportunity to display openness to his curiosity and concerns. In fact, this routine of "talking at lunch" may have been created by Buddy's mother for this very reason.

4. *The Emergent Nature of Routines*

This example demonstrates how the very predictability of routines provides a framework for producing, displaying, and interpreting cultural knowledge, values, and beliefs. We see how quickly the participants move from a basic question about blood to a discussion of a wide range of cultural facts, values, and relationships. Although the general framework of the routine itself (talking at lunchtime) is recurrent and predictable, what emerges in this talk (extensions and embellishments of the routine) is not. What we see here is that children, as they become part of their cultures, have wide interpretive latitude in making sense of their places in the world. Thus, almost any everyday routine interaction is ripe for children to refine and extend their developing cultural skills and knowledge.

5. *Remaining Ambiguities*

As in most cases involving young children, confusions are addressed but not resolved in routines. In some cases, the confusion may increase. However, the structure of routines allows participants to move ahead (in this case to go on with lunch) while the confusions are left behind to be pursued at other points in time.

From Individual Progression to Collective Reproductions

As we discussed earlier, most theories of child development focus on the individual child. These theories take a **linear view of the developmental process.** In the linear view, it is assumed that the child must pass through a preparatory period in childhood before he or she can develop into a socially competent adult. In this view, the period of childhood consists of a set of developmental stages in which cognitive skills, emotions, and knowledge are acquired in preparation for adult life (see Exhibit 1.2).

EXHIBIT 1.2

The Linear View of Development

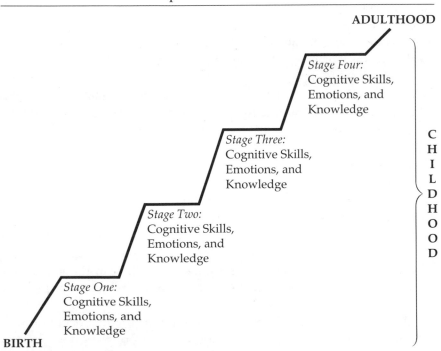

Interpretive reproduction views children's evolving membership in their cultures as *reproductive* rather than linear. According to this **reproductive view,** children do not simply imitate or internalize the world around them. They strive to interpret or make sense of their culture and to participate in it. In attempting to make sense of the adult world, children come to *collectively produce* their own peer worlds and cultures.

The Orb Web Model

The notion of interpretive reproduction can be presented graphically in a way that captures its productive-reproductive characteristics. The key is to use a model that captures interpretive reproduction as a spiral in which children produce and participate in a series of embedded peer cultures. I've found the "spider web" to be an effective heuristic device or metaphor for conceptualizing interpretive reproduction (Corsaro, 1993). Of the different varieties of webs that spiders produce, the orb web, produced by common garden spiders, is the most useful for my conceptual needs. There are a number of features of the orb web that make it a useful metaphor for conceptualizing the process of interpretive reproduction. Let's look at Exhibit 1.4. The radii or spokes of the model represent a range of locales or fields that make up various social institutions (family, economic, cultural, educational, political, occupational, community, and religious). The fields illustrate the diverse locations in which institutional interaction or behavior occurs (Bourdieu, 1991). For example, family interaction takes place in a wide range of actual locales such as the home, the family car, in neighborhood parks, and at family reunions, weddings, funerals, and so forth, while educational activities take place in classrooms, libraries, gymnasiums, music practice rooms, and many other locations. It is important to note that these institutional fields (the radii of the web) exist as stable but changing structures upon which children will weave their webs. Cultural information flows to all parts of the web along these radii.

At the hub or the center of the web is the family of origin, which serves as a nexus of all cultural institutions for children. Children enter the culture through their families at birth. Thus, families are very important to the notion of interpretive reproduction. Children in modern societies, however, begin to participate in other institutional locales with other children and adults who are not family members at an early age. It is in these institutional fields, as well as in the family, that children begin to produce and participate in a series of peer cultures.

The differently shaded spirals represent four distinct peer cultures, which are created by each generation of children in a given society:

EXHIBIT 1.3
The Orb Web Model

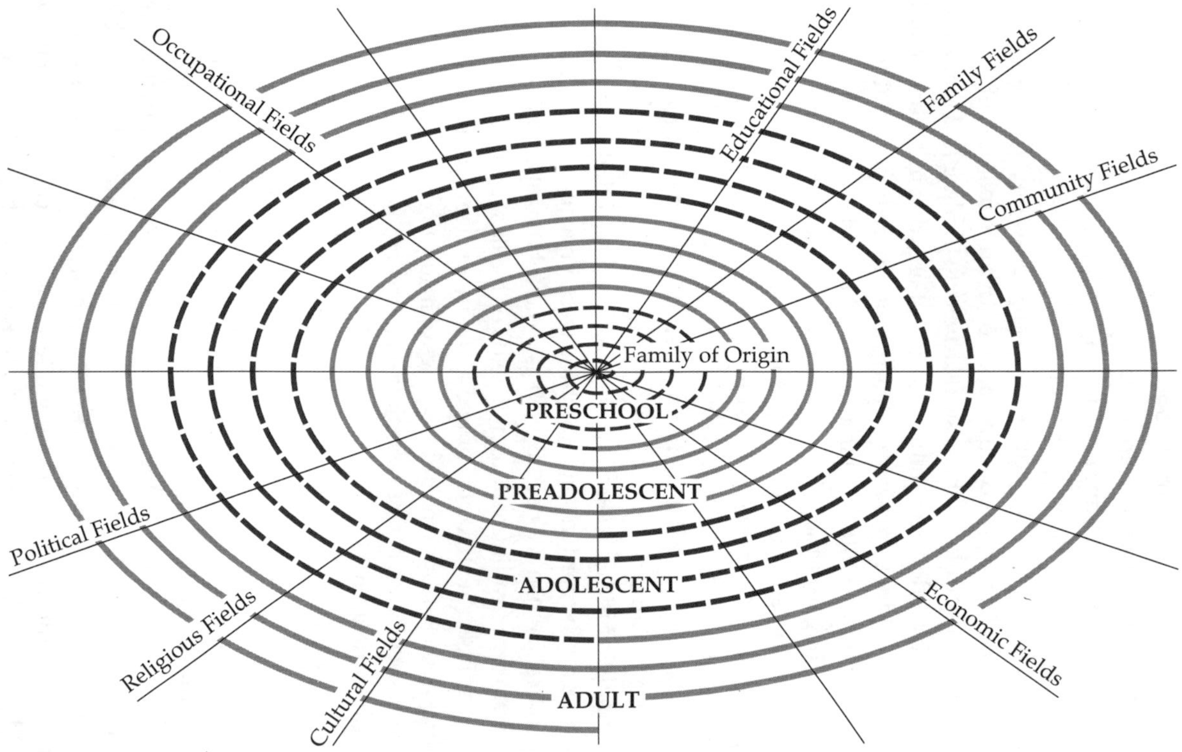

Community Fields
Family Fields
Educational Fields
Economic Fields
Family of Origin
PRESCHOOL
PREADOLESCENT
ADOLESCENT
ADULT
Occupational Fields
Cultural Fields
Political Fields
Religious Fields

preschool, preadolescent, adolescent, and adult. Although aspects of peer culture may be passed on to younger children by older children, peer cultures are not preexisting structures that children encounter or confront. It is in this sense that these cultures differ from the institutional fields (radii) upon which they are woven. While affected by the many experiences that occur through interactions with the adult world and encounters in institutional fields (or crossings of the various radii), children's peer cultures are innovative and creative collective productions. In this sense, the webbing or spirals of peer cultures are collectively spun on the framework of the cultural knowledge and institutions they come in part to constitute.

These collective, productive, and innovative features of children's peer cultures are captured in the basic features of spiraling and embeddedness in the orb web model. Peer cultures are not stages that individual children pass through. Children produce and participate in their peer cultures, and these productions are embedded in the web of experiences children weave with others throughout their lives. Therefore, children's experiences in peer cultures are not left behind with maturity or individual development; rather, they remain part of their live histories as active members of a given culture. Thus, *individual development is embedded in the collective production of a series of peer cultures which in turn contribute to reproduction and change in the wider adult society or culture.*

Finally, it is the general structure of the model that is most crucial. As is the case for the garden spiders, whose webs vary in terms of number of radii and spirals, when we use the web as a model for interpretive reproduction, the number of radii (institutional fields or locales) and the nature and number of spirals (the makeup or age diversity of peer groups and cohorts, the nature of the encounters and crossings of institutional locales, and so on) varies across cultures, across subcultural groups within a particular culture, and over historical time.

Children's Two Cultures

Although the orb web model is useful for visualizing the nature of interpretive reproduction, like any metaphor it tends to reify a highly complex process; in other words, it regards as concrete something that is, in fact, an abstract concept. However, the model does capture the idea that children are always participating in and part of two cultures—children's and adults'—and these cultures are intricately interwoven. To capture the complexity of children's evolving membership in these two cultures we need to examine their collective activities with each other and adults. We also need to consider children as part of a social group that has a place in the larger social structure. Here our focus will be on childhood as a structural form that has a permanent place in society. In this book we will continually shift back and forth between these micro and macro levels, examining both children and childhood.

Summary

Until recently sociology has paid relatively little attention to children and childhood. The neglect or marginalization of children in sociology is clearly related to traditional views of socialization, which relegate children to a primarily passive role. Most of these theories were based on behavioristic views of child development that have been severely challenged by the rise of constructivism in contemporary developmental psychology. Best represented in Piaget's cognitive developmental theory and Vygotsky's sociocultural approach, constructivism stresses the child's active role in her development and her eventual participation in the adult world. Although constructivist theories of individual human development provide sociology with a lens for refocusing our images of children as active agents, these theories primarily focus on developmental outcomes and fail to seriously consider the complexity of social structure and children's collective activities. Interpretive reproduction provides a basis for a new sociology of childhood. Interpretive reproduction replaces linear models of children's individual social development with the collective, productive-reproductive view that is illustrated in the orb web model. In the model, children spontaneously participate as active members of both childhood and adult cultures. In Chapter 2 we will extend the notion of interpretive reproduction by examining its relation to structural approaches to children and childhood.

2

The Structure of Childhood and Children's Interpretive Reproductions

In my ethnographic research in preschools in the United States and Italy my goal is always to discover the children's perspectives, to see what it is like to be a child in the school. To do this I have to overcome the children's tendency to see me as a typical adult. A big problem is physical size; I am much bigger than the children. In my early work I found that a "reactive" method of field entry into children's worlds works best. In simple terms, I enter free play areas, sit down, and wait for the kids to react to me. (I should point out that this is pretty much the opposite of what most adults do in such settings. Teachers, parents, and other adults normally do not sit down in play areas, and when they enter it is usually to ask questions, give advice, or settle disputes. In short, they are more active in their dealings with children.) I find that the reactive method works, but in American schools it normally takes some time. After awhile the children begin to ask me questions, draw me into their activities, and gradually define me as an atypical adult. Size is still a factor, however, and the children come to see me as a big kid, often referring to me as "Big Bill."

When I have used the reactive method in Italian preschools, things have gone somewhat differently. To the Italian children, as soon as I spoke in my fractured Italian I was peculiar, funny, and fascinating. I was not just an atypical adult but also an incompetent one—not just a big kid but sort of a big, dumb kid (Corsaro, 1996). This gets us to the point of my story: I began to see what it was like for children when those around you assume you are incompetent, incomplete, and in need of training. For example, long after my Italian improved, I was still teased about my mistakes and failure to understand something someone had said. The youngest kids in the schools especially enjoyed this teasing, often saying: "Bill, *lui capisce niente!*" ("Bill, he doesn't understand anything!") Of course, the children knew this was not true, but they enjoyed turning the tables on an adult. The issue runs deeper than this, however. The children often extended my incompetence in language to other areas of social and cultural knowledge. Once on a field trip to a zoo that had scale models of dinosaurs, I pointed out to a small group of kids (in very good Italian, I might add) that the dinosaur we were looking at had lived in the same place that I now lived in the United States (I was certain I was right about this because the map accompanying the exhibit clearly indicated as much). The kids laughed uproariously and one, Ramano, said, "Bill, he's crazy! He says the dinosaur lived in the United States." Then, pointing to the dinosaur, he added, "But you can see it lived right here!"

It was a new experience for me to be on the receiving end of the power differential between kids and adults. Adults, of course, are quick to dismiss children's insights, knowledge, and contributions to the culture all the time. We usually do not do this in a mean way (although the ill treatment of children in modern society seems to be increasing); it is more that we take children's perspective for granted and our own views as the truth. In this chapter I want to challenge this tendency by focusing on childhood as a structural form and children as social agents who contribute to the reproduction of childhood and society through their negotiations with adults and their creative production of peer cultures with other children.

Assumptions of the Structural Perspective

In a series of theoretical papers stemming from his work on the international project "Childhood as a Social Phenomenon," the Danish sociologist Jens Qvortrup (1991, 1993a, 1993b, 1994a, 1994b) has outlined a structural perspective to the study of childhood. The approach is based on three central assumptions: (1) childhood constitutes a particular structural form; (2) childhood is exposed to the same societal forces as adulthood; and (3) children are themselves coconstructors of childhood and society. Let's examine each of these assumptions.

Childhood as a Structural Form

We first discussed the notion of **childhood as a social form** in Chapter 1, noting that childhood is both a period in which children live their lives and a category or part of society, like social class. We also discussed that while childhood is a temporary period for children, it is a permanent structural category in society. Qvortrup further develops the notion of viewing childhood as a structural form by contrasting it with perspectives that focus on childhood only as a period of life. He places these perspectives in three general categories. The first is the typical psychological view, which is individual- and personality-oriented. In this view childhood is forward-looking or anticipatory, and is determined by an adult perspective. The second is the psychoanalytic view, which is also individual- and personality-oriented, but here the interest in individual adulthood requires the *retrospective* examination of the individual's childhood experiences. A third view is the life course perspective. This perspective is a mix of individual and nonindividual approaches, in that it follows single individuals from childhood to adulthood or vice versa while at the same time stressing the impact of historical and societal events. All of these views are similar to the traditional theories of socialization we discussed in Chapter 1 in that (1) they focus on the anticipatory outcomes of childhood (that is, children becoming adults), and (2) they consider childhood and adulthood as necessarily belonging to different historical periods.

Qvortrup argues that by conceptualizing childhood as a structural form we can move beyond these individualistic, adult-oriented, and time-bound perspectives to pose and answer a wide range of sociological questions. Consider just a few possibilities: How is childhood alike, different from, and related to other age groups at any given time and place? (For example, consider the interrelations of childhood, adulthood, and old age in the 1950s compared to the 1980s in the United States.) How has the conception and nature of childhood changed over different historical periods in particular societies (for example, childhood in the 1890s compared to the 1990s in the United States)? How do conceptions and the nature of childhood vary across cultures at particular points in time (for example, childhood in the 1990s in Western industrial societies compared to non-Western developing societies)? We will examine these and related questions in detail in Chapters 3, 4, and 10. Let's now move to a consideration of the general effects of societal forces on childhood.

Societal Effects on Childhood

A key feature of Qvortrup's structural approach is that it sees childhood as integrated in society (Qvortrup, 1991, p. 14). Children in their particular childhoods are, like adults, active participants in organized activities (for example, they engage in economic production and consumption). They both affect and are affected by major societal events and developments. Consider, for example, recent changes in Western societies such as higher divorce rates, greater female participation in the labor force, and lower fertility levels (especially among the middle and upper classes). Sociologists have increasingly documented the effects of these factors on the family and to some extent on individual children. But how are the lives of children, that is, contemporary children's childhoods, affected by such changes? Furthermore, how might children, through their collective activities, contribute to society's accommodation to such changes?

We will examine children, families, and social change in Chapter 4, but first let's address one of the issues posed above, the interrelations of different age groups in a given society and how these may change over time. In particular, how has increased longevity due to modern technology affected the interrelations of the generations and the lives of children in American society? Let's consider the case study of the new American grandparent.

The New American Grandparent

In their book *The New American Grandparent*, sociologists Andrew Cherlin and Frank Furstenberg chart the modernization of "grandparenthood." They note that a number of trends such as changes in mortality, fertility, communication, transportation, retirement, Social Security, and standards of living have transformed grandparenthood since World War II. As a result, "more people are living long enough to become grandparents and to enjoy a lengthy period of life as grandparents." Further, note Cherlin and Furstenberg, grandparents "can keep in touch more easily with their grandchildren; they have more time to devote to them; they have more money to spend on them; and they are less likely still to be raising their own children" (1986, p. 35).

Cherlin and Furstenberg interviewed grandparents to pursue the effects of this modernization of grandparenthood and to examine grandparenting styles, careers, and the effects of divorce on grandparenting. They also studied the influence of grandparents on grandchildren. For this topic the authors supplemented their interviews of grandparents with survey items from a larger study of adolescent grandchildren and their parents. Here the findings were somewhat surprising. Even though grandparenthood has seemed to change for the better, there was little evidence from the grandchildren's responses that greater involvement by grandparents had any major impact on their lives. In qualification of these findings, Cherlin and Furstenberg recognize the limits of their survey data, noting that surveys can "not reveal the subtle forms of influence that occur when grandparents and grandchildren interact over long periods of time" (1986, p. 182). Nevertheless, they argue that the results are persuasive and lead them to see grandparents in America as "volunteer firefighters" who are "required to be on the scene when needed but otherwise keep their assistance in reserve" (1986, p. 184).

Like most traditional sociological research that involves children, Cherlin and Furstenberg's study focuses on the effects of a social phenomenon (in this case grandparenting) on *individual children*. Although their acknowledgment of subtle forms of influence hints at the complexity of the worlds of children and their grandparents, the authors fail to push their study to consider fully children's perspectives. For example, they do not consider the possible counterpart of the conception of grandparenthood, which we can term "grandchildhood." Just as adults are grandparents, children are grandchildren, and as the nature of grandparenting changes so does the nature of being a grandchild. The very difficulty of the word, *grandchildhood,* is due to the tendency of social scientists to think of children as individually affected (as dependent variables) rather than as agents of complex collective actions.

Surely the intergenerational lives of grandchildren have changed in ways that parallel those of their grandparents. We can consider a whole new set of vantage points: styles of being a grandchild; grandchild careers; and variations in these styles and careers by gender, class, race, and ethnicity. An important factor to keep in mind in this regard is the influence of parents on their children's lives as grandchildren (or for that matter the lives of their parents as grandparents). At least for younger children, for instance, parents control access to grandparents, and they both actively and reactively support children in their interpretation and appreciation of their interactions with grandparents. Finally, children's interactions with grandparents occur often in multigenerational settings (for example, in the presence of grandparents, parents, aunts, uncles, and cousins). These occasions provide an ideal setting for priming activities in which children are prepared for transitions into a variety of social relations in their lives. One such family obligation—to serve as the adult child caretaker of elderly parents—may indeed be a long and demanding one for the present generation of children.

Children's Activities and Contributions to Society

Like all theories that focus primarily on how the structural features of society affect individual societal members, a structural approach to the sociology of childhood runs the risk of undervaluing how the collective actions of individuals (including children) can affect society. Qvortrup is well aware of this tendency, and he argues that "children are themselves coconstructors of childhood and society" (1993, p. 14). While acknowledging the historical trend of an increasing sentimentalism and overprotectiveness of children as noted by Zelizer (1985) and others, he challenges their accompanying contention that children have moved from being useful to useless. On the contrary,

Qvortrup maintains that children have always been useful and that it is the *nature* of their contributions to society that have changed (1991, pp. 25–26). A wonderful example of Qvortrup's point in this regard is research conducted by the anthropologist Enid Schildkrout (1975) in her study of a certain African culture.

Age and Gender in Hausa Society

In her study of Hausa culture in the Nigerian city of Kano in the 1970s, Schildkrout found that children were essential in maintaining an institution known as *purdah*. Purdah relates to Hausa beliefs about male/female interaction and places specific limits on both men's and women's spatial mobility. The vast majority of married Hausa women in Kano were in purdah, which meant that they generally did not leave their compounds except to visit relatives or close female friends, to attend ceremonies for births, marriages, and funerals, or to go for medical treatment or visit the sick. Men also did not have free access in and out of each other's house. A man could not, for example, enter the household of his younger married sister. Adhering to the rules of purdah meant there was very little daily interaction between men and women, even between spouses, because most men worked away from their homes.

Although purdah strongly affects the spatial mobility of adults, "Hausa children enjoy a freedom that no other group in the society commands—the right to wander in and out of people's houses. Children are not expected to observe formal greetings behaviour, and they casually walk into the houses of neighbours, relatives, friends, and even strangers, to look for playmates, to make purchases, to offer things for sale, or to carry messages" (Schildkrout, 1975, p. 124). Children's freedom in this regard is essential for the institution of purdah because if this were not the case, women (except for the very wealthy, who could replace children with paid labor) could not remain in purdah and still carry out their domestic responsibilities. Furthermore, children's freedom allowed women to be involved in independent economic activities. With their own children or those of relatives or neighbors to serve as street traders and messengers, "women sell cooked food outside their houses, and may invest in other commodities such as detergent, kola nuts, sugar, salt, fruit—just about anything that can be transported on a tray and sold in small quantities" (Schildkrout, p. 119). Money from these economic ventures serves as insurance for divorce, which is frequent; it also can supplement the income of husbands. As a result of the experiences in this cash economy of adults very early in life, many girls and boys develop their own "children's economy." They use allowance money provided for their work for their mothers and for running errands for other adults to set up their own small businesses. "By ten, many girls cook for sale on their own. With initial help from their mothers, or other adult female relatives, who may give them a cooking pot, charcoal, or a small stove, they purchase small amounts of ingredients and prepare various snack foods. These are then sold in very small quantities to other children" (p. 128). It is clear that Hausa women's and men's sex roles could not be defined as they were without the children performing roles that were distinct from but complementary to those of adults.

By the time this study was published in 1975, Schildkrout found that the development of Western educational beliefs and increasing primary school enrollment was viewed by adult members of the Hausa culture as threatening the institution of purdah and the complex socio-economic relations and complementary roles of adults and children in these relations. Although very few people objected to what were seen as the long-term benefits of Western education, the resistance that did exist was "very often based upon those very realistic appraisals of its immediate socio-economic consequences" (p. 133).

Although this case study is generally in line with functionalist views of society, which we criticized earlier in Chapter 1, there is an important difference in this particular case from traditional functionalist views of children and socialization. In the Hausa culture, children do not simply internalize the norms of their society like those in line with purdah and then behave in accordance with them in later life. On the contrary, children are active contributors to society in that they cooperate with adults in the enforcement of norms and values. In the process of carrying out activities related to purdah children do, of course, come to understand its significance, and in this way they contribute to societal maintenance.

Overall, the above case study vividly illustrates the ways in which children serve as active contributors to society, and how children and adults are complementary participants in the social system. Qvortrup points to other activities of children from industrialized societies—in school, the workplace, the home, and also in organized sports, play and leisure settings—through which children make similar contributions.

Children's schoolwork. In line with historians and sociologists of education, Qvortrup notes children's movement from primarily agricultural labor in preindustrial society, to a wide range of types of work during the transition to industrial capitalism (on farms, in factories, in mills, on city streets), and finally to formal schooling in modern industrial societies. He argues, however, that this last movement should not be seen as a break from the past, because schooling is a continuation of children's work (albeit of a different type); it is an investment in the future economic health of any modern society. Furthermore, schooling has some immediate payoff in that children, along with their teachers, are coproducers of knowledge. This point is especially true in modern societies where children and youth spend long periods of time (stretching well into young adulthood) in educational institutions.

The notion of schooling as work is not widely recognized by adults, including social scientists. Qvortrup links this "collective amnesia" regarding the usefulness of schoolwork to the bureaucratic nature of schools—to their focus on functioning as accrediting devices that shape immature and unskilled children into productive adults. Such views are clearly related to the traditional theories of socialization and child development; the focus is on preparing children for their future as adults, rather than appreciating their present contributions.

Children's work outside the home. Given the amount of time children in Western societies spend on schoolwork, opportunities for work outside the home would seem to be limited. In fact, youth employment has declined in much of Western Europe and in Japan. This trend has not occurred in the U.S., however, where there has been a steady rise in labor force participation by youth (Harrisson, Reubens, & Sparr, 1983). In developing countries the pattern is somewhat different because children have always worked either for their families or for others to supplement family income. Although educational expansion has somewhat curtailed the number of hours children and youth can work, demanding work with long hours normally supplements school work for even young children in these countries.

In theory, children's work outside the home should have positive benefits. It can, for example, add variety to childhood experiences and prepare children for future work roles. However, for both developing and industrialized societies, children and youth who work outside the home today seem to gain little from the experience and are often exploited (Greenberger and Steinberg, 1986). We will return to discuss why work outside the home is seldom beneficial for children in contemporary society in Chapter 4.

Children's work in the home. As more and more women have entered the work force, the study of domestic labor or housework has become an important research topic in American sociology. Most studies document the heavy work demands and stress on dual-income and single parent families, most especially for women. In fact, study after study documents that women perform most of the housework in what Arlie Hochschild (1989) terms the "second shift." Beth Shelton (1992), for example, found that in 1987 employed women spent an estimated thirty-three hours a week on housework compared to employed men's twenty-two hours a week.

In many of the early studies of domestic labor carried out in the 1970s and early 1980s, children were seen primarily as sources of additional work for mothers. However, more recently researchers have begun to take children's contributions into account. Most of these studies do not use children as respondents, but rather parental (usually mother's) reports of children's work in the home. Nonetheless, most of the studies reported a similar pattern, with younger children (eight-to-thirteen-year-olds) contributing two to four hours a week to domestic chores and older children (fourteen-to-eighteen-year-olds) six to nine hours a week. In accounting for differences by age, the studies also consistently documented gender differences, with girls contributing more domestic labor than boys. Moreover, chores were highly gender typed, with girls doing cooking, cleaning, and other indoor tasks and boys more often engaging in outdoor tasks such as yard work. In a recent study of parental reports of the household labor of five-to-eighteen-year-old children, Sampson Blair found that "daughters perform significantly more total labor than sons (5.62 versus 4.63 hours) per week" and that daughters spent "the majority of their time in those tasks traditionally defined as 'female-dominated'" (1992, pp. 187–188).

An interesting aspect of these studies is how the relation between children and domestic labor is conceptualized. Although psychologists often consider the effects of such labor on children's cognitive, emotional, and social development (see Goodnow, 1988), sociologists focus primarily on adult members of the family and on implications for the reproduction of current gender inequalities. In neither case do we learn much about *children's* perspectives on household chores or how domestic labor relates to other features of children's daily lives. We will return to pursue these topics in Chapter 4.

Children's play and leisure activities. In his book *Childhood's Future*, the journalist Richard Louv recounts a episode when he was playing catch with his son in a city park. The park was filling with children's soccer teams and as Louv and his son Jason threw the ball back and forth, they were approached by the mother of one of Jason's classmates. Louv reports the following conversation:

"Whatcha doing? Waiting for a team?" she said with a friendly smile.

"Nope. Just playing catch," I answered, tossing the ball to Jason.

"Killing time, eh?" she said. (Louv, 1990, p. 109)

The above exchange captures the recent trend in Western societies toward the institutionalization of more and more of children's leisure time activities; the woman assumed the father and son wouldn't be in a park with a ball and a mitt unless they were waiting for an organized event to take place. Qvortrup reports that in all of the sixteen industrialized countries participating in the international project, "Childhood as a Social Phenomenon," well over 50 percent of children are involved in organized sports and leisure activities, with many involved in several such activities (1991, p. 29).

Commentators like Louv, Qvortrup, and others challenge the assumption that such activities are voluntary on the part of the children, pointing to the highly structured, closely supervised, and rigidly scheduled nature of what Qvortrup terms "planned spontaneity" (Louv, 1990, pp. 109–116; Qvortrup, 1991, pp. 29–30). Children interviewed by Louv echoed this theme. One fifth-grader commented:

> "I don't really have much time to play at all because I have piano lessons. My mom makes me practice for about an hour every day, and then I have my homework, and that's about an hour's worth, and then I got soccer practice, and that's from 5:30 to 7:00, and then there's no time left to play. On weekends we usually have soccer games, and I have the chores, and then I'm free to play—which is only about two hours, three hours something like that." (Louv, 1991, p. 110)

This child's distinction between planned activities like soccer and piano practice, and "play" is intriguing. Kids seem to have less and less time to be kids. In fact, many commercial establishments (pizza restaurant chains, indoor playgrounds or amusement areas) try to convince parents that they can provide "kid play" for their children. But why aren't kids allowed to find their own fun, to set out on their own play quests in the neighborhood, nearby parks and playgrounds, or even their own backyard?

The major reason for an increase in organized activities for children may well be an accompanying increase in parental concerns regarding children's safety. Given modern conditions, parental preoccupation with children's well-being, even while playing in their own neighborhoods, is understandable. Such fears have been heightened in recent years by the media's reporting and depiction of children as victims of physical and sexual abuse.

There is much debate about the accuracy of descriptive accounts and statistical reports of child victimization (Best, 1990). Nevertheless, there are good reasons for parents to be fearful. Violent crimes against children have increased, and better reporting of child abuse has led to a much more accurate understanding of the extent of the problem. There is little doubt that concerns about the physical safety of poor children in the U.S. and throughout the world are justified. However, the general anxiety about children's safety runs much deeper, beyond big city streets to affluent suburbs and small towns. This uneasiness about our children is probably related to the state of modern societies more generally: We have less time for our children and for family interaction and activities, we do not know our communities and neighborhoods well, and we rely more on the media for information and advice (Stephens, 1993). We will explore this topic more fully in Chapter 9, where we consider children as social problems.

A second reason for the increased institutionalization of children's activities is that structured leisure activities and lessons provide parents with needed child care. In a recent national child care survey in the U.S. conducted by the Urban Institute, Sandra Hofferth and her colleagues found that "many parents use lessons as a way to care for school-age children after school, as well as to expand their academic, physical, social, and cultural skills" (Hofferth et al., 1991, p. 67). The percentage of families relying on lessons for after-school care is highest for households with working mothers, where 22.4 percent rely on such care for their ten-to-twelve-year-old children. This is the most frequent type of arrangement except for "father care," which was 33 percent. Hofferth et al. point out the "two for one" advantage of after-school lessons: The child gets to pursue an area of interest, and at the same time the parent benefits from "child care." The data also suggest that lessons may become a necessary *replacement* for center care as children move from preschool into elementary school. For example, 42.8 percent of families with employed mothers rely on center care (child care at an institutionalized setting) for three-to-four-year-olds; 16 percent for six-to-nine-year-olds; and only 3.2 percent for ten-to-twelve-year-olds; the corresponding figures for families relying on lessons is .6 percent for three-to-four-year-olds, 13.6 percent for six-to-nine-year-olds, and 22.4 percent for ten-to-twelve-year-olds (Hofferth et al., 1991, p. 50). Older children may be more interested in things like piano and tennis lessons; however, it is also true that after-school center care for school-age children is not available in many communities.

A third reason for an increase in organized activities for children may be demographic changes in American families. As social demographer Don Hernandez (1993a, b) recently documented, children have experienced a dramatic shift from large to small families during the past 100 years. For example, notes Hernandez, "the typical child born in 1890 lived, as an adolescent, in a family in which there were about 6.6 siblings, but the typical child born in 1994 is expected to live in a family that is only one-third as large—with 1.9 children" (1993b, p. 418). Although there was a brief lull in this dramatic shift during the baby boom period of about 1945 to 1957, it was more than offset by the baby bust period in later years. As Hernandez notes, this shift has drastically reduced the number of siblings who are available for companionship. Without siblings to integrate them into informal neighborhood activities and children's cultures (or to serve as caretakers and protectors), children find they have to rely more on parents. And for the two reasons we discussed above, parents often turn to organized (and often age-segregated) activities.

Childhood, Children's Activities, and Interpretive Reproduction in Peer Culture

Qvortrup's approach to childhood as a social phenomenon and his emphasis on children as active, coconstructors of their social worlds reflects an important shift away from individualistic views of socialization in which the individual child internalizes adult skills and knowledge. His view leads us to a better understanding of children's place, stake, and importance in both cultural production and maintenance. However, children do not just actively contribute to the adult culture and their own childhoods in a direct way. Children creatively appropriate information from the adult world to produce their own, unique peer cultures. As we saw in Chapter 1, the process of interpretive reproduction enables children to become a part of adult culture— to contribute to its reproduction and extension—through their negotiations with adults and their creative production of a series of peer cultures with other children. Let's turn now to a more detailed discussion of this notion of interpretive reproduction within children's peer cultures.

In Chapter 1 we discussed examples of young children's participation in cultural routines in the family. For example, we considered the importance of parent-infant games like "peekaboo" for providing infants with opportunities to participate in everyday family life and to develop a sense of security in belonging to a social group. Also, in the case study of the two-and-a-half-year-old child (Buddy) and his mother, we saw that the everyday routine of conversation at lunch helped establish a strong emotional bond between mother and son, and it also provided Buddy with numerous opportunities to explore and to learn about his social world. Through their participation in such cultural routines in the family with parents and siblings, young children initiate their **evolving membership in their culture.** We can see this evolving membership as a process in which children refine and expand their place in the culture over time and with experience (Lave & Wenger, 1991). This process continues as children from very young ages begin to participate in cultural routines and other collective activities outside the family. By interacting with playmates in play groups and preschools, children produce the first in a series of peer cultures in which childhood knowledge and practices are gradually transformed into the knowledge and skills necessary to participate in the adult world.

We will consider children's peer cultures in detail in Chapters 5 through 8. However, here I want to stress that children's production of peer cultures is neither a matter of simple imitation nor direct appropriation of the adult world. Children creatively appropriate or take information from the adult world to produce their own unique peer cultures. Such appropriation is *creative* in that it extends or elaborates peer culture; children transform information from the adult world in order to meet the concerns of their peer world. In this way they simultaneously contribute to the reproduction of the adult culture. Thus, children's peer cultures have an autonomy that makes them worthy of documentation and study in their own right.

Three Kinds of Collective Action

In Chapter 1 I referred to the process of creative appropriation as interpretive reproduction. Interpretive reproduction is made up of three types of collective action: (1) *children's creative appropriation of information and knowledge from the adult world;* (2) *children's production and participation in a series of peer cultures;* and (3) *children's contribution to the reproduction and extension of the adult culture.* These activities follow a certain progression: Appropriation enables cultural production, which contributes to reproduction and change. The activities are, however, not historically partitioned. That is, children do not proceed through a specific period in which they appropriate all the needed information to produce a peer culture and only then make contributions to reproduction and change in adult culture. Instead these collective actions *occur both within the moment and over time.* To better understand this idea it is helpful to consider how children acquire and use language. Children do not first learn all the rules of grammar, phonology, and semantics, practice these rules, and only then begin to use them to communicate with others. Instead, children use their developing language skills to communicate at specific moments in time, and they refine and further develop the skills through repeated use in interaction over time. It is the same for the creation of and participation in peer culture. Children appropriate information from the adult world to create and participate in a peer culture at specific moments in time. These same collective actions, through their repetition in peer culture over time, contribute to children's better understanding of the aspects of the adult culture they have appropriated. Further, these repetitions over time can even bring about changes in certain aspects of the adult culture. Let's consider the following case study.

Preschool Children's Secondary Adjustments to Teacher's Rules

In my twenty years of ethnographic research in nursery schools in the United States and Italy, I found that children attempt to evade adult rules through collaboratively produced **secondary adjustments,** which enable the children to gain a certain amount of control over their lives in these settings. According to Goffman, secondary adjustments are "any habitual arrangement by which a member of an organization employs unauthorized means, or obtains unauthorized ends, or both, thus getting around the organization's assumptions as to what he should do and get and hence what he should be" (1961, p. 189).

In my studies I found that children produced a wide variety of secondary adjustments in response to school rules. For example, the children employed several concealment strategies to evade the rule that prohibited bringing toys or other personal objects from home to school. This rule was necessary: Personal objects were attractive to other children just because they were different from the everyday materials in the preschools, and as a result, the teachers were constantly settling disputes about these items. Therefore, such objects could not be brought to school; if they were brought, they had to be stored in the child's locker until the end of the day. In both the American and Italian schools the children attempted to evade this rule by bringing small, personal objects that they could conceal in their pockets. Particular favorites were small toy animals, matchbox cars, candies, and chewing gum. While playing, a child often would show his or her "stashed loot" to a playmate and carefully share the forbidden object without catching the teachers' attention. The teachers, of course, often knew what was going on but simply ignored minor transgressions. The teachers overlooked these violations because the nature of the secondary adjustment often eliminates the organizational need to enforce the rule. Children share and play with smuggled personal objects surreptitiously to avoid detection by the teachers. If the children always played with personal objects in this fashion, there would be no conflict and hence no need for the rule. That is not the case, however; the careful sharing takes place only because the adult rule is in effect. Thus, in an indirect way, the secondary adjustment endorses the organizational need for the rule. We see, then, that children's secondary adjustments (which are innovative and highly valued features of the peer culture, as we shall see later in Chapter 7) often contribute to the maintenance of the adult rules.

The story does not end here, however. The children's secondary adjustments to school rules often led to the teachers' selective enforcement of the rules and, in some cases, to changes in the rules and in the organizational structure of the nursery school. I often found that teachers relaxed the enforcement of school rules because they recognized the creativity of certain features of peer culture. For example, in an American school, teachers first relaxed a rule prohibiting children from moving objects from one play area to another; they allowed the children to use string and blocks from a worktable to create a "fishing" game by dangling the string from an upstairs playhouse to their peers below, who then attached the blocks. The teachers then actually endorsed the secondary adjustment by joining in the play (see Corsaro, 1985, p. 257). In these instances the teachers themselves appear to be engaged in a secondary adjustment to their own rules, and are exposing children to a basic feature of all rules—that is, knowledge of the content of a rule is never sufficient for its application; rules must be applied and interpreted in social context (Wootton, 1986).

Summary

In recent years we have seen the beginnings of a new sociology of childhood, one that breaks free from the individualistic doctrine that regards socialization as the child's private internalization of adult skills and knowledge. In this new approach the focus is on *childhood* as a social construction resulting from the collective actions of *children* with adults and each other. Childhood is recognized as a structural form and children are social agents who contribute to the reproduction of childhood and society through their negotiations with adults and through their creative production of a series of peer cultures with other children. This new view of childhood as a social phenomenon replaces the traditional notion of socialization with the concept of interpretive reproduction. Interpretive reproduction reflects children's evolving membership in their culture, which begins in the family and spirals outward as children create a series of embedded peer cultures based on the institutional structure of the adult culture. Overall, the notion of interpretive reproduction challenges sociology to take children seriously and to appreciate children's contributions to social reproduction and change.

PART TWO

Children, Childhood, and Families in Historical and Cultural Context

Many years ago in my first ethnographic study in a preschool, a four-year-old girl asked me, "Bill, do you remember the good old days?" Now, this was during the early years of my research with young children and I was still getting used to the surprising things children say and ask. Nowadays kids still ask surprising things, but I'm less surprised by this fact and know I do not always have to have a good answer. Back then I thought I did, and I was taken aback. A four-year-old is asking me about the good old days. Whose good old days? I was a lot older than she. But not that old. Where did she hear this line? From her parents? A television commercial? Do her grandpa or grandma talk about the good old days? Does she really expect an answer? All this is going through my head and she's there, smiling, looking up at me.

So, I sort of mumble, "Well, let's see, the good old days. Do you mean—well, like when I was a kid?"

"Ah, the good old days," she said. Then she turned and walked away. It was as if any response I gave would have been sufficient. I was not to take the question so seriously.

When it comes to the study of children and childhood, few psychologists and not many more sociologists have taken questions about the good old days very seriously either. Neither psychologists nor sociologists have routinely placed their work in sociohistorical context. The situation is a little better when it comes to cross-cultural studies of children and childhood, but not much. There are exceptions, but for most psychologists and sociologists, the focus has been on the individual development of children in Western societies from the mid–twentieth century or so.

A new sociology of childhood has to correct this tendency. We need to place the theoretical notion of interpretive reproduction in historical and cultural context. This section of the book will do just that. Chapter 3 explores Ariès's groundbreaking work on the history of childhood. Ariès's subtle and innovative analysis and his bold interpretations of a range of historical materials generated both intense interest in the history of conceptions of childhood, as well as a good bit of criticism. We will look at both the related work and the criticisms. We will also consider several examples from the new history of childhood, which capture the perspectives of children and youth from medieval times to the early twentieth century. Although this review is selective and does not capture many important, recent historical studies of childhood and children, it does place the notion of interpretive reproduction in historical context.

The topic of Chapter 4 is children in families from a global perspective. Here we'll look at how children and childhood are affected by recent social changes in families, and we'll also ponder the growing diversity of families in both industrialized and developing societies. Although much of the work on families fails to consider seriously the activities and contributions of children, we'll focus on research that has directly investigated young children's experiences in families in both Western and non-Western or developing societies. We'll also examine how social changes in Western and developing societies affect childhood. We'll focus on general experiences of children as a social group to discover how their childhoods have been affected by key social and economic changes in families.

3

Historical Views of
Childhood and Children

> In medieval society the idea of childhood did not exist; this is not to suggest
> that children were neglected, forsaken or despised. The idea of childhood is
> not to be confused with affection for children: it corresponds to an awareness
> of the particular nature of childhood, that particular nature which distin-
> guishes the child from the adult, even the young adult. In medieval society
> this awareness was lacking.
>
> *Philippe Ariès,* Centuries of Childhood *(1962, p. 128)*

The above quote, the central claim in Phillipe Ariès's historical account of
family life and the conception of childhood, sparked the attention of historians, who, like sociologists, had long neglected children. Ariès's approach to
the history of childhood was complex and powerful. Using a contingent
sense of time, he traced changes in ideas about the organization of family,
children, and age relations from the Middle Ages to the end of the eighteenth
century. Although Ariès never claimed these stages were inevitable, his book
soon spawned evolutionary theories of the family and conceptions of childhood (deMause, 1974; Shorter, 1977; Stone, 1977) and, in turn, fired heated
debate about the historical evidence for such assertions.

Although a number of elements of Ariès's position are now considered
untenable, his work overall is of major importance for the history of childhood. Most important, he argued that childhood was a social construction
and that historians should take children and their lives seriously. As a result,
a growing number of historians have come to adopt children's perspectives
and voices in their studies of children and childhood.

In this chapter we'll consider Ariès's theory, the related evolutionary
views of others, and the methodological debates about the adequacy of their
evidence and interpretations as presented in the work of Linda Pollock. We'll
then look at several examples from the new history of childhood that capture
the perspectives of children and youth from medieval times to the early
twentieth century. Most current discussions of the sociology of childhood
give only brief mention of children of the past. We will look beyond these

accounts in order to examine a more extensive review of work on the history of childhood and to place the notion of interpretive reproduction in historical context.

Philippe Ariès's *Centuries of Childhood*

For Ariès the "idea of childhood" corresponds to an awareness of the particular nature of childhood, that particular nature that distinguishes the child from the adult. According to Ariès this awareness was lacking in medieval society. That is why, as soon as a child could live without the constant attention of his mother or nanny, he belonged to adult society. Ariès's support for this contention is drawn primarily from his interpretations of medieval art. Children were almost totally absent from medieval paintings, and where they were depicted they looked much like miniature adults. Ariès does, however, notice a gradual change in the depiction of children beginning in the thirteenth century. He points to the introduction, in paintings, of the *putto*, the naked child. These *putti*, or "semi-pagan angels," were not seen as real historic children; rather they were used as ornamental motif in the work of great masters such as Titian. However, the ubiquity of *putti* during this period, argued Ariès, "corresponded to something far deeper than the taste for classical nudity," something that can be ascribed only to a broad surge of interest in childhood (1962, p. 44).

Ariès believes that this first recognition and interest in childhood eventually led to the *coddling period*, which fully emerged in the sixteenth century, when childhood was seen as a time of innocence and sweetness. Children were idolized and valued as a source of amusement or escape for adults, especially women. Consider, for example, this quote from a letter Mme de Sévigné wrote to her son in 1672: "I am reading the story of Christopher Columbus's discovery of the Indies, which is entertaining me greatly; but your daughter entertains me even more. I do so love her . . . she strokes your portrait and caresses it in such an amusing way that I have to kiss her straight away" (Ariès, 1962, p. 130).

The *moralistic period* (from the sixteenth through the eighteenth centuries) was in large part a negative reaction to the coddling period, most especially from scholars and moralists of the time. The French essayist Montaigne wrote: "I cannot abide that passion for caressing new-born children, which have neither mental activities nor recognizable bodily shape by which to make themselves lovable," noting further that he cannot accept the idea of loving children "for our amusement like monkeys or taking pleasure in their games and infantile nonsense" (Ariès, 1962, p. 130). This attitude was taken up and extended by other moralists who emphasized that childhood is a period of immaturity and that children must be trained and disciplined.

Ariès argues that such early writings on morals and education laid the groundwork for the development of child psychology, which has had tremendous influence on conceptions of childhood and child rearing in contemporary times. Thus, Ariès saw a progression from no conception of childhood to coddling, and then to the moralistic period in which childhood is seen as a time for discipline and preparation for adulthood. However, it is a mistake to assume that Ariès feels that this evolution was *inevitable or that it was a positive occurrence*, as some interpreters of his work have done.

For Ariès the modern world is "obsessed by the physical, moral, and sexual problems of childhood," which have developed from moralist propaganda that "taught parents that they were spiritual guardians, that they were responsible before God for the souls, and indeed the bodies too, of their children" (1962, pp. 411–412). Ariès bemoans the removal of the child from adult society, arguing that the "solicitude of family, church, moralists, and administrators deprived the child of the freedom he had hitherto enjoyed among adults. It inflicted on him the birch, the prison cell—in a word, the punishments usually reserved for convicts from the lowest strata of society" (1962, p. 413).

Clearly, then, Ariès does not believe that things have gotten better for children. In fact, Ariès sees the progressive separation of children and adults as part of more general cultural changes that have resulted in separations by social class and race in modern society. He argues that the old society "concentrated the maximum number of ways of life into the minimum of space" and in doing so accepted the mixing of widely different social class groups (1962, p. 415). Modern society, on the other hand, provides "each way of life with a confined space in which it [is] understood that the dominant features should be respected, and that each person [has] to resemble a conventional model, an ideal type . . . ." (1962, p. 415).

Though some have found problems with ambiguity and sweeping generalizations in his work, Ariès generated a great deal of interest in the history of childhood, perhaps even more so because of his bold interpretations and conclusions. His recognition of the contradiction in denying children their freedom, in the name of their own protection and moral education, is directly related to the present-day conception of "children as social problems" that we discuss in Chapter 9.

The Debate Regarding Grand Stage Theories of the Family and Childhood

Ariès offered a constructivist argument about institutional changes and their effects on conceptions of children. He saw these changes as phases of the unique history of Europe involving shifting configurations in the family and educational institutions. For example, he pointed to the general movement from extended families that were very much a part of the surrounding community to nuclear families that were more isolated from the rest of society and the emergence of age-graded schools as having important effects on both conceptions of childhood and the lives of children. Other theorists pushed these ideas much further, proposing grand stage theories of the family (deMause, 1974; Shorter, 1977; Stone, 1977). These theories hold that there are specific, universal, and, in some cases, predestined stages in the evolution of the family, children, and childhood.

For example, deMause (1974) offers a "psychogenic theory of history" in which historical changes in the conceptions and treatment of children result from individual parents working out their own anxieties and psychological problems in their interaction with their children. deMause saw a pattern from the vicious mistreatment of children in medieval times to more humane care and nurturing of children in the present. He maintained that "the further back in history one goes, the lower the level of child care, and the more likely children are to be killed, abandoned, beaten, terrorized, and sexually abused" (deMause, 1974, p. 1).

A number of historians have criticized the work of both deMause and other grand stage theorists and have offered impressive historical evidence in support of their critiques (Garnsey, 1991; Hanawalt, 1993; Pollock, 1983; Shahar, 1990). Perhaps the best known of these critiques is that of Linda Pollock.

In her book *Forgotten Children*, Pollock carefully (at times laboriously) challenges the conceptions of the history of childhood in the work of Ariès and most especially grand stage theorists such as deMause. She is especially critical of the indirect evidence (for example, paintings, philosophical and religious tracts, advice literature, and letters) upon which much of the earlier work on the history of childhood is based. Pollock believes a history of childhood can be pursued with more direct primary sources like diaries, autobiographies, and newspaper reports of court cases regarding child abuse. First, she notes that when direct sources are used, a much less negative picture of childhood emerges. Second, many who have used diaries to supplement less direct sources have done so selectively and anecdotally, which Pollock feels led to a distortion of how children were viewed and treated in the past. Pollock points, for example, to the many references to Puritan Samuel Sewall's accounts in his diary in 1878 of "whipping" his son Joseph as typical of the practice of selective analysis. Although many accounts stress Sewall's report of the whipping as evidence of the strict discipline of the seventeenth century, few note that this is the only statement in a long and detailed diary where Sewall mentions physically punishing his son. Then, there is the importance of considering social and cultural context in interpreting such cases.

As Pollock points out, "parent-child interaction is a continuing process, not a series of isolated events" (1983, p. 66). In the Sewall case, it turns out that the father resorted to physical punishment after several times admonishing his son for inappropriate behavior during prayer and other quiet times within the Puritan household. The actual whipping came about when the boy "threw a lump of brass at his sister, bruising and cutting her forehead" (Pollock, 1983, p. 66).

Aware of the need to examine sources thoroughly and systematically, Pollock undertook an intensive analysis of 500 British and American diaries, autobiographies, and related sources. She found little support for Ariès's thesis that there was an abiding indifference to children, or deMause's contention of widespread mistreatment and abuse of children until the enlightenment of the eighteenth and ninteenth centuries. Rather, Pollock discovered that "nearly all children were wanted, such developmental stages as weaning and teething aroused interest and concern, and parents revealed anxiety and distress at the illness or death of their children" (1983, p. 268). Acknowledging some reports of physical punishment in her materials, Pollock nevertheless concluded that diaries and newspaper reports of abuse suggest that cruelty to children was not widespread and that a "large section of the population—probably most parents—were not 'battering' their children" (1983, p. 268). Finally, Pollock found that the parent-child relationship was not formal and one-sided. Children were close to their parents and were influenced by them, but parents were influenced by their children as well. From these and related findings, Pollock ends her book with the following challenge to historians: "Instead of trying to explain the supposed changes in the parent-child relationship, historians would do well to ponder just why parental care is a variable so curiously resistant to change" (1983, p. 271). Unfortunately, Pollock never developed this idea. As Gillis argues, the book "bulldozes the standard literature, but leaves the task of reconstruction to others" (1985, p. 143).

Pollock does provide some support for the idea of continuity of parental care when she argues that qualitative aspects of care such as protection, love, and socialization are essential for human survival. In the actual analysis of her materials, she began to see, but did not fully develop, the notion that the care and socialization of children as prerequisites for cultural survival must always be culturally constructed through the collective actions of adults and children. There are some weaknesses in Pollock's evidence, though: The diaries and autobiographies are limited primarily to the literate upper classes, the authors may have selectively omitted information that would put themselves in a bad light, and it is possible that some materials may have been edited by others. Even so, her work has been very well received for its careful and painstaking scholarship. Pollock's intensive analysis of diaries allowed her to go beyond the focus on adult sentiments that characterized others' earlier work, and it set the stage for subsequent historical studies of childhood, which attempt to reconstruct the everyday activities and cultural practices of children themselves.

The New History of Childhood

The new history of childhood, like the new sociology of childhood that we discussed in Chapters 1 and 2, focuses directly on the collective actions of children with adults and with each other. In doing so it begins to address a long-ignored defect in the historical record. Even in the historical accounts of authors like Ariès, deMause, and Pollock that we discussed above, the focus remains on *adult* conceptions of childhood, their sentiments toward children, and their methods of child rearing. What is left out is a consideration of "children and adolescents as influential actors in past societies" (West & Petrick, 1992, p. 1). And that is what the new history of childhood is all about. Now let's consider some of the work of these new historians of childhood.

Barbara Hanawalt's Growing Up in Medieval London

Relying on evidence from court records, coroner's rolls, literary sources, and books of advice, Barbara Hanawalt captures the lives of London children and youth in the fourteenth and fifteenth centuries. Hanawalt grounds her discussion of the rights, treatment, and everyday activities of children in careful exploration of the evidence. However, she also dramatizes these facts in what some see as a daring historical narrative style. At the end of each chapter in her book *Growing Up in Medieval London*, Hanawalt pens composite stories about real children that summarize the main points of the chapter. Let's look at some of Hanawalt's main themes.

Treatment of children and their quality of life. Hanawalt acknowledges that life in fourteenth- and fifteenth-century London was difficult for children and adolescents. The mortality rate among infants and young children was high and there were many dangers from disease and accidents. However, she notes that "play, rather than serious work, was still very much part of children's lives" (1993, p. 66). She also disputes the notion that it was common practice to neglect or abuse young children, that there was a general callousness about the death of children, or that there was no conception of children beyond the infancy period. First, she notes that no court records show widespread abandonment or infanticide and that the ecclesiastical court records for London reveal allegations of fewer than one infanticide case

per year (1993, p. 44). Second, Hanawalt acknowledges that it is safe to assume that children spent a good part of their first year of life swaddled and
in cradles. However, she goes on to point out that, given the cold and damp
environment, swaddling prevented chills and kept the children from crawl-
ing about the filth of London or moving outside onto dangerous streets.
Third, Hanawalt produces numerous examples illustrating that young children clearly were seen as being different from adults and requiring different
treatment. In one court case, for example, a mother complained that a man
had wrongfully made her seven-year-old daughter a servant with a seven-
year contract. The mayor's court agreed and returned the child to her mother
"out of charity for the youth of the infant"(1993, p. 66). Hanawalt points to a
second case where neighbors came to the rescue of a child being beaten by
adults. This boy was carrying water near a shop when he was accosted by a
cook and a clerk. Neighbors intervened, but the cook and clerk said they
could beat the boy if they liked. A fight ensued with the neighbors defending the boy (whom they did not know), and the clerk and cook were beaten
up. Later the vanquished bullies sued but lost the case. Neighbors and the
court felt that they deserved the beating they received for mistreating the
youth (1993, p. 67).

Finally, Hanawalt presents a great deal of data on the laws and procedures regarding the care of orphans. The laws and courts monitored the fortunes of orphans, overlooked their estates, and guarded against any abuse or
mistreatment by foster parents. In fact, Hanawalt argues that "London's laws
granted medieval orphans more protection than our own courts give today's
children" (1993, p. 89).

The play of young children and youth.　Hanawalt maintains that London adults
knew that children must and would play. Children "played ball and tag, ran
races, played hoops, and imitated adult ceremonies such as royal entries,
Masses, and marriages" (1993, p. 78). Sadly, much of Hanawalt's support
for claims about children's play come from court or coroner's records of
injuries and deaths. She reports how one young boy fell to his death
when he climbed out a window to retrieve a ball that had landed in the
gutter when he had been playing with it earlier. In another case a seven-
year-old boy was playing with two other boys on pieces of timber when
a piece fell on him and broke his right leg. Using one of her composite
stories, Hanawalt presents a moving account of a third case. In the composite, Hanawalt dramatizes the story of eight-year-old Richard Le Mazon.
Richard was on his way back to school from his midday meal when he joined
up with friends to play a favorite and daring game—hanging by the hands
from a beam that protruded from the side of London Bridge. Richard was
feeling brave on his turn in the game, "but when he swung himself out on

the beam, he felt his hands slipping. As Richard plummeted toward the river, he prayed to St. Nicholas to save him, promising that he would always obey his parents. His satchel pulled him down, and Father Thames claimed another victim" (Hanawalt, 1993, p. 82).

Children's participation in public celebrations and folklore. In addition to the games the children organized among themselves, the urban environment of many cities, including London, prompted a number of parades and pageants that involved children and certainly entertained them. Some celebrations were reserved for children. The most notable was that of the boy bishops, which coincided with St. Nicholas Day. St. Nicholas was a favorite of young students because of a legend about two young boys on their way to study in Athens. One of the boys' fathers had instructed them to stop and visit Bishop Nicholas in the city of Myra. When the boys arrived in Myra, they decided to spend the night at an inn and visit the Bishop the next day. The innkeeper, seeing the boys' wealth, killed them and cut them into little pieces to sell as pickled pork. Bishop Nicholas had a vision of the murder and rushed to the inn. He reprimanded the innkeeper and sought his forgiveness from heaven. Nicholas's wish was granted, and the pieces of the boys emerged from the brine tub and reassembled. The Bishop sent the boys off to Athens amid great rejoicing (Hanawalt, 1993, p. 79).

In the boy bishop celebration, Hanawalt argues, it is the bishops rather than the boys who get disassembled. The best scholar from each school is elected to impersonate the bishop, and the rest of the boys form his clergy. The boys take over the church for the services and sermon, ousting the real bishop. As Hanawalt notes: "It was one of those medieval, world-turned-topsy-turvy events. The boys, whose life seemed all discipline, were given a taste of the power to discipline" (1993, p. 79). The boys traveled in style with ceremonial capes, rings, and crosses, and their clergy stopped at parish homes for offerings, gracious meals, and gifts. It is no wonder that Richard Le Mazon looked forward to the event and aspired to be the boy bishop.

The importance of Hanawalt's study. Hanawalt's historical work on children in medieval London is important for a new sociology of childhood for several reasons. First, it challenges prior work, which claimed that children were treated harshly in the medieval period and that they were forced to enter adult society at an early age with little opportunity to have or enjoy their childhoods. Second, Hanawalt's detailed descriptions of children's play, games, and involvement in public rituals and celebrations show that children created and participated in their own peer cultures as far back as the fourteenth century. Especially interesting in this regard was the children's fascination with St. Nicholas and their clear enjoyment of the boy bishops celebration. In activities like the boy bishops ritual, children gained control over adult authority and celebrated their autonomy in a highly public fashion. As we will see in Chapters 5 through 8, children's challenging of adult authority is also a key feature of the peer cultures of children in contemporary societies. Overall, these aspects of Hanawalt's study demonstrate the value of taking children seriously as active agents in their cultures.

Slave Children in the Pre–Civil War South

Recently, several reports have attempted to reconstruct the lives of slave children, including an article by Lester Alston (1992) entitled "Children as Chattel" and another by David Wiggins (1985) entitled "The Play of Slave Children in the Plantation Communities of the Old South, 1820–1860." These authors rely on narratives, testimonies, autobiographies, and diaries. The bulk of the data comes from the 1936–1938 Federal Writer's Project, which compiled the slave narrative collection. As Wiggins points out, there are some inherent problems with narratives from the Federal Writer's Project. Because nearly two-thirds of the former slaves who were interviewed were eighty or more years old, there is the obvious concern of failing memory. A second problem relates to "the question of whether longevity was the result of unusually good rather than typical treatment as slaves" (1985, p. 174). Also, in recalling childhood memories (probably the best of times for most slaves), there may be a tendency to paint a more favorable picture (especially when compared to memories of their adult lives). Possible biases, procedures, and methods of the predominately white southern interviewers may also come into play. Wiggins argues, however, that the narratives do represent the voices of slaves themselves rather than the speculations of commentators. Let's take a look at the nature of childhood in slavery based on these historical records.

The nature of childhood in slavery. As Alston notes, "children were born into slave communities that were as distinct from the African communities of their forebears as they were from the social communities of their white owners. Their experiences of childhood were shaped by an African American slave subculture that, by the time of the Civil War, was four to six generations old and was peopled by parents and elders who themselves had been born on these shores into slave families and slave communities" (1992, p. 208). A sense of community was central to both adult slaves and their children. Wiggins notes that members of slave quarters viewed themselves "as a familial group" with a "common need to stay together no matter what the circumstances" (1985, p. 174).

Slave mothers worked in the fields until shortly before their babies were born. They were then given a "lying-in period" of just a few days to a few weeks to spend with their newborns before returning to the regular sun-up-to-sun-down work schedule. After that time, care of the infants was given over to older slave women who often functioned as wet nurses. When the children reached toddler age (around two) they were placed in the care of siblings and other children in the slave community. This type of communal child rearing was continued by the practice of having slave children eight to twelve years old tend to younger children (Alston, 1992, p. 211).

Wiggins reports similar patterns of communal child rearing and links it to the work requirements for slave children. Slave children were not expected to work full-time in the fields until about the age of thirteen. Alston argues that this delay was for economic and not humanitarian reasons. He points out that "the (economic) reality was that many slave holders believed that a slowed maturity during childhood guaranteed maximum productivity later, that work during childhood weakened the foundation for physical health in adulthood, and that a slow breaking-in reduced the trauma of going to the fields and facing the whip" (Alston, 1992, p. 360; also see Genovese, 1974, pp. 504–5). During this transition period slave children were expected to perform chores such as hauling water, fetching wood, tending gardens, cleaning the yards, and feeding livestock. The care of younger children was seen as part of these work obligations. An especially interesting aspect of this pattern of communal child care primarily by older siblings and children in the slave community is its striking similarity to child care practices in many regions of contemporary Africa (see Harkness & Super, 1992).

Children's activities and play in slave communities. There was more to the everyday lives of slave children than chores and caretaking. They also had some freedom to explore their physical world and to play. Older children especially had a good deal of autonomy. Boys and, less often, girls also made good use of their explorations by hunting and fishing with peers during the day and with their fathers at night to supplement the quarters' food supply. Not only was hunting and fishing enjoyable, but also it generated feelings of self-worth in the children because of their contributions to the family table. Perhaps more important, such activities also provided limited shared interaction and support between fathers and their children.

Slave children engaged in both traditional and improvised games. They were especially attracted to dramatic role play, a type of play commented on by Hanawalt in her study of children in medieval London. Both Wiggins and Alston believe the evidence strongly suggests that slave children attempted to relieve particular anxieties and fears through the medium of dramatic role play. They especially liked to emulate social events such as church services, funerals, and auctions (Alston, 1992, p. 225). One former slave from Texas described the game of auction, where one child would become the auctioneer and conduct a simulated slave sale. The fact that slave children knew early on that they themselves could be sold and separated from their families certainly displays the power of such play for dealing with fears and anxieties. In another game, "Hiding the Switch," several children would look for a switch hidden by another child. The one who found the switch ran after the others attempting to hit them. The relation of this type of play to certain brutal treatment of adults in many slave quarters should be obvious.

The slave children played a number of organized games like jump rope and various chasing games. However, Wiggins reported the apparent absence of any games that required the elimination of players. "Even the various dodge ball and tagging games played by the children contained designed stratagems within their rule structure that prevented the removal of any participants" (1985, p. 181). Wiggins links this finding to real fears among these children that members of their family (and eventually they themselves) could be "indiscriminately sold or hired out anytime" (1985, p. 181).

Although slave children also frequently participated in games and played together with the white children of the plantation, "a caste system frequently operated within the 'play world' of the slave and white children just as it did in the everyday affairs of the plantation community" (Wiggins, 1985, p. 184). Interview data from the Federal Writer's Project indicates that the white children often took the role of master of the plantation or overseer of slave workers in their play with slave children. Still, slave children were not passive in their play with white playmates. They often took great pride in standing up to the plantation children and especially in outwitting them in verbal play and physical contests. In fact, Wiggins reports that most slave children felt both morally and physically superior to white children. "'We was stronger and knowed how to play, and the white children didn't,' recalled Felix Heywood of Texas" (Wiggins, 1985, p. 185).

Slave children and the new sociology of childhood. The work of Alston and Wiggins contributes importantly to our understanding of the lives of families and children in slavery. It captures the major roles children played in building and maintaining strong communal bonds in slave communities under extremely challenging circumstances. Especially important were older children's contributions to the care and socialization of younger children, which is very similar to child care practices in contemporary African societies. These historical studies also provide insights into how children's play and games can provide secure arenas in which children can deal with anxieties and fears that can be extremely difficult to confront directly. As we will see in Chapters 5 through 8 many routines in the peer cultures of children in contemporary societies serve these same functions. Overall, we see, as we did with the work of Hanawalt, that the documentation of children's activities and lives in the past contributes a great deal to our understanding of history and of children in present-day societies.

American Pioneer and Immigrant Children at the Turn of the Century

Two recent historical studies bring to life the exciting, challenging, and rapidly changing worlds of the American frontier at the end of the nineteenth century and of American cities in the early twentieth century, from the perspectives of children and youth. Elliott West (1992) describes the lives of children who migrated to and settled with their families on the Great Plains (Nebraska, Kansas, the Dakotas, and Oklahoma) in the period from about 1880 to the turn of the century. He relies primarily on diaries to tell the children's stories, but he also makes good use of interviews, autobiographies, and written "reminiscences" of a wide range of the children's experiences. David Nasaw's (1985) study covers approximately the period from the late 1890s until about 1920 and focuses on children's lives in cities across the nation, with a concentration on the large urban areas of the Northeast. The children Nasaw describes were for the most part preadolescents, lower working class, ethnic, and recent immigrants to the United States. His primary materials include detailed reports of children's work activities by child reformers, oral histories, and autobiographies, but he also uses secondary sources such as biographies and novels to supplement and extend his interpretations. These two studies document the important roles children played in their families' economic survival, and they identify the importance of children's autonomy and pioneering spirit as they became the first generation to grow up in a new world.

Children's contributions to family and societal production. The Euro-American conquest of the frontier plains in the last half of the ninteenth century was accomplished primarily by hardworking families. Children contributed significantly to the central tasks of *production* (the breaking, plowing, planting of the land, and caring and harvesting of crops) and *subsistence* (providing food and clothing and caring for daily needs) in bringing about the transformation of the vast plains region. In fact, West argues that children "generally labored at a wider variety of tasks than either mothers or fathers" and in that sense were "the most accomplished and versatile workers of the farming frontier" (1992, p. 30).

Although men usually carried out the physically taxing work of breaking the thickly rooted sod, children were intricately involved in the remaining phases of production. As West notes, the revolution in agricultural technology during this period allowed children to take over some jobs that were previously carried out only by men. Boys and girls as young as eight plowed fields in the spring. West quotes Percy Ebbut, who, as a young child, noted observing full-grown men having much difficulty using old-style plows in his native England, while he "plowed acre after acre from the time I was twelve years old" with a new steel-tipped plow in the fields of his family farm in Kansas (1992, p. 28).

Once fields were plowed and crops planted, children were responsible for their care and protection. They worked "as living scarecrows, patrolling the fields for hours a day, disbursing the grazing cattle and horses, and shooing away the whirling birds that threatened to devour the family's future" (West, 1992, p. 29). Finally, children played a major role at harvest time, with their contributions increasing and becoming more diverse with the advent of new methods. For example, when the horse-drawn thresher arrived, "a small girl might lead the animals around the circle, while one brother cut the bands of sheaves about to be threshed and another kept the machine cleared of straw to keep it from clogging" (West, 1992, p. 29).

The children's contributions to the families' subsistence was probably even more important than their work in farm production. Girls and boys helped in preparing and caring for gardens. However, it was mainly girls who helped with household chores (cooking, cleaning, and so on) and mainly boys who tended to farm chores (tending cattle, haying, and so on). Both boys and girls supplemented the family food supply by gathering wild plants, fruit and berries, and by hunting and fishing. Adults, according to West, had little time for hunting. Children, on the other hand, "some as young as seven or eight," stalked and killed "antelopes, raccoons, ducks, geese, deer, prairie chickens, bison, wild hogs, and, above all, rabbits" (West, 1992, p. 30). As was the case for the slave children discussed earlier, the children of the frontier felt a sense of autonomy, as well as pride for their contributions to the family—all while they were having fun!

Like the children on the plains frontier, working-class urban children contributed in important ways to the economic health of their families. At the turn of the century most working- and lower-class children of American cities moved from full-time work to schooling because of child labor laws. However, these children continued to work both in and outside the home for the majority of their nonschool hours. Like farm children, these girls and boys worked in a wide variety of jobs. Some of these jobs were the urban equivalents of those performed by children of the plains frontier. In addition to foraging for food (in this case discarded and decaying fruits and vegetables, and stale bread and bakery goods) urban children also scavenged backyards, alleyways, train yards, construction sites, and most especially city dumps for anything of value: rags, old furniture and dishes, bottles, tires, pieces of wood, metal, and coal. At first glance, scavenging and junking in inner cities would seem much less enjoyable than collecting berries, hunting, and fishing on the frontier. However, as Nasaw observes, children felt a sense of autonomy scavenging in the streets and dumps. He cites the photographer Lewis Hine, who observed that dumps (especially those that contained only nondecaying refuse) were natural meeting places for children. "Since no adults frequented the dumps except the hoboes, who were seldom any trouble," noted Hine, the children could do as they pleased: run and chase, dig for buried treasure, build forts, "start a warming fire or throw rocks at old bottles without raising the ire of property owners or the cops'" (as quoted in Nasaw, 1985, p. 93).

Although girls engaged in scavenging and in the types of work we discuss below, their primary work responsibilities kept them near or in the home. Because they lacked modern conveniences, their work responsibilities were many and varied, and were extremely challenging. Household chores required hours of preparation and multiple steps:

> The laundry had to be done by hand from beginning to end: sorted, soaked, rubbed against the washboard, rinsed, boiled, rinsed again, wrung out, starched, hung to dry, ironed with irons heated on the stove, folded, and put away. Cooking involved not only preparing the food and cooking it but hauling coal for the fire, dumping the ashes afterwards, and keeping the cast-iron stove cleaned, blacked, and rust-free. Housecleaning was complicated by the soot, grime, and ashes released by coal-burning stoves and kerosene and gas lamps. Shopping had to be done daily and in several different shops; there were no refrigerators to store food purchased earlier in the week and no supermarkets for one-stop marketing. (Nasaw, 1985, p. 105)

The household work did not end here, however, as many families had boarders to look after and took in "homework" (usually involving sewing or sorting of various goods) from jobbers and contractors. This work was done by mothers, but always with help from daughters. In addition to helping with all these demanding chores, girls as young as seven years old assumed their major responsibilities as "little mothers" (Nasaw, 1985, pp. 101–114). These girls took full responsibility for younger siblings, often while tending to other chores like shopping. "In many working-class families," argues Nasaw, "the babies and small children were effectively raised by their older sisters" (1985, p. 107).

Unlike the plains frontier, where technology expanded the role of children in family production and income, in American cities at the turn of the century technological change, industrialization, and growing urbanization continually created and eliminated part-time jobs outside the family for children (Nasaw, 1985, pp. 39–47). Early in the period, retail businesses and working-class children were perfectly suited for each other. Children needed and wanted part-time work, and shopkeepers and department store owners needed children to run errands, carry messages, and deliver goods. For example, in large department stores "cash" boys and girls carried the item sold and the customer's money to an inspector, who took the money and sent the children back with a wrapped package and change. By the turn of the century, however, these jobs were all eliminated as the "pneumatic tube [a device in which receipts and money could be transferred by air pressure from sales clerks to cashiers], followed swiftly by cash registers at each sales counter, made the children superfluous" (Nasaw, 1985, p. 43).

As quickly as jobs were eliminated, however, children were able to find others. Many jobs were created by the rapid rate of urbanization. With the expansion of streetcar lines and the growing concentration of white-collar workers in central cities, retailers gained an ever-increasing number of customers. Many children were willing to work for retailers in a range of capacities. Others, however, struck out on their own to practice capitalism without the constraints of bosses, supervisors, or even regular hours. Nasaw refers to these children as the "littlest hustlers" who sold candy, gum, fruit, flowers, and just about anything their adult customers would buy. Many of the adults on the streets of the big cities—businessmen on their way to and from work and well-to-do patrons of large department stores—were very different from the adults of the working-class, immigrant neighborhoods of the children.

Perhaps the most famous of all the little hustlers were the "newsies" whose rise and fall is captured in the following case study.

The Newsies

David Nasaw (1985) notes that the rise of a new generation of newspaper hustlers was a product of the boom in afternoon circulation that had been building through the 1880s and 1890s but took off during the Spanish-American War. The morning papers that had been the mainstay of the industry had, by the turn of the century, been eclipsed by the late editions. By 1900, "evening papers, bought on the way home from work, outnumbered morning papers . . . about three to one" (pp. 62–63). Because of such growing demand and the fact that the customers came to the paper rather than vice versa, twentieth century newsies were able to transform what was once full-time work into part-time jobs that conveniently fit their after-school work hours.

Newsies bought papers from circulation managers of various publishers and worked as independent contractors. Thus, they had a great deal of autonomy "to set their own schedules, establish their own pace, and work when and where they chose" (p. 67). In fact, argues Nasaw, they "experienced more autonomy at work than in school or at home" (p. 67). Still, newsies had to sell all the papers they contracted for in order to make a profit; adult distributors had no pity on children who could not get the job done. The boys (and some girls) had to come up with a "stake" to buy their initial supply of papers, and often borrowed money from parents, siblings or friends. The profits from the first batch of papers were then used to keep going and, in most cases, to begin a profitable career as a newsie. Physical, cognitive, and social skills had to be developed and sharpened in order for a child to become a successful newsie. Newsies also developed strategies to pitch their wares successfully. One such strategy was the well-known "Extra! Extra! Read all about it!" chant, which was designed to capture the attention of potential customers. In most cases, real news was simply exaggerated a bit for extra impact, but newsies were not above true fabrication (Nasaw, 1985, p. 78).

Newsies also often used the "last paper ploy," pretending to be hungry, cold, and exhausted as they conned sympathetic adults to buy the last paper. Once the customer moved out of sight, another paper was pulled out and the routine was repeated. Newsies also had a wide range of strategies to cajole tips from customers, often by claiming to lack needed change.

Newsies were so good at their trade that they were in great demand and were often courted by the major newspaper publishers. In fact, the newsies became so powerful and organized that they formed a union and went on strike against the major New York publishers Joseph Pulitzer and William Randolph Hearst in 1899 in protest of a rise in the prices of papers. The publishers did not take the strike seriously at first, but as the newsies held the line and garnered public support, the publishers decided to offer a settlement. As Nasaw notes, by "unionizing and striking to protect their rights and their profits, the children were behaving precisely as they believed American workers should when treated unjustly" (1985, p. 181). Thus, the children were playing an active and major role in their own socialization in preparation for the adult world they were about to enter.

Autonomy, activity, and social reproduction. In Chapter 1 we discussed the notion of interpretive reproduction and the idea of children's evolving membership in their culture. As illustrated in the orb web model, children enter the culture through the family, but come to collectively produce and participate in a series of peer cultures. In this view children do not simply develop as individuals; they collectively produce peer cultures and contribute to the reproduction of the wider society or culture. The cyclical processes in the weaving of the web are always situated in cultural time and space. Major cultural or societal changes create reverberations in the web that are experienced differently across generations. Especially important is the idea that children often contribute to two cultures (children's and adults') *simultaneously.* Children of the plains and cities of turn-of-the-century America, like the Hausa children studied by Shildkrout (1975), whom we discussed in Chapter 2, were active, here-and-now contributors to their families' subsistence.

The experiences and perspectives of parents and children on the plains frontier and in American cities at the turn of the century aptly demonstrate how the process of interpretive reproduction unfolds. In both cases families were relocated in new worlds. Adults continued to weave their webs, but their foundation consisted of new cultural fields that brought with them new demands and challenges. The demands of this new place and time were, however, always perceived and acted upon through a lens that focused on past experiences in other places and times. Adult migrants to the frontier and immigrants to the big cities of a new country had high hopes for a new beginning and better lives for themselves and their children. They could not and did not, however, leave their pasts behind—they always retained memories of "family, friends, the millions of details that made up the familiar world of their origins" (West, 1992, p. 32). These adults tended *to retrospect on their pasts* in dealing with challenges of their new world, including the raising of their children.

The children of the plains frontier and the cities were, on the other hand, highly engaged in weaving their webs from a present-day perspective. They were native to the frontier and the city "with no memory, no longing, no historic commitment to another land, another way of life" (Nasaw, 1985, p. 195). As West notes, "They were not 'far from home,' they *were* home" (1992, p. 33). As a result they actively engaged their worlds with energy, excitement, and true pioneer spirit. When not caught up in the moment, children of the frontier and city did not look back, but looked forward, spurred on by goals and dreams that were developing in their childhoods.

As we noted earlier in discussing the orb web model, one of its most instructive features is that it reminds us that we do not leave experiences in childhood behind with maturity and development. "We live our lives," argues Nasaw, "moving forward to catch the possibilities we set before us as children." In this sense, the lessons the children learned on the city streets and frontier plains of turn-of-the-century America "were not interred with their childhoods, but were cast forward to frame their perceptions of the society they would join as adults" (1985, p. 198).

Summary

The major goal of this chapter has been to place the new sociology of children into historical context. In doing so we examined Ariès's highly original and groundbreaking work on the changing conceptions of childhood and children's changing place in society from the Middle Ages to the eighteenth century. Ariès saw a general movement from a lack of awareness of an idea of childhood, to a coddling period where children were idolized and valued as a source of amusement for adults, to a moralistic period in which childhood was seen as a period of training and discipline in preparation for adult life. Ariès did not see these changes as inevitable, but rather related to shifts in institutional arrangements in European societies such as the move from extended to more nuclear families and the emergence of age-graded schools. Overall, Ariès bemoaned the general separations by class and race that have occurred in modern societies.

Unfortunately, many others working in the area of the history of childhood and the family concentrated primarily on Ariès's ideas of changes in conceptions of childhood, pushing them much further to propose grand-stage theories of the family. These theories maintain that there are universal (and, in some cases, predestined) stages in the evolution of the family, children, and childhood. This work has been criticized by Pollock and other historians for its sweeping claims, its reliance on indirect evidence (such as paintings, religious tracts, and letters), and its unsystematic historical analysis. In her own work, relying on more direct sources (such as diaries, newspaper reports, and court records), Pollock found a great deal of support for the idea of continuity in conceptions of children, parental care, and parental-child relations over time. Although Pollock does not offer a satisfactory theoretical explanation for such continuity, her work, along with that of Ariès, influenced many other historians to focus more directly on children's collective actions and contributions to past societies and to seek out sound historical evidence which bore on these concerns.

We referred to this work as the new history of childhood and examined several examples, including Hanawalt's study of children in medieval London, the research of Alston and Wiggins on slave children in the Pre–Civil War South, West's study of pioneer children on the American Great Plains in the 1880s, and Nasaw's depiction of children in American cities at the turn of the century. The historical narratives in all these studies bring children to life and show that they were influential actors in past societies. However, the importance of these studies goes beyond their documentation of children's contributions to the historical record. They are also vitally important for seeing children as actively contributing to societal production and change while simultaneously creating their own child cultures. In this sense, they help us better understand the notion of interpretive reproduction introduced in Chapter 1 which stressed the importance and complexity of children's collective actions in both the adult world and in their own peer cultures.

4

Social Change, Families, and Children

Examining Changes in Families from the Children's Perspective

In Chapter 3 we placed the new sociology of childhood in its historical context. In this chapter our focus will be on children in families. We'll look at how children and childhood are affected by recent social changes in families, and we'll examine the growing diversity of families in both industrialized and developing societies. Increased divorce rates, the rise of single-mother and blended families, the increase in nonmarital births, and the growing gap between the rich and poor all have had profound effects on children. Some lament what they see as the breakdown of the traditional *family* and family values; others argue that *families* are going through an important period of adjustment and redefinition.

Although children are often used to frame the discourse, the voices of children are seldom heard amidst the polemic posturing on both sides of the debate. Furthermore, the effects of changes in families on children's everyday lives are seldom considered. We often hear the refrain from conservatives that we must cut government spending (most especially for welfare programs) for the future of our children. However, there seems to be much less concern for children's lives *today*—for their childhoods—especially the childhoods of working-class and poor children. This focus on children's futures serves as an excellent example of what the Finnish sociologist Leena Alanen (1990) has referred to as "children negatively defined." By this she means that children are defined primarily by what they are going to be and not by what they presently are. We will return to join this debate about children's lives and futures in the last three chapters of the book.

Some sociologists who take a more liberal position argue for the redefinition of families. They focus primarily on adults' adjustments to changing family roles, especially those made by women. Ruth Sidel (1986) has demonstrated that women and children often come last; by this she means that they are most negatively affected by postindustrial change. Still, one yearns to hear more of the voices of young children in theoretical and empirical work by those who call for family redefinition. Sociologist Judith Stacey (1991) impressively traces the attempts of two working-class families to cope with domestic upheaval by carving out wide-ranging, supportive kin networks. Stacey's research focused primarily on two women whose children were grown and had started families of their own. These grown children often were still dependent on their parents and in-laws, and on each other as they struggled with unemployment, drug addiction, family conflict and abuse, and failed aspirations. We learn much about the adult kin in these two families, but the young grandchildren are rarely identified by gender or name, nor are they given the opportunity to present their perspective of their families' lives. At one point some of the grandchildren are referred to as being part of a "too rapidly increasing brood" (Stacey, 1991, p. 202); at another point they are called "contraceptive failures" that "ensnared [their mother] in a family life that was a continual series of traumas and abuse" (Stacey, 1991, p. 225). Surely such an example of "blaming the victim" is no more acceptable when applied to children than it is when applied to women.

Undoubtedly, Stacey does not intend to blame children for their circumstances, and she is not alone in her oversight of children's perspectives. All those who comment on the difficulties families face in contemporary societies must step back a bit from their struggles to preserve or redefine postindustrial families to appreciate more fully *how these struggles affect the childhoods of children of the present.*

Our goal must be to bring children back into our conceptualizations of social change and families. In this chapter, we will consider some of the research on young children's experiences in families in both Western and non-Western or developing societies. We will focus on work carried out primarily in the United States and some Western European societies and in several developing societies, most especially Africa. We'll also examine how social changes in Western and developing societies are affecting childhood. Here the focus is less on specific children and the texture of their everyday lives and more on general experiences of children as a social group to discover how their childhoods have been affected by key social and economic changes in families since the turn of the century.

Children's Everyday Lives in Families

Most studies on children in families concentrate primarily on socialization and on developmental outcomes. For example, there is a long history of research in psychology on the effects of attachment and emotional bonding, socialization practices and parenting styles, family disruption, and the role of media events in the family on individual development. Sociologists who study families have also investigated these topics, but they usually view them as intervening variables that are affected by social, structural, and cultural conditions and by the processes of social change. Although they are important, we will not review studies such as these; instead we will examine studies that investigate children's actual experiences and participation in family life. We look first at such studies in Western, industrialized societies.

Studies of Families in Western Societies

A few months after my daughter learned to walk, she liked to practice her new mobility by climbing up and onto what seemed to us to be very dangerous places. My wife and I often took to removing her from atop chairs and other furniture, placing her back on solid ground, and admonishing her about the danger of such behavior. After several repetitions of such episodes, I heard her call out to me one day, and when I turned to look she was standing at the very top of the back of a large cushioned chair. I gasped and jumped up to get her down, but I still had to chuckle at the large smile on her gleeful face. She was clearing communicating, "Hey Daddy, look what I did this time!"

In her book *The Beginnings of Social Understanding*, psychologist Judy Dunn links episodes such as this one to children's development of humor, referring to the incidents as "amusement of forbidden acts." In her observational studies of young children's behavior in the family, Dunn found that such amusement of forbidden acts increased dramatically from about 1.5 incidents in two hours at the age of four months to an average of 6.1 in two hours at the age of fourteen months (Dunn, 1988, p. 154). Perhaps more important, the children were four times more likely to express amusement at their own transgressions than they were to express it at those of other people. We can see that a key feature of children's peer cultures, one we discussed in Chapter 2—to challenge the authority of adults—begins at a very early age.

Dunn is one of a very few psychologists or sociologists who actually study young children in the family in Western societies. As Dunn notes, children rarely have been studied in the world in which they develop or in a context in which we can capture the subtleties of social understanding. There are at least two reasons for the lack of research on children's everyday life in the family. The first is methodological, and the second has more to do with ethics and practicality. In the social sciences, research methods are normally of two different types: positivist or interpretive. Positivist approaches stress the importance of investigating causal relations between social and psychological variables and in formulating and testing hypotheses under controlled conditions. Interpretive approaches stress the importance of meaning or interpretive understanding of social processes (that is, what the processes "mean" from the perspective of the social participants involved) and favor the direct study of these processes in natural settings. The positivist thrust of most social science has led researchers to carry out their studies of children in experimental settings with precise controls that give them the ability to test specific hypotheses. However, even researchers who take an interpretive approach rarely have studied children in the family in Western society. The lack of study of family interaction and process even by interpretive researchers is related to how the privacy of family life is valued in most Western societies. Researchers face a good deal of resistance and must confront challenging ethical issues when attempting to set up camp in the family. Still, we are beginning to see more observational and ethnographic studies of the family, and we are learning more about children's participation in family life. In this respect Dunn's work on young children's involvement in family life with parents and siblings is groundbreaking (1988; Dunn & Kendrick, 1982). It represents one of the few attempts in developmental psychology to examine closely the importance of interpersonal relations in the context of family life for young children's social and emotional development.

Dunn used a combination of observational and interview methods to capture key processes in children's socioemotional development between the ages of one and three. Dunn found strong evidence for the rapid growth of assertive and resistant behavior by children in their second year in dealings with parents and siblings. These behaviors, in turn, led to conflicts and the display of emotions. Dunn relates these findings to children's discovery of misbehavior (including emotional displays) as a means of gaining control over their parents. Dunn further develops the theoretical significance of these findings by arguing that the "urgency of self-assertion in the face of powerful others increases along with the child's understanding" (1988, p. 176). Indeed, according to Dunn, children's self-interest drives much of their behavior in these early years. Dunn argues, however, that it is not that young children simply want their way; it is rather that they want to be effective members of their families. In this view "children are motivated to understand the social rules and relationships of their cultural world *because they need to get things done in their family relationships*" (1988, p. 189).

In addition to Dunn's research, many important studies of adult-young child interaction in families have focused on language development. Many of the early studies in this area were restricted to tape recordings of children's spontaneous language use over the first three years of life. The aim was to document children's development of the form and function of language. Later studies moved to a broader focus on children's development of communicative competence through their involvement in everyday cultural routines in families with both parents and siblings (Dunn & Kendrick, 1982;

Haight & Miller, 1993; Heath, 1983; Miller, Potts, Fung, Hoogstra, & Mintz, 1990; Ochs, 1988; Schieffelin, 1990; Schieffelin & Ochs, 1986; Zukow, 1989).

In Chapter 1 we discussed the importance of language and children's involvement in everyday cultural routines for interpretive reproduction. Recent work by the psychologist Peggy Miller and her colleagues brings these theoretical notions to life through the careful observation and analysis of language practices in families. Miller examines *narrative practices*, the term she uses to describe stories that provide family members with "widely available means by which" they "create, interpret, and publicly project culturally constituted images of self in face-to-face interaction" (Miller, Potts, Fung, Hoogstra, & Mintz, 1990, p. 294). Miller and her colleagues argue that children develop "a means of expressing and understanding who they are through their routine participation in culturally organized narrative practices in which personal experiences are recounted" (1990, p. 295). The emphasis on collective practices is important. Unlike conventional approaches, which focus on how various experiences in families affect children's individual development, *this interpretive approach stresses children's active involvement in the joint creation of family experiences through their very participation in families*. We learn not only about potential outcomes, but also about how children participate in and contribute to the creation of their own childhoods in families. Let's look at an example from Miller's research in working-class families in the eastern United States.

Amy Sticks Up for Her Mom

In the following story, told in the presence of twenty-three-month-old Amy and her five-year-old cousin, Kris, Amy's mother, Marlene, relates to the researcher an event involving her boyfriend, Johnny, whom Amy habitually calls "Daddy." The story focuses on Amy's clever, assertive retort to Johnny's efforts to prod her into teasing her mother (bold words indicate stress).

Mother:	Johnny told her the other night, he says to her, "Isn't your mother a creep?"
Amy:	Mar! Mar!
Mother:	And he kept tellin' her all these things and she says: "**Na** huh." She says, "**You** are, Daddy. **You're** the creep."
Researcher:	(Laughs)
Mother:	That's what she told him. He like to come off that chair.

Amy:	(Now sitting close to her mother on the sofa) Mar!
Mother:	Yeah.
Amy:	Yeah.
Mother :	Yeah, he says, "Tell your mother she's a creep." And finally she's just sittin' there takin' it and takin' it and he said, "Tell her, tell your mother she's a creep." That's when she said, "**Nuh** uh, Daddy." She said, "**You're** the creep."

Source: Adapted from Miller, Potts, Fung, Hoogstra, & Mintz, 1990, p. 296

A number of elements in this case study are important for understanding how such narratives can be seen as excellent examples of interpretive reproduction in families. Telling stories about young children relays information about the importance and organization of their experiences. Thus, by "consistently telling stories about some experiences rather than others, caregivers convey which ones are reportable. By creating a particular rendition of the experience, they show what the component events are, how the events are related, and what is important about them" (Miller, Potts, Fung, Hoogstra, & Mintz, 1990, p. 297). For example, Miller found in her work with these working-class families that they valued their children being able to stick up for themselves, especially in response to frequent adult teasing (Miller, 1982; 1986). In fact, such teasing was viewed as good preparation for interaction with peers and other adults. In this case, Amy not only resisted Johnny's playful teasing but also demonstrated "quick-witted assertiveness" (especially for a two-year-old), which was the main "point" of the story (1990, p. 297).

Such narratives also are multifunctional. The mother is able to convey to Miller the developing communicative competence of her daughter, the nature of her close relationship with her boyfriend (Amy calls him Daddy and feels comfortable in teasing him, and Johnny accepts being put in his place), and her valuing of assertiveness in her child. Amy is present throughout the story and seems attentive to the fact that she is being singled out in a positive way, "as someone whose experiences are tellable" (1990, p. 297).

In this and other studies Miller pursued the implications of such narrative practices by examining cases where children intervened in narratives produced by their parents. She found that by the age of two-and-a-half, children were four times more likely to intervene and make comments in stories about themselves than in other stories. She also found that children appropriate stories they have heard and reproduce them in other settings (Miller, Potts, Fung, Hoogstra, & Mintz, 1990, pp. 298–305; also see Miller & Sperry, 1988; Miller & Moore, 1989).

Overall, in this important observational work of Dunn, Miller, and others, families are conceptualized as local cultures (see Gubrium & Holstein, 1990) in which young children actively participate, contribute to their own socialization, and affect the participation of adults. Such capturing of important productive-reproductive processes in families is made possible by the use of interpretive ethnographic methods. Earlier we noted that interpretive research methods stress the importance of meaning and understanding social processes from the participants' perspectives. Interpretive ethnographic methods involve the careful entry into natural settings like families and peer groups, observing over long periods of time, and capturing the meaning of social processes from the perspective of those studied. Such methods are becoming more common in research on families and children in Western societies. However, they have long been employed by anthropologists to understand family life and socialization processes in non-Western cultures. It is to a consideration of such research that we now turn.

Studies of Families in Non-Western Societies

A number of recent, important, cross-cultural studies of early socialization in the family share a definite affinity with the work of Dunn and Miller. A central feature of this work is the focus on children's development of communicative competence through their involvement in everyday cultural routines within families (Briggs, 1992; Ochs, 1988; Schieffelin, 1990; Schieffelin & Ochs, 1986; Watson-Gegeo & Gegeo, 1986).

Elinor Ochs's (1988) study of culture and language development in a Samoan village captures many of the strengths of this cross-cultural research. Ochs maintains that participants in verbal interactions draw on linguistic and sociocultural knowledge to create and define what is taking place in any given interactive event. For example, Ochs notes that findings from studies of middle-class families in the United States illustrate that American adults do not hesitate "to guess" at what children are trying to communicate in situations of ambiguity. In such instances, adults offer up reformulations of unclear speech for children to confirm or disconfirm. Although clarification frequently occurs in adult-child interaction in Samoa (and in some rare cases involves guessing and reformulation), Samoan adults show a clear preference for a "minimal-grasp" strategy in which they "initiate clarification of children's utterances through quizzical expressions, statements of nonunderstanding, WH questions [for example, "Where's Daddy," "What are you doing"], and other directives, to elicit from the child a reformulation of all or part of the unclear utterance or gesture" (Ochs, 1988, p. 136).

Although this difference in strategies of clarification may seem minor or even trivial, it is reflective of major differences between Samoan and American society and demonstrates how children's conversations with caregivers are socially and culturally organized. The white middle-class American style of clarification reflects our society's beliefs that a speaker's *intentions* are critical to the interpretation of his utterances or actions. This is evident in the American legal system, where the notion of intent is important in the characterization of crimes and accompanying sanctions. Ochs argues that this orientation "leads members to take seriously and pursue establishing an individual's motivations and psychological states" (1988, p. 141). Samoans generally display a strong dispreference for guessing at what is going on in another person's mind, and in the Samoan legal arena actions are "assessed almost exclusively in terms of social and economic losses and disturbances" (1988, p. 141). However, personal intentions are important in communicative situations when the speaker is of high social status. At political meetings, for example, high chiefs and high-status orators are entitled to voice personal opinions. In these situations, those of lower status often *guess* about personal intentions when ambiguities arise. Such guessing rarely is directed toward lower-ranking individuals, such as those involved in caretaker-child interactions. In fact, given the low status of children, such guessing is seen not only as inappropriate but also as not worth the time. Because Samoans believe that children learn by listening to and watching (over and over) indications that their actions or responses need clarification, adults elicit redoings and resayings through simple clarification requests.

Although work on sibling relations in Western societies has appeared only recently, there is a long history of the study of sibling interaction in other societies (Harkness & Super, 1992; Nsamenang, 1992a; Weisner & Gallimore, 1977; Zukow, 1989). In a fascinating study of socialization practices of the Kalui people of Papua New Guinea, Bambi Schieffelin (1990) found clear differences in the way mothers encouraged interaction between same-sex and opposite-sex siblings. Same-sex siblings are encouraged to cooperate, and mothers urge younger children to seek the help and company of older siblings just as they urge older children to comply with the wishes of their younger siblings. However, cooperation is not fostered between opposite-sex siblings, and younger brothers are actually encouraged to tease, provoke, and even hit their older sisters.

Schieffelin argues that these differences in parental socialization practices not only affect the nature of sibling relations, but also prepare children for sibling relations, gender identities, and male-female relations in adult life.

Whereas men in Kalui society establish cooperative and egalitarian roles with other men (especially brothers), they are socialized to develop an orientation of entitlement regarding the attention and support of women. Schieffelin refers to this process as men coming to "feel owed." Women, on the other hand, are given less attention as children and "learn quickly that 'feeling owed' as a general orientation is neither valued nor appropriate for them" (1990, p. 248). As a result women are the givers of the society, "responding to the appeals and demands of others, particularly men and children; less often women" (1990, p. 249).

In Africa the long tradition of having multiple caregivers for young children is captured in the proverb "It takes a village to raise a child." This idea runs counter to Western theories of child development, which support the notion of *attachment*. These theories hold that the child must establish a strong bond with a primary caretaker (normally the mother) for healthy emotional development. In their study of the Efe (Pygmies) of Northeastern Zaire, Edward Tronick, Gilda Morelli, and Steve Winn (1987) documented a distinctive pattern of multiple caretaker child care. Efe infants spend a large percentage of time away from their mothers, who return to work in the fields only a few days after giving birth. At the work site, child-care responsibilities are generally shared by several individuals. The infants are nursed by several women, including the mother. In fact, argue Tronick, Morelli, and Winn, "almost all females attempt to comfort a distressed or fussy infant." Such comforting "includes allowing the infant to suckle and often occurs in the mother's presence. But if unsuccessful the infant is returned to the mother" (1987, p. 99).

Given certain ecological factors, such as the low temperature of the forests in which they dwell, the small size of the infants, cultural values, and their unique cultural history, some researchers see many highly beneficial physical, emotional, and social outcomes of multiple caregiving by the Efe (Tronick, Morelli, & Winn, 1987, p. 104). These researchers propose that multiple caretaking in the Efe "may function to teach infants about culturally appropriate styles of interactions as well as to expose infants to the culture's valuation of cooperation, mutual support, and gregariousness" (1990, p. 103).

Similar patterns of multiple caregiving, most especially of young children by older siblings and peers, can be seen in other parts of Africa. Bame Nsamenang describes traditional child care in Cameroon in West-Central Africa as a "social enterprise in which parents, kin, sometimes neighbors and friends, and older children were active participants" (1992a, p. 422). He notes, however, that fathers are never assigned routine caretaking duties, and once the children are weaned mothers turn most of the care over to older siblings or peers. The typical pattern is for fathers to be involved in animal husbandry, clearing and fencing farmland, and building dwellings, while mothers are responsible for childrearing, food production and processing, and homekeeping. This pattern bears striking similarity to the one described by Alston and Wiggins in their work on child care by slave children in the Pre–Civil War South of the United States, which we discussed in Chapter 3.

The younger, five-to-six-year-old Cameroonian children take on progressively demanding chores such as running errands, fetching water and firewood, and tending animals under the direction of older children. Nsamenang points out the strong communal ethos of these groups and notes that peer cultures involving both work and play emerged. He argues further that this pattern of peer socialization and training "seemed relevant and appropriate for the requirements of a subsistent, agrarian economy. The close texture of traditional life and the courtesies and human warmth it engendered and fostered, supported individuals and families" (1992a, p. 426).

Similar patterns of multi-age peer caregiving have been documented in the East African countries of Kenya, Tanzania, and Uganda. In these societies infants as young as one to three months are often turned over to child nurses, usually young girls between six and ten years of age. These child nurses serve as primary caregivers; the mothers normally return to full-time agricultural work (Harkness & Super, 1992). Although these caretaking practices may seem neglectful by Western standards, the actual pattern of caregiving by child nurses and mothers is quite indulgent. In fact, a comparative study of the caretaking behavior of American mothers and the Kipsigis of Kenya showed "that the African babies received three times the *amount* of attention of the U.S. babies, whereas [the] mothers' *rate* of attention in both samples were similar" (Harkness & Super, 1992, p. 453, italics added). Furthermore, East African caretakers believe that infants should be responded to quickly when they are fussy. As Harkness and Super note, "it would be unthinkable in the East African context for a baby to cry itself to sleep; this U.S. custom is considered abusive by East Africans" (1992, p. 453). Finally, as was the case for indigenous caretaking practices in Cameroon, the responsibilities given to older siblings and peers in caring for younger children are seen as an "*apprenticeship system* in which women and men are well trained in parental roles by the time they actually have children of their own" (1992, p. 454). Here we see a parallel to the "little mothers" of turn-of-the-century American cities, which were described by Nasaw in Chapter 3. Unfortunately, the comforting sense of traditional community and collective responsibility that occurred as a result of these indigenous child-care practices have recently been disrupted by major economic and social changes in Africa and much of the Third World (Bradshaw & Wallace, 1996).

The Effects of Recent Socioeconomic Changes on Children and Childhood in Western Societies

In Chapter 1 we saw that children enter into their society or culture through the family and that families play a central role in children's early lives. As we saw in Chapter 3, the structure of the family and family processes were both alike and different on the plains frontier and in large cities in turn-of-the-century America. Both frontier and big city families were large, and children were expected to begin to contribute to their families' economic well-being from an early age. Children in frontier families were directly involved in the subsistence economy of the farms, while city children contributed their labor both at home and in employment as newsies, delivery boys and girls, and scavengers. American families have changed dramatically since the turn of the century, and these changes have brought about major transformations in the everyday lives of young children. The most dramatic changes have been the decline of two-parent farm families and change in family size, coupled with an increase in mothers' labor force participation and in the number of mother-only families. Although this book focuses primarily on childhood up to and including preadolescence, in considering these trends in family structure we will focus on adolescence as well. Let's discuss each of these changes in turn.

The Rapid Decline of Two-Parent Farm Families

As we discussed earlier, the shift from an agricultural to an industrialized economy in Western societies brought about major changes in families. In the United States these economic changes led to a dramatic family reorganization in a relatively short period of time. In 1830 nearly 70 percent of children lived in two-parent farm families, but by 1930 this percentage had dropped to less than 30 percent. During the same 100-year period, the number of children living in nonfarm families with breadwinner fathers and homemaker mothers increased from 15 percent to 55 percent, and in 1930 this was the most prevalent type of family organization (see Exhibit 4.1). Children no longer worked side by side with their parents and siblings, contributing to the family livelihood. Now fathers spent their workdays away from the home while mothers remained home to care for their children and perform domestic work (Hernandez, 1994, p. 4).

This change did not mean, however, that children and youth no longer worked. It was the *nature* of children's work that changed. For example, there was an almost complete reversal of teenage employment in what Ellen Greenberger and Laurence Steinberg (1986) term the "old" workplace (crafts,

EXHIBIT 4.1

Children Aged 0–17 in Farm Families, Father-as-Breadwinner Families, and Dual-Earner Families: 1790–1989

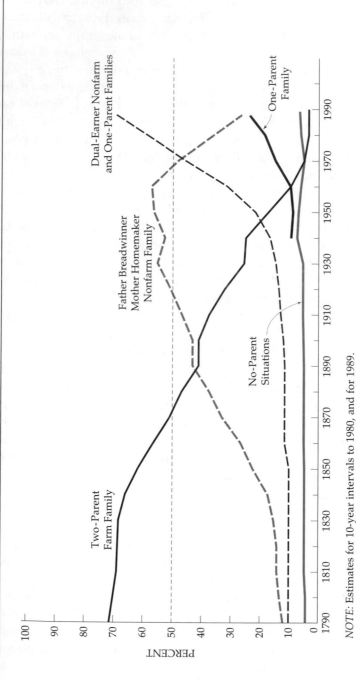

NOTE: Estimates for 10-year intervals to 1980, and for 1989.

Source: Hernandez, 1993a, p. 103. Copyright © by Russell Sage Foundation. Reprinted with permission of Russell Sage Foundation. (Original data from Census PUMs for 1940–1980, CPS for 1980 and 1989, and Appendix 4.1.)

factory, and farm) and the "new" workplace (service and sales) in the United States between 1940 and 1980. Today in industrialized societies fewer after-school and summer jobs are available that provide the kinds of experiences that enhance childhood and adolescence or prepare children and youth for the transition to adulthood. In fact, two jobs in particular (store clerks and food service workers) constituted "the core of the new adolescent work-place" for in-school workers in the 1980s (Greenberger & Steinberg, 1986, p. 63). It is a safe assumption that this trend has continued to grow in the 1990s.

On an intuitive level most adults believe that for today's youth, work—even though clearly different from that of the past—is still valuable and clearly preferable to many other activities. Greenberger and Steinberg present a set of observational, interview, and survey findings that clearly challenge this view. They found, for example, that "working is more likely to interfere with than enhance schooling; promotes pseudomaturity rather than maturity; is associated in certain circumstances with higher, not lower, rates of delinquency and drug and alcohol use; and fosters cynical rather than re-spectful attitudes toward work" (1986, p. 235). They link these negative ef-fects to the fact that the new youth workplace is educationally irrelevant, economically unnecessary, and largely age-segregated.

Of course, many American children and youth have to work to supple-ment meager family incomes. These youth have less opportunities in sales and service positions as compared to middle-class youth, however, because many service and retail businesses have relocated from downtown areas to suburban shopping malls in American cities. In fact, low-income minority youth face high rates of unemployment, and many of those who do find work tend to work thirty-five or more hours per week while continuing their schooling (Lewin-Epstein, 1981). Limited employment opportunities for poor youth in the United States has led some criminologists to argue that a significant percentage of criminal activity, especially that related to the drug trade, can be seen as a form of employment (see Hagan, 1994).

The Decline in Family Size

Children also have been affected by a dramatic shift in family size during the past 100 years. Although there was a brief lull in this shift during the baby boom period of 1945 to 1957 (see Exhibit 4.2), it was more than offset by the baby bust period in later years. (This trend toward lower fertility and smaller families is even stronger in most European countries.)

This shift in family size has drastically reduced the number of siblings who are available for companionship. Without siblings to integrate them into informal neighborhood activities and children's cultures, children find they

EXHIBIT 4.2

Median Number of Siblings in a Typical American Family, 1865–1994

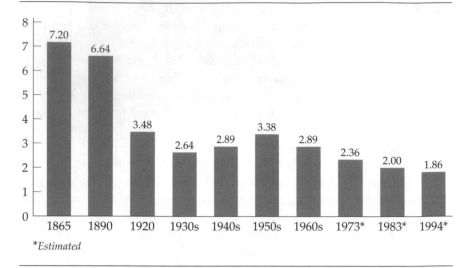

*Estimated

Source: Hernandez, 1993, p. 34, copyright by Russell Sage Foundation. Reprinted with permission
of Russell Sage Foundation.

have to rely more on parents. Because parental work demands have also increased, especially with many more mothers working, there has been a resulting increase in the general institutionalization of children. Many children
now enter child care and early education institutions shortly after birth, with
the majority of American children now spending several years in such institutions before entering elementary school. Also, as we discussed in Chapter
2, parents in contemporary American society often enroll their children in
lessons and organized activities. These often serve a dual function, providing child care and also serving as a substitute for the interactions with siblings and parents that occurred more routinely in the large families of the
past.

The Rise in Mothers' Labor Force Participation

Another major change in families began in the 1940s and reached its peak in
the 1990s: the dramatic rise in mothers' labor force participation. As we see
in Exhibit 4.3, mothers' labor force participation increased at a steady rate of
about 10 percent each year, from 10 percent in 1940 to nearly 60 percent
in 1990. In addition to creating a need for child care institutions and for
children's leisure activities, the increase in mothers' labor force participation also affected the nature of children's lives when they were at home

EXHIBIT 4.3

Proportion of Children with Mothers in the Labor Force

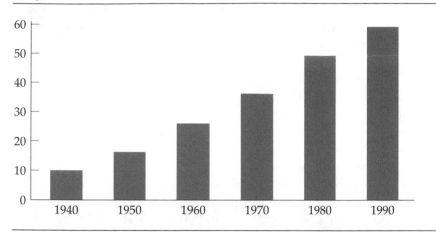

Source: Hernandez, 1993a, p. 109; 1993b, p. 9.

with parents, especially regarding children's contributions to work in the home. As we discussed in Chapter 2, the increase in mothers' labor force participation often meant that mothers now had two jobs—one in and another outside the home. However, work in the home changed for children and youth as well, and it is important to examine these changes from the perspectives of children.

Take, for example, studies of the relation between family structure and children's household work. The findings from these studies are mixed. In several studies it was found that children help to pick up the slack when both parents or the single parent is working (Blair, 1992; Solberg, 1990). However, these and other studies suggest that in families where mothers work outside the home, gender differences in children's contributions are magnified: Daughters contribute more and perform more gender-typed tasks (Hilton & Haldeman, 1991). In fact, one study (Benin & Edwards, 1990) found that sons actually contributed less in dual-earner families than they did in traditional families, and that the gap between sons' and daughters' contributions was greater (10.2 hours of work per week for daughters compared to only 2.7 hours per week for sons).

The authors of reports such as these almost always interpret such findings from the parents' perspective. For example, they suggest that sons get by with doing less because of the "stereotyped assumption that their daughters can perform housework tasks well, whereas their sons cannot" (Benin & Edwards, 1990, p. 370). Others maintain that hard-pressed, stressed-out mothers have less time to argue with and nag their sons into action, so they pass the work on to daughters or do it themselves. But what of the children's perspectives? In one study, after first noting that the median number of hours of housework per week was *only* about six for older girls, the authors noted, "On top of schoolwork, homework, and extracurricular activities, chores can add a significant additional demand on children" (White & Brinkerhoff, 1981, p. 792). However, neither this study nor *any of the other studies* I could locate ever controlled for or *even considered* the effects of children's work outside the home. This was true even in those studies where it appears such information was present in the database used.

We know from our earlier discussion of youth employment that for adolescents, the amount of paid work undertaken outside the home is often extensive. Some studies of youth employment report that boys work longer hours than girls—21.1 mean hours per week for male high school seniors compared to 17.8 for girls (Lewin-Epstein, 1981, p. 74). This difference surely may contribute to gender differences in hours worked in the home; boys are home less often and therefore have less time available for working in the home. Wendy Manning, however, found in a more recent study that the number of hours worked outside the home did not differ by gender (1990, p. 189).

Although the evidence suggests that adolescent females may be working even harder than male adolescents overall, the key issue is that adolescent work in school, at home, and on the job is not appreciated as it should be in sociological research. In their study of teenage workers, Greenberger and Steinberg lamented the amount of time youth invested in outside work, noting that "the student with a half-time job is a very busy person, who commits, at the minimum, fifty hours to school and work; and if after-school activities are substantial, sixty hours or more" (1986, p. 22). This estimate does not include housework. If we factor in chores at home, along with assigned homework, eating, and sleeping, we find that about 18 of the 168 hours in a week are available for leisure and related activities. If housework is the "second shift" for parents (especially mothers) then it must be the "third shift" for adolescents (especially daughters).

Not surprisingly, one of the few studies of parental attitudes toward children's work found that "helping around the house was the domain of greatest disagreement," and children who worked outside the home "were significantly more likely to disagree about helping than nonworkers were" (Manning, 1990, p. 194). Here again, however, the findings were based on parental reports, and the children's behaviors and attitudes were filtered through the perspectives of parents.

Studies of children's perceptions of housework are rare. In her ethnography of adolescent girls growing up in South London, Helena Wulff found that girls begrudgingly accepted the necessity of helping with chores. However, the girls often offered up complaints like the following: "Parents can be mean when it comes to housework, especially mums. You have to hoover the whole house and polish the furniture" (Wulff, 1988, p. 150). In an innovative study of children's housework, Anne Solberg first collected questionnaire data from 800 schoolchildren (ages ten through twelve) from across Norway and then followed up with intensive interviews of ten families living in Oslo. The results from the survey were quite similar to the American studies discussed above concerning number of hours worked, gender differences, and so on. However, the interview study revealed some fascinating insights regarding the children's perspectives. The children were more likely to accept and even enjoy housework in homes where duties were divided up in an egalitarian way, with all family members taking turns fixing evening meals, rotating the laundry and so on. Also, children felt that being responsible for certain chores after school gave them more independence. They especially liked the control and run of the house for a few hours and would often intermesh play and socializing with peers and chores. According to Solberg, the children's negotiated use of domestic space in these instances gave them a sense of autonomy, while the parents—although not aware of all that may have occurred while they were away—expressed pleasure at their children's ability to look after themselves and get some work done at the same time (1990, pp. 134–135).

The Rise in Mother-Only Families

A final major change in family organization in Western societies is the marked increase in mother-only families. The proportion of mother-only families increased from 6.7 percent in 1940 to about 10 percent in 1970, and then to 20 percent in 1990 (see Hernandez, 1994, pp. 9–10). The reasons for this increase are complex and vary significantly by race for American families. However, they relate primarily to divorce and to out-of-wedlock births. The primary effect of this trend on children and childhood is profoundly negative; a large proportion of children in the United States have been thrust into poverty in the last twenty years, and the poverty rates are much higher for children from mother-only families than they are for other family structures (Hernandez, 1994; Rainwater and Smeeding, 1995). Although the topic is subject to much debate, there clearly are negative social and psychological consequences for children born out of wedlock and for those from divorced families as well. We will return to discuss the debate regarding these negative outcomes in Chapter 10, where we consider the social problems of children.

The Effects of Recent Socioeconomic Changes on Children and Childhood in Developing Societies

Industrialization and modernization in the Third World has been both rapid and uneven. Although industrialization brought economic growth and improved quality of life to some developing countries in the 1970s, a range of social, economic, ecological, and epidemic problems (especially ethnic violence, external indebtedness, drought, and AIDS) have more than reversed these gains in the last twenty years. How have these problems affected the lives of children? As York Bradshaw has noted, most international development research has "either ignored children or relegated them to a secondary status," which is highly "unfortunate because children represent one of the most vulnerable groups in most societies" (1993, p. 134). We will return to discuss Bradshaw's documentation of this neglect, and the negative effects modernization has wrought for many Third World children, in Chapter 10. Here we briefly consider how the disruption of traditional family structure, along with the indigenous family processes and practices brought on by modernization, affect the everyday lives of children.

Let's consider the work lives of the Poomkara youth of a rural Kerala village in South India, where changes regarding educational expectations for children often clash with traditional views of children's labor. The anthropologist Olga Nieuwenhuys (1993) notes that schooling has become popular in Kerala (and among members of the lower castes in general) because it is believed to be a way of escaping caste discrimination (by obtaining certification for government service). However, the underlying assumption of Kerala's educational policies is that while attending school "rural children would continue to work in support of themselves and their families in their spare time" (Nieuwenhuys, 1993, p. 105). In fact, both the state and parents see education "as a matter of personal endurance, gift and luck of the child, that is, as a child's frontier" (Nieuwenhuys, 1993, p. 105). This frontier is clearly challenging for Indian secondary school children, because adults assume little responsibility for helping them with school expenses such as transportation, food, supplies, and clothing. Children must pay for these expenses from meager allowances and from wages they earn from parents and other adults for their work. Furthermore, parents still consider it to be the children's primary duty to assist in daily work routines.

Although Nieuwenhuys points to some positive aspects of this difficult combination of schooling and work for the Indian youth (for example, increased independence and self-reliance), there are many negative aspects. Schooling has increased competition among children, a factor that threatens the solidarity of the communities. Also, many children fail at school, and this generates feelings of inferiority. However, as Nieuwenhuys argues, "the most insidious and ill-understood effect may very well be the high level of drudgery" the children face in dealing with demands of school and work, which leaves them with little time for play and leisure (1993, p. 108). It is easy to see how Poomkara youth would come to appreciate Qvortrup's contention that education "is another type of work for children."

Let's return now to our earlier consideration of African families. In Cameroon, modernization and sociopolitical changes have affected the indigenous practice of collective child care by siblings and peers. Many contemporary Cameroonian adults and children "spend a greater part of their waking lives in schools, offices, farms, or marketplaces, [as well as] remote places, pursuing careers or performing a variety of activities and services that were previously unavailable" (Nsamenang, 1992a, p. 437). These changes make it very difficult for Cameroonians "to be their brother's keepers as they were during the old order" (1992a, p. 437).

Both mothers and children in Cameroon must make difficult adjustments. As was the case for the Poomkara youth discussed above, Cameroonian children must accommodate their new school demands with their traditional work and caretaking responsibilities. Such accommodation can be extremely demanding. In some cases preadolescent children are temporarily withdrawn from school to care for younger siblings; they return when their siblings reach school age. In other cases, "some elementary school pupils bring along their younger siblings to school, while busy parents in the Bamenda Grassfields sometimes encourage their toddlers to sneak into classrooms in their neighborhoods in order to have the watchful attention of teachers and peers" (Nsamenang, 1992a, p. 433).

Similar problems of accommodation to modernization and to Western economic and educational practices have been reported for East African families (see Harkness & Super, 1992). Recognition of these difficulties, especially for children, has led to a questioning by some African social scientists of a too rapid acceptance of Western practices (Serpell, 1992). Such recognition has led many to argue that Africans may best aspire "to become more modern by being less Western" (Wober, 1975).

Summary

In this chapter we built on our earlier discussion of the new history of childhood by examining how recent economic, social and cultural changes have affected families and children. Our goal has been to better understand these changes from the perspectives of the children themselves. We addressed this goal in two ways: (1) by examining children's everyday lives in families, and (2) by considering how childhood as a structural form (that is, how the general experiences of children as a social group) has been affected by recent social and economic changes in families. In both cases we placed our analysis in a comparative perspective by including consideration of children, families, and childhood in both Western and developing societies.

In our review of studies of children's experiences in families in Western societies we saw the utility of conceptualizing families as local cultures in which young children actively participate, contribute to their own social development, and affect the participation of all other family members. Studies of children's family lives in developing societies demonstrate a similar pattern of children's active participation, but these studies challenge many Western assumptions about the nature of parent-child and sibling relations. In many non-Western families, care of young children is seen as much more of a collective or community concern rather than as an individual responsibility. Although parents (especially mothers) are always primary caregivers in these societies, kin, siblings, and older children play major roles. In African societies we saw that these collective child care practices, which entail giving responsibilities to older siblings and peers, serve as an apprenticeship system in which women and men are trained for parental roles.

Our analysis of the effects of recent socioeconomic changes on childhood examined a series of changes in families in Western societies from the middle of the nineteenth century to the present, including the rapid decline of the two-parent farm family, the decline of family size, the rise of mothers' labor force participation, and an increase in mother-only families. The decline in two-parent farm families means that children no longer work side by side with parents and siblings, contributing to the family subsistence. Rather, fathers spend their work days away from home while mothers remain at home to care for children and to perform domestic work. Children continue to work, but the nature of their jobs centers around family chores and, in the teen years, outside employment in a narrow range of service and sales jobs. The decline in family size has meant fewer siblings available for companionship and for integration in neighborhood peer cultures, which are themselves less extensive than in the past. As a result of these changes, children find they must rely more on parents. However, parental work demands also increased in the period between the 1940s and the present. With many mothers working, there has been an increase in the general institutionalization of children in a range of child care programs, after-school programs, and sports, music, and art programs. The increase of mothers' labor force participation also means that children (especially preadolescent and adolescent females) are expected to contribute more to work in the home. Finally, the marked increase in mother-only families resulting from divorce and out-of-wedlock births since the 1950s has had negative effects on a large proportion of children in the United States in that many of these children have been thrust into poverty.

When looking at the nature of socioeconomic changes on childhood in the developing countries we concentrated primarily on the effects of modernization on the indigenous practice of collective child care by siblings and peers and on the tension it creates between education and work for children. Child care now becomes more of a social problem as collective care is less viable in increasingly industrial and service economies (compared to traditional agricultural subsistence economies). Preadolescent and adolescent children feel the loss of their childhoods as they struggle to meet new educational demands and continue to perform their child care duties and other work in families and villages.

Many of the recent socioeconomic changes in Western and developing societies have resulted in children's increased separation from adults, and their increased dependence on each other. This trend has brought about the development of extensive and complex peer cultures, which play a major role in the everyday lives of young children and preadolescents. It is to an examination of these peer cultures that we turn in the next part of the book.

PART THREE

Children's Cultures

As I noted in Chapter 2, my acceptance into the peer culture of Italian preschool children early on was related to my limited competence in Italian. In fact, given my struggling hold on the language at the time and my general lack of knowledge of the local school and peer cultures, I was in many ways like the three-year-old Italian child who enters preschool for the first time. Over time, like the younger children in the mixed-age group of three-to-five-year-olds, I developed as a participating member of the local culture.

After a month or so in the school, I was starting to feel that I had some of the everyday routines and activities down. But I was still on the periphery of things, still an outsider. Then something important happened. I was sitting on the floor with two boys, Felice and Roberto, racing some toy cars around in circles. Felice was talking about an Italian race car driver as we played, but because he was talking so fast I could understand only part of what he was saying. At one point, however, I clearly heard the phrase *"Lui è morto,"* and I knew this meant "He's dead." I guessed that Felice must be recounting a tragic accident in some past grand prix event. At that moment I remembered a particular phrase that I had learned in my first Italian course: *"Che Peccato!"* ("What a pity!"). Hearing me produce the expression, the two boys looked up in amazement and Felice said, "Bill! Bill! *Ha ragione! Bravo Bill!"* ("Bill! Bill! He's right! Way to go, Bill!"). *"Bravo Bill!"* Roberto chimed in, and then I heard Felice calling out to other children in the school. Several of the children came over and listened attentively as Felice repeated the story of the tragic accident and then added, "and Bill said, *'Che peccato!'"* The small group cheered and some even clapped at this news. Not in the least embarrassed by all the attention, I felt good—*like one of the group.* I was no longer an outsider trying to gain membership. I was doing it. I was part of the action! (Corsaro, 1996).

In this part of the book I want to try to capture what it is like to be a part of children's cultures. I want to take you beyond *cognitive* awareness to a deep *emotional* appreciation of children's memberships in their peer cultures. Chapter 5 defines the notion of children's peer culture and consider its main elements in detail. Until recently, much of the research on peer relations and culture has focused on the outcomes (both positive and negative) of peer interaction for individual development. The orientation of much of this work was either functionalist (in which culture is defined as shared values, beliefs, and artifacts) or cognitive (in which culture is a set of organizing principles that people keep in their heads and that guide behavior). Chapter 5 breaks from this tradition by viewing children's peer cultures as worthy of study in their own right and as essential components of cultural reproduction more generally. The approach to children's culture is interpretive, with an emphasis not only on shared values and concerns, but also on public, collective, and performative aspects of social life. Chapter 5 also addresses the importance of children's early exposure to symbolic and material aspects of peer cultures in the family.

Chapters 6 and 7 examine basic features of the initial peer cultures of preschool and early elementary school children. Chapter 6 examines the basic themes of communal sharing and control in initial peer cultures as children develop a sense of group identity. Chapter 7 charts how children's negotiations and conflicts bring about social differentiation in initial peer cultures and also the elaboration of those cultures.

Chapter 8 examines how peer groups provide a secure base for older preadolescents as they attempt to make sense of and deal with new demands regarding personal relations, sexuality, and identity development. Everyday activities in peer cultures enable these youths to explore collectively a wide range of confusions and uncertainties that accompany their growing autonomy and individual responsibilities.

5

Children's Peer Cultures and Interpretive Reproduction

Examining Peer Culture from Children's Perspective

As we discussed in Chapter 1, a major change in children's lives is their move outside the family. As we have seen, the timing and nature of children's movement from the family into a society of peers varies over time and across cultures. In discussing these issues, I am using the term *peers* specifically to refer to that cohort or group of children who spend time together on an everyday basis. My focus is on local peer cultures that are produced and shared primarily through face-to-face interaction. (Of course, such local cultures are part of more general groups of children, which can be defined in terms of age or geographical boundaries—for example, all three-to-six-year-olds in the United States.) Children produce a series of local peer cultures that become part of, and contribute to, the wider cultures of other children and adults within which they are embedded. These processes vary over time and across cultures, and the documentation and understanding of these variations should be a central topic in the new sociology of childhood.

Much of the traditional work on peer culture has focused on the outcomes (positive and negative) of experiences with peers on individual development. Most of this work has a functionalist view of culture; that is, culture is viewed as consisting of internalized shared values and norms that guide behavior. In line with the notion of interpretive reproduction, we need to break away from this traditional view of peer culture. First, although the study of individual development (or how the child becomes an adult) is important, children and their peer cultures are worthy of documentation and study in their own right. In simple terms, *kids are deserving of study as kids*. Second, children's culture is not something kids carry around in their heads to guide their behavior. Peer culture is public, collective, and performative (Geertz, 1973; Goffman, 1974). Therefore, in line with our interpretive approach, I define **children's peer culture** as *a stable set of activities or routines, artifacts, values, and concerns that children produce and share in interaction with peers* (Corsaro & Eder, 1990).

In this chapter we'll discuss the importance of peer cultures for interpretive reproduction. We'll begin by considering how children's peer cultures fit into the general model of interpretive reproduction. We'll then go on to discuss the importance of children's experiences in their families to their transitions into initial peer cultures. Finally, we'll consider symbolic and material aspects of children's cultures.

Central Importance of Peer Culture in Interpretive Reproduction

In Chapters 1 and 2, we noted that from the perspective of interpretive reproduction the focus is on children's place and participation in cultural production and reproduction rather than on children's private internalization of adult skills and knowledge. Central to this view is children's participation in cultural routines. Routines, rather than individuals, are analyzed. It is through collective production of and participation in routines that children's evolving memberships in both their peer cultures and the adult world are situated. Children's participation in adult-child routines often generate disturbances or uncertainties in their lives. Such disturbances (including confusion, ambiguities, fears, and conflicts) are a natural outcome of adult-child interaction, given the power of adults and the cognitive and emotional immaturity of children. Although children play an active role in the production of cultural routines with adults, they most often occupy subordinate positions and are exposed to much more cultural information than they can process and understand. Surely many confusions, fears, and uncertainties are addressed as they arise in adult-child interaction. However, it is an important assumption of the interpretive approach that important features of peer cultures arise and develop as a result of children's attempts to make sense of, and to a certain extent to resist, the adult world.

From the perspective of interpretive reproduction, children's activities with peers and their collective production of a series of peer cultures are just as important as their interaction with adults. Further, certain elements of peer culture also affect adult-child routines in the family and other cultural settings. We see, then, that children's participation in adult-child routines in the family and other settings, and their participation in the routines of peer cultures, both influence their evolving membership in their children's culture and in the adult world.

Children's Transition to Initial Peer Cultures

Families play a key role in the development of peer culture in interpretive reproduction. Children do not individually experience input from the adult world; rather, they participate in cultural routines in which information is first mediated by adults. In children's early years most of these adult-child cultural routines take place in families. Thus, initial peer cultures do not arise from children's direct confrontations of the adult world. As children venture out from the family, they are aimed in *specific directions*, are prepared for interaction with distinct *interpersonal and emotional orientations*, and are armed with particular *cultural resources* that are all derived from earlier experiences in their families. Let's take a look at some of these family influences.

Family Influences on Children's Entry Into Initial Peer Cultures

Decisions about children's initial interactions with peers, including the nature of these interactions, are first made within families. Parents normally decide when children first move outside families and what types of peer settings and institutions their children will enter (for example, neighborhood play groups, day care centers, or early education programs). The nature and timing of these decisions relate to cultural conditions, values, and practices; they vary across cultures and within cultures over time. We saw in Chapter 4, for example, that in many non-Western societies, children move as toddlers into multiage peer care groups or are cared for primarily by older siblings. As we saw in our discussion of Nasaw's *Children of the City* in Chapter 3, young sibling care by "little mothers" was the norm among the working class of major cities in turn-of-the-century America. Sibling care probably was still common in the United States, especially in lower- and working-class families, at least into the 1950s, and it still exists today.

Beginning in the 1960s, the need for out-of-home care increased dramatically in Western societies as more and more women entered the workforce. Most countries in Western Europe were quick to respond to the demands for needed child care. Child care and early education programs expanded dramatically in Western Europe, especially for three-to-five-year-olds. In Italy, for example, nearly 90 percent of all three-to-five-year-olds attended government-supported early education programs in 1986 (Corsaro & Emiliani, 1992). In the United States, on the other hand, most parents believed until recently that preschool children are better cared for at home (Mason & Kuhlthau, 1989). Such values now, however, clearly conflict with the reality of the American economy, and by 1990 the majority of three-to-five-year old children of working mothers were cared for outside the home (Hofferth et al., 1991). Still, both the government and parents remain ambivalent about young children moving outside the family before they reach the age when formal schooling begins.

Children's participation in decisions about nonparental care or early education in preschool programs is limited. Once children enter child care or early education settings, however, their experiences in those settings and in

routines with parents that evaluate their performance and progress can prepare them for coming transitions to formal schooling. For example, in our
interviews of Head Start parents, Katherine Rosier and I found that mothers
frequently drew their children's attention to coming changes in their lives.
One mother reported a story about her son, who she had constantly reminded, "You're doing great in Head Start this year and you'll be going to
kindergarten when you're five years old." The day after his fifth birthday in
May, the boy awoke, dressed, and announced to his mother, "Well I'm ready
to go to kinnygarten, Momma, walk me to kinnygarten." When his mother
said he had to wait until autumn, he protested, "But I don't wanna go to
Head Start no more, I'm five years old!" (Corsaro & Rosier, 1994, p. 7).

Interpersonal and Emotional Influences

Young children's relations with adults (teachers, coaches, counselors, and
others) and peers in settings where peer cultures emerge are, in many ways,
affected by earlier parent-child interactional routines in families (Parke &
Ladd, 1992). Children seek in adult caretakers and peers the emotional bonds
and feelings of security they first established in families (Giddens, 1991;
Ladd, 1992). It could be argued that this striving to maintain the sense of security first established in families is the basis of children's formation of peer
cultures. It is most certainly a strong factor in children's valuing of participation and communal sharing in their peer cultures and friendship relations.
We will examine the processes of sharing and friendship in initial peer cultures in Chapter 6. Here it is useful to consider how children's transitions
from families to peer groups affect their relations with others and their developing conceptions of friendship.

When children first arrive in preschools, they soon realize that their conceptions of ownership, possession, and sharing, which are based on their earlier experiences in families, are often not compatible with the interactive
demands of preschools. Ownership is more tangible at home; some things
belong to young children, other things to their siblings, and still other things
to their parents. Problems with sharing these possessions, especially in families with one or two children, are most likely to occur when the young child
has a visitor. On these occasions, the child is expected to share her or his
possessions with playmates. Although children may resist, they soon
learn that such sharing is temporary. Actual ownership of the objects is
never challenged.

In preschools things are different because all the toys and educational
materials are communally owned. Thus, use of the toys and materials de-
pends on negotiations for their temporary possession. It is in the course of
these negotiations that children attempt to establish joint ownership of ob-

jects and of the play itself within a small group, and to protect their sharing of the play against the intrusions of others. We will examine children's tendency to *protect their interactive space* in the next chapter, but here let's consider its more general significance in terms of children's transitions from families to preschools.

In preschools, children are, in a sense, *anchoring* ownership to themselves and their playmates when they verbally mark off a specific area of play as shared and protected from others ("We're playing here. Nobody else can come in."). One result of these negotiations is a more advanced notion of ownership, one that goes beyond matching objects to individuals. Now children begin to see that some objects can be owned in common and shared with others in specific interactive events (Corsaro, 1988).

A second process in the protection of interactive space relates to children's conceptions of friendship. Although there are no ethnographic studies of how parents arrange and encourage interactions between their preschool children and their peers in homes, recent observational studies and surveys of parents provide suggestive data about these processes (Ladd, Profilet, & Hart, 1992; Lollis, Ross, & Tate, 1992). We know from these studies that parents do arrange and supervise informal play groups. We also know that parents use a number of strategies for encouraging play and discouraging conflict. However, none of the research looks closely at how these strategies relate to parents' actual talk about friendship with their children in such situations. Therefore, we must rely on indirect evidence and on some of my own informal observations to speculate about parents' talk about friendship in these situations.

It would appear from experiences in families that children come to see friends as other children with whom they come into contact. Adults tend to associate friendship and sharing ("Anna is your friend who has come to play and you should share your toys with her"). As a result, children's early conception of "friend" is primarily as a label for certain other children they know who have been designated as such by parents. In preschools, as we've discussed, sharing and friendship are often tied to children's attempts to generate and protect shared interactive events. The concept of friend is no longer simply a label that is applied to a specific child. Rather, the notion of friendship relates to *observable shared activities*—playing together in specific areas and protecting the play from other children. Thus, children tend to mark the shared experience with phrases like, "We're friends, right?" and to dissuade the access attempts of others with the words, "You can't play, you're not our friend" (Corsaro, 1979, 1985).

As we noted earlier, one outcome of children's involvement in adult-child routines is the generation of disturbances or uncertainties for children. One source of such uncertainty is the simple fact that children are exposed to much more cultural information than they can process and understand. Unfortunately, disturbances also arise from the stress, conflicts, and even violence young children experience in their families. As psychoanalytic theorists point out, such experiences are especially emotionally stressful for young children who can not understand why those who they love so much can act in such unreasonable ways (Bettelheim, 1976). In such situations children will often turn inward and blame themselves for parental failings. The activities and routines of peer culture can serve as therapeutic havens for confronting and dealing with anxieties from negative experiences in the family. Fantasy play with peers is especially important in these cases, because it enables children to gain control over disturbing events and anxieties (Garbarino et al., 1992).

Symbolic Aspects of Children's Cultures

By **childhood symbolic culture** we mean various representations or expressive symbols of children's beliefs, concerns, and values (Griswold, 1994, p. 3). Three primary sources of childhood symbolic culture are children's media (cartoons, films, and so on), children's literature (especially fairy tales), and mythical figures and legends (Santa Claus, the Tooth Fairy, and others). Information from these three sources is primarily mediated by adults in cultural routines in the family and other settings. Children, however, quickly appropriate, use, and transform symbolic culture as they produce and participate in peer culture. In this chapter we primarily will consider the characteristics of symbolic culture and children's exposure to it. We'll discuss children's transformation and use of symbolic culture capital (that is, the specific items of symbolic culture that children possess and share) in their peer cultures in Chapters 6 through 8.

The Media

Most studies on the content of children's television programing involve criticism of its violence, lack of educational value, sexism, and appeal to hedonism (see Seiter, 1993 for a review). We know little, however, about how children negotiate with parents for access to children's television and other media, how they communicate with parents and peers about what they see, and how they appropriate, use, and extend information from the media. Ellen Seiter's (1993) analysis of toy-based videos for girls (*My Little Pony*) and boys (*Slimer and the Real Ghostbusters*) is an important exception. She argues that such programs are much more complex than middle-class parents assume. We will return to discuss Seiter's analysis of the toys on which these programs are based when we consider adult contributions to children's material culture.

For most people, the mere mention of children immediately brings the Disney company and its vast empire of theme parks, movies, videotapes, and books to mind. Yet, the few studies by scholarly researchers that have examined the Disney company and its products have focused primarily on the company's marketing strategies, vision of childhood, and repackaging of classic fairy tales for mass consumption (Bell, Haas, & Sells, 1995; Giroux, 1996; Hunt & Frankenberg, 1990; Kline, 1993; Tatar, 1992). Disney's influence is seen as so great that some have voiced concern over its recent merger with ABC and its growing control over the global media market. Yet, the role that Disney images, characters, and stories play in children's lives in the family and peer group remains relatively unexplored.

Literature and Fairy Tales

Numerous textual analyses of children's books and fairy tales from a number of different theoretical perspectives exist. Perhaps the most well known is Bruno Bettelheim's (1976) *The Uses of Enchantment,* which presents a psychoanalytic interpretation of classic fairy tales. Maria Tatar (1992) relies on Stanley Fish's (1980) notion of *interpretive communities* to criticize Bettelheim, other scholars of children's literature, and much of children's literature itself. Interpretive communities are practices or strategies we share as members of a community for organizing our experiences. They, in turn, preconstrain our construction of the meaning of texts. Tatar notes that most children's literature and nearly every study of it *address the interpretive communities of adults.* Tatar and others (see Lurie, 1990) attempt to remedy this situation by focusing on subversive children's literature, staying close to the surface level of the story, and attempting to adopt children's perspective. By subversive children's literature, Tatar and Lurie mean stories in which children successfully challenge adult authority and in the process make adults look foolish. A classic example of such literature is *Pippi Longstocking* by the Swedish author Astrid Lindgren. However, Tatar, Lurie and others will always fall short in capturing children's perspectives, because their analyses *do not include children (or adults and children) constructing their interpretive communities over time.*

One recent exception is a case study of two young girls, Lindsey and Ashley, which "demonstrates the innumerable ways in which books and other written texts lay beneath much of the everyday life of their family" (Wolf & Heath, 1992, p. 195). The case study is the result of a collaboration between Shelby Wolf, social scientist, lover of literature, and the mother of the girls, and Shirley Heath, anthropologist, linguist, and longtime ethnographer of literacy in children's everyday lives (see Heath, 1983). Wolf was the ethnographer in this study, observing the role of literature in the lives of her girls from their birth until Lindsey was nine and Ashley was six. Beginning shortly after Lindsey's third birthday, Wolf's ethnography became more focused and rigorous as part of her master's thesis, and she began routinely to tape record reading sessions with both girls and to take notes on the children's extension of their experiences with the texts into their daily lives.

Wolf and her husband read a wide range of books with their girls, from classic fairy tales to adult fiction like *To Kill a Mockingbird*. What most interests us is the mediational processes in which children acquire symbolic culture and how they use such symbolic culture in their everyday lives. In this regard, Wolf and Heath's analysis of their materials is richly textured with many wonderful instances of the symbolic culture of this family. The authors point out that the children played an active part in the readings. Although fascinated by stories with giants, dragons, monsters, and evil queens, the girls would, for example, often admonish their mother to "talk the dragon in a normal voice" because it was too scary. Wolfe reports a frequent routine that occurred after readings of frightful stories in which she and her husband would hear Lindsey rummaging about in her room.

> Her door would open and we would hear a loud clump. Then another and another. The door would close and we would hear her bedsprings squeak in final surrender. Curious, we would creep up the stairs, only to discover several of her "scariest" books lying abandoned outside her door. (1992, p. 138)

The longitudinal design of the case study allowed the authors to capture historical patterns in which information was first shared in reading sessions and then later reproduced, often in the voice and words of the original characters, in appropriate contexts. What children consider to be appropriate contexts, however, can at times be a revelation to adults, because children often achieve "potential recognitions of their own understanding of some element of literature in a totally new and unpredictable way" (Wolf & Heath, 1992, p. 122). Furthermore, "children's visual, logical, musical, and linguistic insights can exceed those of adults, since children, when they read literature, may be motivated by their quest for transformative powers to make the external world conform more fully to their wishes" (1992, p. 122). This insight, which is clearly in line with our notion of interpretive reproduction, is nicely captured in numerous examples in which "Lindsey and Ashley transformed literature for their own purposes in negotiating attention, affection, and reason with adults and each other" (1992, p. 8). One memorable example of such transformation occurred as part of Lindsey's and Ashley's response to a deserved punishment. The two girls had been quarreling and three times interrupted their mother's writing. Having lost her temper, Wolf reports:

> I flung the dusty kitchen rug out the door and sent Lindsey up the stairs for the vacuum cleaner. I stationed Ashley at the sink to do the breakfast dishes. Both girls eyed me resentfully, but I ignored their pleas and went back to work. After a while, I realized that it was much too quiet and descended the stairs again, expecting the worst.
>
> Instead, they were both happily scrubbing the kitchen floor. "I'm Laura and Ashley is Mary," Lindsey explained. "We're playing *Little House in the Big Woods*, and we've got to get the cabin clean for our mom!" (Wolf & Heath, 1992, p. 156)

In this example, argues Wolf and Heath, the girls "made their tasks acceptable by moving into the rules of the Wilder girls' world, where children obeyed their parents instantly and rarely squabbled" (1992, p. 156).

Although Wolf and Heath studied just one family and two children, their work provides a wealth of information on how children are exposed to and appropriate symbolic culture through literature. It also reminds us of the obvious but infrequently acted-on truth: Children are the best sources for understanding childhood.

Mythical Figures and Legends

A good part of the symbolic culture that children bring with them as they enter communal life with peers is drawn from cultural myths and legends. Especially relevant are mythical figures like Santa Claus, the Tooth Fairy, and the Easter Bunny, who are central to childhood culture and lore. A virtual legion of other imaginary figures inhabit children's literature and media. Parents introduce these mythical characters to children and regularly interweave them into their childhoods through what are often deeply cherished rituals. Furthermore, the meanings of these family rituals are enhanced by the subroutines that make up their overall structure—subroutines that are ripe for embellishment in the local cultures of the families. For example, most families produce the general Easter Bunny ritual, but often vary the subroutines of its production. Eggs may be colored in different ways and at different times, they may be hidden inside the home or outside in the yard on Easter morning, there may be a variety of rules children follow when hunting for the eggs, and so forth. Thus, when children come together in neighborhoods, preschools, and kindergarten and elementary school classrooms and playgrounds, their joy and wonder in the embracement of these mythical figures is doubly exalted. They discover not only shared and valued childhood symbolic culture capital, but also a myriad of variations for expressing and appreciating their shared wealth.

We are all familiar with family rituals regarding Santa Claus, the Tooth Fairy, and the Easter Bunny in American culture. Before turning to some recent and very interesting research on such myths and legends in our own culture, though, let's briefly look at the role such legends play in family rituals in two other societies. We begin with an example that is both geographically and culturally distant from our own society: *Gaingeen,* a bogey that appears among the Murik of Papua New Guinea. We then move closer to home to discuss *la Befana,* a witch from Italy.

Gaingeen.   Anthropologist Kathleen Barlow studied the Murik, a fishing and trading society of Papua New Guinea. The Murik are, according to Barlow, "fervently animistic" in that they believe in a number of "spirits who display human-like tendencies toward mischief, deceit, and irritability" (1985, p. 2). One of these spirits is *Gaingeen,* who appears sporadically in the village to chase and beat children, "if he can catch them, which he seldom does" (1985, p. 3). Gaingeen never speaks, but rather conveys his intentions through threatening gestures such as kicking and shaking the spears and sticks he always carries with him.

Infants and toddlers first encounter Gaingeen when parents or older siblings carry them out to observe the bogey during one of his appearances in the village. The young children often are terrified and cling tightly to whoever is holding them. Some parents go right up to Gaingeen and hand him their child (see Exhibit 5.1).

Gaingeen comes to play an important part in caretaker-child routines in Murik households. Murik caretakers prefer to use indirect tactics like distraction to get young children to stop crying or to dissuade them from undesirable behaviors. Once Gaingeen has been introduced, he is frequently called upon for this purpose.

> Mothers who want to wean a child call, *"Gaingeen* you come o! She/He wants to nurse again here." Older siblings hurry their dawdling juniors along the path saying, "Yeay! Hurry up! *Gaingeen* is coming!" Grandmothers recall wandering toddlers from doorways and windows, "Eeee! *Gaingeen, Gaingeen!"* (Barlow, 1985, p. 4)

As children grow older, they learn that Gaingeen usually does not come every time he is called. Still, he may appear, and the young child will always look around to see if Gaingeen is coming when caretakers call his name.

When children are about four years old, they normally venture outside the home to play in mixed-age groups in the village under the care of older siblings. In these instances they tag along with the older children, who sometimes make Gaingeen costumes and engage in a form of approach-avoidance

EXHIBIT 5.1

Gaingeen Holding a Child

Photo by Kathleen Barlow.

play, which we will discuss in the next chapter. When the younger children see their older siblings wearing costumes, they realize that the real Gaingeen, the one they have seen in the village, may be someone in costume as well. They are still afraid of Gaingeen, but they now become suspicious. Could he also be an older child or an adult in a costume?

Eventually, when the children are seven years old or so, the "secret of the mask figure is revealed and the children discover he is an adolescent boy wearing a costume" (Barlow, 1985, p. 1). Despite this demystification, Gaingeen remains an important figure in play and learning throughout childhood. As we will see in the next chapter, the children appropriate Gaingeen and create their own peer routines in which he plays a central role in their attempts to deal with more general fears and anxieties.

La Befana. In Italy children are fascinated by the mythical character *la Befana.* La Befana, who is believed to have originated in Southern Italy, is a witch who flies about on a broom bringing presents to children on January 6th, at Epiphany. (Epiphany is a church festival commemorating the coming of the Magi as the first manifestation of Christ to the Gentiles.) According to legend, the three wise men stopped to ask la Befana for directions on their way to Bethlehem. They also invited her to join them. La Befana told them she was too busy sweeping and sent them away. Afterward, she was filled with remorse and tried to follow. She couldn't catch them and has been flying around Italy ever since, looking for the Christ child. She leaves presents at the house of every child in case one of them is the Savior.

EXHIBIT 5.2

La Befana

This legend seems to have been altered somewhat in contemporary times, with parents warning their children that la Befana does not leave presents for bad children. She is said to slide down chimneys on her broom, delivering presents to good children and filling their stockings with sweets, while bad children get switches or a lump of coal. Some mothers even tell their naughty children to behave or la Befana will steal them away. Many children, however, come to see la Befana as more than a benevolent arbiter of good and bad behavior. They view her as someone who, like *Babbo Natale* (the Italian Santa Claus), always comes through in the end with presents for all children.

In my observations in Northern Italy, I found that children look forward to receiving gifts at Christmas from Babbo Natale, but they are just as excited about la Befana coming several days later. Parents often actively promote the legend by constructing images of the witch in their homes, yards, and neighborhood parks. Like Gaingeen, some of la Befana's appeal to children is the fact that she is both mysterious and frightening. In fact, Italian preschool children frequently debate the power of various threatening figures like witches. In one preschool I studied, children frequently talked about *la Strega* (the witch). One little girl, Antonia, explained to me that witches do not really exist, that they are *per finta* (for pretend). But she later pointed out that *"la Strega e il Dracula sono gli amici"* (the witch and Dracula are friends).

Antonia's view of la Strega symbolizes the children's attraction to monsters. Monsters do not really exist, but we can pretend they do. And this pretense often has a tinge of reality, especially if the threatening agents are introduced by parents and are part of cultural legends, like la Strega and Gaingeen. These fascinating and threatening figures are appropriated from the routines and rituals in the family and are reproduced as part of routines in peer culture by the Murick and Italian children. We will return to look at the nature of these routines and their importance in peer cultures in Chapter 6.

The Tooth Fairy. What of children's mythical and fantasy figures in the United States? How are they introduced to children in the family, and how do they become part of children's symbolic culture? In her book *Flights of Fancy, Leaps of Faith*, Cindy Dell Clark (1995) went directly to children and parents to explore the rituals and meanings of Santa Claus, the Tooth Fairy, and the Easter Bunny.

Perhaps the central insight in Clark's analysis is that children actively participate in and contribute to the dynamics of these mythical legends and rituals. Clark argues that children influence the interactive process of culture in two ways: (1) "the symbolic association of children with certain cultural values (including nature, as well as the capacity for wonder and awe) gives them implicit influence within ritual practices," and (2) "children directly affect cultural practices through their own actions" (1995, p. 103). Let's look at how these cultural processes are demonstrated in one of the mythical figures Clark investigated, the Tooth Fairy.

Although many cultures have shed-tooth rituals, "the Tooth Fairy is largely a Western custom, having evolved in the cultural melting pot of the United States" (Clark, 1995, p. 10). The ritual surrounding the Tooth Fairy involves a rite of passage. In a traditional sense it is a reward for the physical pain and mental anguish that can accompany losing baby teeth. Clark found that most of the children she studied placed their lost teeth in a special receptacle, a Tooth Fairy pouch, to wait for the Tooth Fairy to replace it with money. Such pouches are often handcrafted items that are embroidered or hand-sewn. They call attention to the feminine aspect of the ritual, with the Tooth Fairy (always a female) representing the healing and therapeutic mother comforting and rewarding children for their loss. But the ritual is prospective as well as retrospective. In retrospectively celebrating the loss of the tooth shortly after it has occurred, the ritual also marks the beginning of an occurrence that will have many repetitions (the loss of additional teeth in exchange for money from the Tooth Fairy). In this way the ritual encourages children's awareness of ongoing transitions in their lives and helps prepare them for these changes.

Tooth loss and the Tooth Fairy ritual coincide with another important change in children's lives—their entry into formal schooling during kindergarten or first grade. Children are now deeply embedded in an initial peer culture and are becoming aware of their movement over the next few years into middle childhood and preadolescence. With this transition will come more personal autonomy and more responsibility. Clark has no direct data on activities in peer culture, but she does point to children's valuing of the power and independence that money from the Tooth Fairy can provide. One child remarked how having money made him "feel like a new person," and another observed, "I like carrying around my own money. I feel more grown up and special" (1995, p. 19).

Undoubtedly, children share similar observations with their friends and see their loss of teeth, participation in the ritual, and acquisition of money as signs of maturity. The ritual is especially appealing to children of this age because of its repetition or reoccurrence, and because of the inevitable accumulation of wealth. Clark notes that when she talked to children about money from the Tooth Fairy, they "were prone to run and fetch their stash of cash and to finger through it, Scrooge-like, while showing it to me" (1995, p. 19). Finally, Clark's reference to kindergarten and first-grade teachers' practice of keeping charts marking the occasion when children lose teeth also supports the notion that the ritual is highly valued in peer culture.

Let's now return to Clark's argument regarding children's active partici-pation in the production of the Tooth Fairy ritual. The beginning of sec-ond dentition occurs when children are six or seven, a period of transition marked by children's movement from families to formal schooling. Clark maintains that adults (especially mothers) actively support the magical fairy as a way to keep children young, to extend their belief in fantasy. As a result, the spotlight in the ritual is on children whose sense of wonder and awe is reassuring to parents who would rather they not grow up too fast. Children, on the other hand, with their successive shedding of baby teeth and grow-ing embeddedness in peer cultures, come to view the process in a different lens, with a "more mature focus" (1995, p. 105). With the loss of baby teeth and the accumulation of material cash wealth, children feel older, more in-dependent, and more like their peers.

As Clark suggests, the process also involves children's gradual under-standing of the underlying essence of faith and trust as represented by the belief in mythical figures like the Tooth Fairy and Santa Claus. These mythi-cal figures serve as what British psychiatrist D. W. Winnicott (1951) called *transition objects* in children's growing separation from their parents, in whom they have invested blind faith and trust. In the end, children do not so much discover that the Tooth Fairy is really Mom and Dad as they come to realize that their firm belief in the Tooth Fairy has been an expression of their faith in the unconditional love of their parents. They also discover that the seeds of this faith can be passed on through their participation in the same cultural rituals with their own children.

Material Aspects of Children's Cultures

By **childhood material culture** I mean clothing, books, artistic and literacy tools (crayons, pens, paper, paints, etc.), and, most especially, toys. Children can, and often do, use some of these objects to produce other material arti-facts of childhood cultures (for example, pictures, paintings, block structures, improvised games and routines, and so on). Much of the research related to children's material culture focuses exclusively on toys. Most of it is carried out by psychologists; it is quantitative (experimental and quasiexperimental) and is designed to test hypotheses regarding the effects of specific content or features of toys on children's individual development. For example, a great deal of research exists on toys and gender stereotyping and the effects of war toys on aggressive behavior (Carlsson-Paige & Levin, 1987; Goldstein, 1994). Such a focus is too narrow and too similar to that of the research on sym-bolic culture. Very little of this research examines parent-child interaction regarding negotiations over the acquisition or use of toys or children's play with toys. To find such research we need to turn to the work of historians and marketing researchers.

It is useful to consider a central theme running through the work on children's material culture. Studies by historians and marketing researchers show that as children develop as individuals, they collectively and creatively appropriate, use, and infuse toys with meaning, both in families and in their peer cultures. These findings are in line with the notion of interpretive reproduction in that they demonstrate the importance of children's collective actions and how these actions contribute to the productions of innovative peer cultures as well as to reproduction and change in adult society. The main reason historical and marketing studies identify the importance of the children's collective actions is because their research designs (which are more qualitative and interpretive in nature) do not close themselves off from such possibilities in order to test how toys affect individual development.

Historical Studies of Children's Material Culture

As Brian Sutton-Smith has argued, the "predominant nature of play throughout history has been play with others, not play with objects" (Sutton-Smith, 1986, p. 26). Objects were often incorporated into play, but were second in importance to the social aspects of play. As a result almost any physical object that could enhance a play theme would do. These objects, sometimes referred to as "playthings," varied over time, from sticks and stones to tires, tin cans, and coat hangers. Such objects were transformed to fit the arising themes of play and did not have fixed meanings. According to Mergen (1992, p. 88), however, two new attitudes toward toys emerged in the 1870s. First, children began to develop a desire for the accumulation of toys for their own sake, with material possessions indicating the status of the owner. Second, toys began to be seen as defining the identity of the child and childhood culture.

Historical studies based primarily on the analysis of autobiographies capture how these two attitudes toward toys often overlap. An excellent example of such overlap is Formanek-Brunell's (1992) study of dolls and doll play in the nineteenth century. Doll play before the Civil War was infrequent and was linked to learning and developing sewing skills and other kinds of domestic training. In the decades after the war, things were quite different. Middle- and upper-class girls were "encouraged by adults to imbue their numerous dolls with affect, to indulge in fantasy, and to display their elaborately dressed dolls at ritual occasions such as tea parties and while visiting" (Formanek-Brunell, 1992, p. 108). Although girls certainly adopted this attitude toward their dolls to some degree, they did not simply internalize the adult values as part of feminine socialization. To the contrary, the girls often had a different agenda as they *appropriated* and used the dolls "for purposes other than training in the emotional and practical skills of mothering" (1992, p. 108). In the autobiographical data, women report rebelling against sedate tea parties as girls by sliding their dolls down banisters atop tea trays and, in another case, wreaking havoc on their tea party "by smashing their unsuspecting dolls to bits" (1992, p. 123). In fact, the physical mistreatment and even torturing of dolls was commonly mentioned in the memoirs. Most of these accounts involved the acts of boys, usually brothers, with the girls often looking on more in fascination than horror. One woman remembered, "When my brother proved my doll had no brains by slicing off her head, I felt I had been deluded; I watched him with stoicism and took no more interest in dolls" (1992, p. 121). Still, girls themselves also carried out such mistreatment, often in response to imagined misbehavior on the part of their dolls. For example, an article in a girl's magazine on doll play in 1908 reported a "four-year-old girl disciplined her doll by forcing it to eat dirt, stones, and coal" (1992, p. 122).

Such behavior was often seen by adults of the time as the expression of repressed anger. In fact, adults encouraged a form of play that many might find horrific or at least in bad taste today: the enactment of doll funerals. According to Formanek-Brunell, doll funerals were much more frequent than doll weddings among middle-class girls in the 1870s and 1880s. She points out that "mourning clothes were packed in the trunks of French lady dolls, and Fathers constructed doll-sized coffins for their daughters' dolls instead of the more usual doll houses" (1992, p. 117). One woman remembered that, "No day was too short for a funeral, just so they [my friends] all got home for supper" (1992, p. 123). Such play was not seen as morbid but was viewed as helping to develop the nurturing and comforting skills that often were needed in a time when many relatives and friends died young. Girls, however, did not simply imitate proper comforting behavior in their doll funerals. Girls often changed the emphasis from cathartic funerals to ritualized executions or harrowing accidents that led to death. (Again, the adult model was appropriated, not simply internalized.)

It is important to keep in mind that autobiographical data of this type have certain validity problems (such as, the faulty or selective memory of the author) and that they allow for limited generalizability given the upper-class backgrounds of most of the authors. Regarding generalizability, many working- and lower-class girls could not afford store-bought dolls, let alone the luxury of destroying them. Still, these historical materials provide direct evidence and therefore lead to more valid conclusions than does simply inferring the nature of play from the mere existence or content of toys. As Mergen notes, "toys have meaning only when children play with them," and if toys "are meaningful to the child they will be reused and remembered" (1992, p. 106). It is the symbolic meaning and value children attach to toys that most interests market researchers, whose main aim is to understand children as consumers of toys and other material goods. It is to this work that we now turn.

Marketing Studies of Children's Material Culture

Developmental and educational psychologists who study children's material culture normally focus on the effects of various play objects and toys on children's cognitive and social development. They rely most often on quantitative, quasiexperimental or experimental studies to estimate the educational value of toys and how play with various toys might contribute to children's cognitive growth and structure. In this approach, less attention is paid to children's toy preference or to the actual processes of children's play with the toys. Market researchers, on the other hand, have little interest in scientifically documenting the effects of toys on children's development (except in cases where they aim their goods at parents; here they do not hesitate to cite scientific research). Their research, argues Kline, "is both pragmatic and proprietary, but that in itself hasn't prevented the cultural industries from gaining insight into contemporary children's everyday experiences of play, fiction and leisure" (Kline, 1993, p. 18). Relying on more qualitative methods such as focus groups, informal interviews, and direct observation, these researchers "don't bother to observe comatose children in the classroom being battered with literacy; they study them at play, at home watching television or in groups on the streets and shops" (Kline, 1993, p. 18). What they discover is that aspects of children's symbolic and material culture, such as "daydreams, hero worship, absurdist humour and a keen sense of group identity"—which academic researchers (and most adults) may see as "meaningless distractions or artefacts of immaturity"—are important attributes of children's cultures (Kline, 1993, p. 18). As Kline notes, marketers make good use of these insights in their strategies for selling things to children, whom they see as highly informed and powerful consumers (1993, p. 18). One thing market researchers have discovered is that one appeal of certain toys and media products is the very fact that children realize that *adults will not like such products and even see them as schmaltzy or disgusting and gross*. This point relates to our earlier discussion of how children desire to gain control over their lives and challenge the power of adults.

In her book on children's consumer culture, *Sold Separately*, Ellen Seiter (1993) develops many of these basic themes. Seiter rightly notes that in contemporary American society it is mothers who most often ultimately decide on their children's consumption of symbolic and material culture. Today's mothers "may object to children's consumer culture, but they often give in to it as well, largely because of the usefulness of television programs and toys as convenience goods for caretakers of children" (Seiter, 1993, p. 8). In doing so, mothers often feel guilty that they are relinquishing their children to a superficial and hedonistic consumer culture.

Like Kline (1993), Seiter does see a certain value in children's consumer culture. She stresses especially the communal nature of children's shared culture with friends and classmates, and its "strong imagination of community." Here, Seiter extends Kline's argument to point out that adults too "invest intense feeling in objects and attribute a wealth of personal and idiosyncratic meanings [to] mass-produced goods" (1993, p. 9). After all, is a sweatshirt with a Chicago Bulls or Indiana Hoosiers logo any more educational (or less expensive) than one with Mickey Mouse or Tweety Bird?

Seiter's point about similarities between adult and child consumer culture relates to our earlier discussion regarding the tendency of adults to evaluate children's activities prospectively. In other words, we adults most often take a linear view of development; we are concerned with how the present experiences of children contribute to their futures as adults. But surely in terms of symbolic and material culture children have some right to enjoy their childhoods!

Children's consumer culture does, of course, have some negative attributes. Parents are rightly concerned about the effects of their children's preferences for repetitive play with toy guns or grossly disproportioned Barbie dolls. In fact, Seiter argues that many aspects of children's media and toys promote negative images in regard to class, race, and gender in American society. On the other hand, she also notes that educationally endorsed and politically correct toys are often very expensive and can be elitist. She points, for example, to European-produced toys like Playmobil's Victorian Dollhouse. The dollhouse retailed at $185 in 1993 and came with a description that introduces the character 'Vicki,' a little girl from a good home who lived during the turn of the century. . . . Vicki's family belonged to 'high society,' because after all her father was the Chancellor of Commerce. Naturally, you can understand that Vicki should be raised by a governess" (Seiter, 1993, p. 218). Ouch! My daughter got one of these dollhouses for Christmas when she was seven; however, I never heard her talk about Vicki and the governess. Of course, my daughter also owns and plays just as often with her inexpensive Gumby, Tweety Bird, and My Little Ponies.

Seiter likes My Little Ponies. In fact, her content analysis of episodes of toy-based cartoons such as *My Little Pony* and *Slimer and the Real Ghostbusters* (popular children's television programing in the mid-1980s) revealed more positive than negative aspects.

> My critical reading of *My Little Pony* and *Ghostbusters* [has] revealed extensive
> borrowing from adult gendered genres, such as soap opera, romance, science
> fiction, and horror. Children learn a great deal about the conventions of these
> adult genres from watching children's television, which imparts to them a lot
> of information about popular culture and about dominant ideologies of gen-
> der. The girls' cartoons are filled with many 'prosocial' messages routinely
> delivered to children, such as the importance of cooperation, kindness, and
> acknowledging the feelings of others. The boys' cartoons, despite their vio-
> lence, also convey many deep-rooted cultural principles, such as the notion
> that the strong (usually men) have an obligation to protect the weak, that the
> use of force can be justified, that people need to learn to check their emotions,
> and, perhaps above all, that male bonding is fun. (Seiter, 1993, pp. 188-89)

Studies of children's consumer culture such as Kline's and Seiter's are important because they take children—their perspectives, preferences, and
shared cultures—seriously. They also look at children's consumer behavior as embedded in a complex interactive system. In this system children
are dependent on parents (usually mothers), but they are active negotia-
tors in decisions regarding the purchase of toys and their access to the
media through television and movies. However, a glaring omission in
this work is adults' and children's joint participation in children's consumer
culture. Parents watch television and rented movies or purchased cassettes
with their children, play games, and engage in other leisure activities with
them in the home. They also frequently take their young children to movies,
amusement parks, museums, zoos, parks, and playgrounds. Yet very little
research exists on parental-child interactions in such settings, which may
constitute a large part of young children's time with their parents. (I
could find only one study of parent-child exploration of Disneyland or
Disneyworld, a major element of children's culture in America) (Hunt &
Frankenberg, 1990). Finally, although studies of children's consumer culture tell us a great deal about children's preferences and their roles in the
consumer decisions, they only rarely and very narrowly explore children's
actual use, refinement, and transformation of symbolic and material goods
within peer cultures.

Summary

In this chapter we explored the concept of children's peer culture and how it
relates to interpretive reproduction. We defined peer culture as a stable set of
activities or routines, artifacts, values, and concerns that children produce
and share in interaction with peers. This view of peer culture is in line with
interpretive reproduction in that it stresses children's collective actions,

shared values, and their place and participation in cultural production. Families play a key role in the development of peer culture in interpretive reproduction. Children do not individually experience input from the adult world; rather they participate in cultural routines in which information is first mediated by adults. However, once children begin to move outside the family, their activities with peers and their collective production of a series of peer cultures become just as important as their interactions with adults. Further, certain elements of peer cultures also affect adult-child routines in the family and other cultural settings.

In this chapter we focused on children's introduction to elements of peer culture in the family. Children's peer cultures are affected by adults, most especially in adult-child routines in families, in two ways. First, important features of peer cultures arise and develop as a result of children's attempts to make sense of and to a certain extent resist the adult world. Second, children's experiences in the family prepare them for entry into initial peer cultures in that parents arrange for and structure their children's early interactive experiences with peers, provide them with emotional support and foster interpersonal styles or orientations, and introduce them to both symbolic and material aspects of children's culture. We examined children's introduction to symbolic and material aspects of peer culture in the family in some detail. We saw that parents introduce children to symbolic culture (that is, various representations or expressive symbols of children's beliefs, concerns, and values) by the way they control and encourage their children's access to media, literature, and mythical figures and legends. Parents introduce children to material culture (that is, books, artistic tools, and toys) through their purchase of and their encouragement of certain types of play with such cultural objects. In line with interpretive reproduction we reviewed studies which attempted to capture how parents and children collectively negotiate access to material culture, and interpret and use symbolic and material culture, in everyday routines and rituals in the family. In this review we noted that children often extend and transform symbolic and material culture that they first attain in the family in their interactions with peers. We now move to a discussion of children's production of preschool and preadolescent peer cultures in Chapters 6 through 8.

6

Sharing and Control in Initial Peer Cultures

How do peer cultures come about? How are their elements shared and passed on to other groups? How do individual children come to produce and participate in a series of peer cultures? Although children's sense of belonging to a peer culture extends to a wide range of social-ecological settings, the direct study of peer interaction and children's peer cultures is relatively recent. Most studies have been confined to a single setting over a limited period of time (usually a year or so at the most). Very few studies have followed children as they make transitions from the family to the peer group or from one peer culture to another. Therefore, it's difficult to answer all of these questions. Still, some patterns have emerged that allow us to begin to address these issues.

We can conceptualize peer cultures as general subcultures of a wider culture or society such as the United States, Italy, or Kenya. Most work on peer subcultures, however, focuses on particular micro or local cultures that are part of a wider network. The advantage of the notion of local culture is that it allows us to focus on culture as something that is directly produced and shared in face-to-face interaction. As Fine (1987) argues, we can study children's peer cultures as shared universes of discourse rather than as groups defined simply in terms of age or geographical boundaries.

Children are introduced to elements of a more general peer culture and to particular local cultures in the family—through interaction with older siblings, from television and other media, and even from parents. We discussed some of the priming activities in the family that prepare children for the transition to the peer group in Chapter 5. However, children actively enter and become participants in and contributors to local peer cultures for the first time as they move outside the family into the surrounding community. This initial peer culture may take the form of loosely structured kin and neighborhood groups. However, in Western societies (and more and more in developing countries) children are moving into organized child care and educational settings at earlier ages. Given the amount of time that young children normally spend in these settings and the intensity of interaction, they often serve as a hub in an interlocking network of peer settings or localities. It is through intensive, everyday interaction in this hub that the first local peer culture develops and flourishes.

Except for a few recent studies of children's play groups in neighborhood settings in Western societies (Berentzen, 1984; Goodwin, 1990) and communal, multi-age child care and play groups in non-Western countries (Harkness & Super, 1992; Martini, 1994; Nsamenang, 1992b) most research on children's peer cultures has occurred in settings like preschools, playgrounds, and classrooms of elementary schools, as well as baseball fields and other locales for organized sports and leisure activities. Although there is clearly a need for studies focusing on a wider range of cultures and settings within cultures, the available research serves as a highly valuable starting point for a better understanding of children's cultures. Recent research has identified specific peer processes, routines, concerns, and values. The studies suggest that peer cultures emerge, develop, and are maintained and refined across the various social settings that make up children's worlds.

Central Themes in Children's Initial Peer Cultures

Although a wide range of features of the peer cultures of young children have been identified, two central themes consistently appear: (1) Children make persistent attempts to *gain control* of their lives and (2) they always attempt to *share* that control with each other. In the preschool years the overriding concerns are social participation and challenging and gaining control over adult authority. These two themes are illustrated by the way young children's routines relate to their concerns with physical size. For young children, interactive settings are characterized by the children's looking up to those adults with power and authority (see Corsaro, 1985; Denzin, 1977). As a result of this recurrent need to look up to the adult world, young children are deeply concerned with physical size. They come to value "growing up" and "getting bigger." In fact, for young children the distinguishing characteristic between themselves and adults is that adults are bigger. This difference in size is a fact I have never completely overcome in many years of ethnographic work with young children. As I noted in Chapter 2, it is the primary reason that many of the young children I have studied have labeled me "Big Bill"—someone who is not a typical adult, but is too big to be a kid.

The best support for the claim that children value "being bigger" is their preference for and their routines of play in areas of nursery schools where they are, in a very real sense, *bigger*. When playing on climbing structures or in playhouses, children routinely climb to the top levels, where they can look down on others, especially adults. Another attraction of these climbing structures is that they are not easily entered by adults since they are scaled to the size of the children. A frequent play routine in the climbing bars in all the nursery schools where I have observed is for children to race each other to the top, where they then look down and call out, "We are bigger than anybody else!" Such chanting is often aimed at adults. For example, in one instance I recorded, several children in an American preschool climbed to the highest level of a playhouse in the outside yard. One of the children, Dominic, yelled out to a teaching assistant, "Willy! Willy! Hi, Willy!" Willy looked up and waved to Dominic. Then Eva and Allen yelled out, "Willy! Willy! Willy!" Soon the three children were joined by two others, Beth and Brian, and all five children began to chant in unison: "Willy! Willy! Willy! We are bigger than you are!" This chanting continued for several minutes and Willy seemed slightly uncomfortable with all the shouting. He laughed, shook his head, and moved inside the school. I had been standing near the climbing house during this episode and I felt a great deal of sympathy for Willy. In fact, I began to worry that the children would begin taunting me next. Therefore, I moved slightly away from the climbing house to sit on the ground near the slide, where I greeted children as they descended.

The themes of control and communal sharing are evidenced in a wide range of routine activities in the peer cultures of young children. In this chapter we'll focus on children's sharing, on friendship play, and on routines related to children's communal attempts to gain control over adult authority. In Chapter 7 we'll consider routines that relate to conflict and differentiation in the peer culture of young children.

Friendship, Sharing, and Social Participation

We will begin our analysis of communal play routines by first examining young children's friendships, sharing, and social participation in peer culture. We'll then move on to consider play routines related to children's attempt to gain control over adult authority. Let's first look at friendship and sharing among peers, beginning with the earliest of peer relations among toddlers.

Play Routines Among Toddlers

Until recently, most studies of peer relations among toddlers have involved observing children in laboratory settings or in small play groups in homes. For example, Mueller (1972) documented how cooperative play with toys serves as a basis for the emergence of social interchanges during the second year. With further language development these interchanges are expanded to become shared routines among toddlers who have a history of interaction. They may serve as the beginnings of friendship and a peer culture (Budwig, Strage, & Bamberg, 1986; Vandell & Mueller, 1980).

Studies of peer relations among toddlers in daycare settings are rare and have been restricted primarily to recent work in Italy and France. Stamback and Verba (1986) have verified the existence of numerous and lengthy episodes of common activities among children from thirteen to twenty-six months in French *crèches* (child care and education centers). Although the overall organization of the episodes varied, there was a common structure in which shared meaning was established and then a theme elaborated. Tullia Mussati has documented stable peer relations in the Italian *asilo nido* (a child care program for children from six months to three years). In one study Mussati and Panni (1981) describe the initiation and solidification of ritual play and how the children share knowledge of the basic structure of the rituals and the pleasure of their shared enactment.

In our study of peer interaction in an *asilo nido* in Bologna, Italy, Luisa Molinari and I found that the children produced several play routines during the first two months of observation that were elaborated over the course of the school year. One routine we call the "little chairs" nicely captures the flavor of play among toddlers. The routine occurred in a large room that contained a number of small chairs (*seggiolini*) for the children to sit in for various activities and during meetings and group projects. The routine begins with one or more of the children pushing the little chairs to the center of the room. Once underway, other children join the play by bringing other chairs or using those already put on line. The following case study is a summary of a short segment of the *seggiolini* routine that Luisa Molinari videotaped in the *asilo nido*.

The Little Chairs Routine

Arianna and Giorgio approach the chairs and Arianna says, "I'll take the white chairs." The two children then begin pushing the chairs to the middle of the room and are joined in the activity by Stella and Franca. Meanwhile, two other children, Tommaso and Marco, who were watching while standing near the window, take two chairs and push them into the long line created by the other children.

Soon several other children join the play. At one point Stella says, "This is not well done!" and she moves some chairs closer together in the line. The children now begin walking on the line of chairs, which prompts Stella to tell one of the teachers that their construction is "well done."

EXHIBIT 6.1

Children arrange *seggiolini*.

EXHIBIT 6.2

Children walk on *seggiolini*.

Now a number of children are walking on the chairs and moving onto a table, where they jump down and run to the other end of the line and start again. At one point Marco sways and says, "I'm falling, I'm falling" but then quickly rights himself and laughs at his pretend crisis. One child, Elvira, kicks at a chair and knocks it from the line. She is immediately reprimanded by Stella, who then returns the chair to its proper place. The children now begin walking in different directions on the structure, and as they cross paths Tommaso pushes Stella. Stella shouts, "Tommaso always pushes me" to Arianna, who is waiting for her at the end of the line. The play continues until one of the teachers announces that it is now time to begin a planned activity.

Source: Adapted from Corsaro & Molinari, 1990, p. 218

In this case study we see that all of the children participate in the routine to some degree. During the routine the teachers often warn the children to be careful, but they intervene only if they fear an injury may occur. In interviews the teachers told us that although they had some misgivings about the play, they did not want to restrict it, noting how much the children enjoyed their innovative creation. Along these lines, it is noteworthy that Marco incorporates the adult concerns into the routine by pretending to fall and then carefully righting himself. In fact, the children were well aware of the teachers' concerns and often reassured them. We can see, for example, how Stella tells a teacher that the design of the chairs is well constructed and, therefore, not dangerous. Moreover, the children often comfort each other when minor injuries occur and avoid asking the teachers for help even when there are disagreements. We can see that the routine gives the children a sense of control over their physical environment and the authority of the teachers.

The little chairs routine took a slightly different form every day. However, some rules were always followed. The children (1) were careful to space the *seggiolini* to ensure that a child can easily step from one to another, and (2) avoided taking away chairs from the finished structure. However, some of the younger children did not always respect these rules and were frequently advised of violations by older children. Finally, we found that the older children began experimenting with the design somewhat near the end of the school term. These experiments involved modifications that made the structure more difficult and challenging to walk on.

An important feature of toddler play routines like the "little chairs" is their simple and primarily *nonverbal* participant structure, which consists of a series of orchestrated actions. This simple structure facilitates the involvement of a large number of children with a fairly wide range of communicative, cognitive, and motor skills. The structure incorporates the option of frequently recycling the main elements of the routines. Such recycling allows children to begin and end participation over a lengthy time frame and to embellish or extend certain features of the routines over time.

The simple participant structure of play routines corresponds to a central value of peer cultures: *doing things together* (Corsaro, 1985; Parker & Gottman, 1989). As we noted earlier, adults tend to view children's activities from a "utility point of view," which focuses on learning and social and cognitive development (Strandell, 1994) . Young children do not know the world from this point of view. "For them," notes Strandell, "the course of events of which they are part has as an immediate impact on their existence as children here in space and now in time" (1994, p. 8). It is for this reason that we adults seldom truly appreciate the strong emotional satisfaction children get from producing and participating in what seems to us to be simple repetitive play.

The Protection of Interactive Space and Children's Early Friendships

The peer routines of preschool children (three-to-six-year-olds) go beyond the primary nonverbal coordinated actions of toddlers in that they normally involve highly sophisticated verbal productions. However, gaining access to play groups, maintaining interaction, and making friends are still demanding tasks for preschool children. Gaining access to play groups is particularly difficult in preschool settings since young children tend to protect shared space, objects, and ongoing play from the entry of others.

Protection of interactive space is the tendency on the part of preschool children to protect their ongoing play from the intrusion of others. In my work in preschools I have found that this tendency is directly related to the fragility of peer interaction, the multiple possibilities of disruption in most preschool settings, and the children's desire to maintain control over shared activities. Consider the following sequence, recorded on videotape in one of my studies in an American preschool:

> Richard and Barbara have been playing in the block area for several minutes. They are both building things and are sitting near each other. They have not spoken to each other, however, and they do not appear to be playing together. Another child, Nancy, who entered the area with Barbara, is sitting nearby watching.
> Richard says to Barbara, "We're playing here by ourselves."
> "Just—ah—we friends, right?" Barbara agrees.
> Richard replies, "Right."
> Barbara and Richard now begin to coordinate their activity and build a house together. Nancy stays on the fringes of the activity for awhile, but then moves closer, indicating her intent to join the play. Barbara and Richard resist

her entry bid, telling Nancy she can not play. Nancy returns to her onlooker role for a few minutes, but then gives up and moves to another area.

Resistance of access attempts seems uncooperative or selfish to adults, including parents and most teachers (see Corsaro, 1985). But it is not that the children are refusing to cooperate or are resisting the idea of sharing. In fact, as we see in this example, the defenders of interactive space are often intensely involved in creating a sense of sharing during the *actual course of playing together* and often mark this discovery with references to affiliation ("We're friends, right?"). In simple terms, the children *want to keep sharing what they are already sharing* and see others as a threat to the community they have established.

Children not involved in ongoing play desire entry and want to be a part of shared activities. Because their entry bids are continually resisted, they realize they must be persistent. Over time most children meet the challenge of resistance and develop a complex set of **access strategies**. Consider the following case study involving three four-year-old girls in an American preschool.

Access Rituals in an American Preschool

Jenny and Betty are playing around a sandbox in the outside courtyard of the school. I am sitting on the ground near the sandbox watching. The girls are putting sand in pots, cupcake pans, and teapots. Occasionally the girls bring me a sand cake to pretend to eat. Debbie now comes up to the sandbox and stands near me, observing the other two girls. After watching for about five minutes she circles the sandbox three times and stops again and stands next to me. After a few more minutes of watching, Debbie moves to the sandbox and reaches for a teapot. Jenny takes the pot away from Debbie and mumbles, "No." Debbie backs away and again stands near me, observing the activity of Jenny and Betty. Then she walks over next to Betty, who is filling the cupcake pan with sand.

Debbie watches Betty for just a few seconds, then says, "We're friends, right, Betty?"

Betty, not looking up at Debbie, continues to place sand in the pan and says, "Right."

Debbie now moves alongside Betty, takes a pot and spoon, begins putting sand in the pot, and says, "I'm making coffee."

"I'm making cupcakes," Betty replies.

Betty now turns to Jenny and says, "We're mothers, right, Jenny?"

"Right," says Jenny.

The three "mothers" continue to play together for about twenty more minutes, until the teachers announce cleanup time.

Source: Adapted from Corsaro, 1979, pp. 320-21

In this example, Debbie's efforts to enter the play illustrate a variety of access strategies. First, she merely places herself in the area of play, a strategy I call *nonverbal entry*. Receiving no response, Debbie keeps watching the play but now physically circles the sandbox (what I term *encirclement*). Some researchers refer to Debbie's actions as "onlooker behavior" and argue that it is an indicator of timidity or immature social skills. However, it is important to observe access attempts within their social contexts. Observing entire episodes of interaction, I find that access attempts often involve a series of strategies that build on one other.

In this case, Debbie, when stationary and on the move, carefully makes note of what the other children are doing. With this information she is able to enter the area and *produce a variant of the ongoing play*. Although normally a successful access strategy, it is initially met with resistance in this instance. Not giving up, however, Debbie watches some more, again enters the area, and makes a verbal *reference to affiliation* ("We're friends, right?"). Betty responds positively but does not explicitly invite Debbie to play. Debbie then repeats her earlier strategy, producing a variant of the play, this time verbally describing it ("I'm making coffee"). Betty now responds in a way that includes Debbie in the play, noting that she is also making something (cupcakes). She then goes on to further define the new situation by saying, "We're mothers," which is confirmed by Jenny. Debbie is now clearly part of the play.

Although Debbie is eventually successful, one might wonder why she simply did not go up and say "Hi," "What ya doing?" or "Can I play?" I have found that nursery school children rarely use such direct strategies. One reason is that such strategies call for a direct response, and this response is very often negative. Remember our earlier point about the protection of interactive space. Children fear that others may disrupt the cherished but fragile sharing they have developed. Direct entry bids like "What ya doing?" or "Can I play?" or the frequently heard, "You have to share!" actually signal that one does not understand what kind of sharing is going on and therefore may cause trouble. The developmental psychologist Catherine Garvey characterizes such requests for information as the three "Don't's" in her guidelines for successful play entry: "Don't ask questions for information (if you can't tell what's going on, you shouldn't be bothering those who do); don't mention yourself or state your feelings about the group or its activity (they're not interested at the moment); don't disagree or criticize the proceedings (you have no right to do so, since you're an outsider)" (1984, p. 164). The "do's" in Garvey's guidelines all revolve around demonstrating that you can play without messing things up: Watch what's going on, figure out the play theme, enter the area, and plug into the action by producing a variant of the play theme. As Garvey notes, it is also a good idea to "hold off on making suggestions or attempting to redirect until you are well into the group" (1984, p. 187).

Again, we see why it is important for adults to take the children's perspective. What may seem like selfish behavior is really an attempt to keep sharing. Further, by actively confronting resistance to their access attempts, children acquire complex strategies that allow them to enter and share in play. There is one more point. The access skills that children develop in this multi-party setting are clear precursors to adult skills that are used in similar settings. Picture yourself at a party. Let's say you have just arrived, gone off to get a drink, been to the bathroom, or some such thing. Now, like the children in the preschool, you do not want to remain alone. What do you do? Do you go up to a group and say "Hi," "What ya talking about?" "Can I talk too?" Probably not. Instead, you probably stand near a group, listen, figure out what they are talking about, and make a relevant contribution to the conversation. In short, you do pretty much what Debbie did in the previous example. There is one difference, however. Adults are not likely to tell the guy who bursts in on a conversation that he "is not our friend" or to "beat it." We may want to, but we send more subtle signals—like ignoring what he has to say. As grown-ups we have learned tact (though it does not always work as well as we might like).

Children's developing knowledge of friendship is closely tied to the social, contextual demands of their peer worlds. Children construct concepts of friendship while at the same time linking these concepts to specific organizational features of peer culture in preschools and other peer settings. Through their experience in preschool, children come to realize that interaction with peers is fragile, and acceptance into ongoing activities is often difficult. Therefore, rather than limiting their social contacts to one or two playmates, the children most often develop stable relations with several playmates as a way to maximize the probability of successful entry and satisfying peer interaction.

For preschool children friendship primarily serves specific integrative functions (gaining access, building solidarity and mutual trust, and protecting interactive space). Friendships are seldom enduring and are rarely based on perceived personal characteristics of playmates (see Corsaro, 1985, pp. 168–169). (It is important, however, to remember the importance of context in this interpretation of my findings; the nature of friendship processes will vary across social and cultural context. We will consider a comparative analysis of friendship processes in three cultural groups in Chapter 7.) It may be that enduring friendships may be more common among preschool children in homes and neighborhoods (Gottman, 1983). Clearly there is a need for long-term ethnographic studies of children's friendships in such settings.

As we've seen, friendship concepts and skills do not arise solely or even primarily as a result of cognitive development or children's individual reflections. Friendships are collectively constructed through children's active involvement in their social worlds and peer cultures, an idea that clearly ties in to the notion of interpretive reproduction. Our earlier discussion of children's transition from the family to the initial peer culture in preschool settings in Chapter 5 is also relevant here. There we pointed out that parents often make the association between friendship and sharing for their children by designating the playmates with whom their children share things as friends. In this sense, two- and three-year-olds are most apt to see friends as those children who are labeled as such by their parents. With experience in initial peer cultures, however, the concept of friendship is transformed from something denoted by a label that is applied to a specific child, to something involving observable shared activity. Friendship means producing shared activity together in a specific area, and protecting that play from the intrusions of others. Thus, children creatively appropriate and extend social knowledge that was first presented to them in adult-child routines. Finally, in protecting their interactive space, children come to realize that they can manage their own activities. In negotiating who is in and who is out, who is one of them and who is not, children begin to grasp their developing social identities. Such differentiation among peers becomes more important throughout the preschool years and is a central process in the peer culture of preadolescents. We will return to this issue of social differentiation in peer cultures in Chapters 7 and 8.

Sharing Routines and Rituals

Although children's cultures are composed of a wide range of behavioral routines, none are perhaps more symbolic of childhood ethos than **sharing rituals**. These collective activities involve patterned, repetitive, and cooperative expressions of the shared values and concerns of childhood. They often involve stylized performances and "constitute ritualized moments which are distinctive to the childhood world in which they are embedded and which punctuate the flow of social exchanges in that world" (Katriel, 1987, p. 306). Sometimes, such stylized performances are embedded in more general peer activities, as seen in Goodwin's (1985) study of African-American girls' negotiations during the game of jump rope and Mishler's (1979) analysis of "trading and bargaining" among middle-class American six-year-olds at lunchtime. Here, however, let us concentrate on ritual performances of Italian children whose overriding purpose of production is to mark communal sharing within peer culture.

The art of verbal negotiation and debate is deeply valued in Italian society. Public discussion and debate (or what Italians refer to as ***discussione****)* is an integral part of everyday life and occurs in bars, public squares, and shopping areas. Children also engage in *discussione* with adults and peers from an early age, and the activity is an important element of peer culture (Corsaro & Rizzo, 1988, 1990; New, 1994). We will return to consider *discussione* among Italian children in the next chapter, when we discuss the importance of conflict in peer culture. For now, let's look at a particular verbal routine, the *cantilena*, which frequently arises in the course of children's discussions in the *scuola materna* (a government-supported preschool program for three-to-six-year-olds).

The *cantilena* is a tonal device or sing-song chant that children produce in a range of verbal activities. The chanting is often accompanied rhythmically with nonverbal gestures such as hitting one's fists or the sides of one's open hands together. Aside from these basic rhythmic features and except that verbalizations normally occur in alternating, nonoverlapping turns, there are no set rules to its production. However, the repetition of lexical items (words or sounds) within turns and key phrases over the course of several exchanges is common. Consider the following example: Several children between the ages of four and six are sitting around a table drawing pictures. One of the children, Nino, suddenly hits his hands together and chants, *"Chi mi da il nero, è per sempre mio amico. Chi mi da il nero, è per sempre mio amico."* ("He who gives me black, is my friend forever. He who gives me black, is my friend forever.") Two children sitting near Nino, Giovanna and Luigi, rummage through a pile of marking pens on the table. Giovanna finds a black one first and hands it to Nino. This routine is repeated several times, with the three children alternating the role of enunciator of the *cantilena*.

It is difficult to capture the effect of the *cantilena* without actually hearing it. In the above example, there is falling intonation in the first part of the phrase ("He who gives me black") ending at the lowest point with the naming of the color, and then rising intonation in the second part ending at the highest point with the word forever. The fall and rise is rather easily produced in this example since a stock phrase about friendship is used. The children, however, often spontaneously produce the *cantilena* in the course of debates where they can often not anticipate the topics of discussion, let alone exact words or phrases. Consider the following case study of Italian children's production of the *cantilena* in a peer discussion.

Italian Children's Production of the *Cantilena* in *Discussione*

Several children (Franco, Paolo, Sara, Nino, Giovanna, and Luigi), who are all about five years old, are sitting around a table drawing. They are in the middle of a *discussione* about the existence of *lupi* (wolves or werewolves) and *fantasmi* (ghosts). After several claims and counters, two of the children, Franco and Paolo, suggest that ghosts do exist and that they live in abandoned houses under the sea. At this point a girl, Sara, initiates a multiturn *cantilena*.

Sara:	*Nelle—le case buie. Stanno nelle buie.* (In the—the dark houses. They stay in the dark.)
Paolo:	*Eh, è vero.* (Yes, it's true.)
Franco:	*E sotto mar—è buio!* (And under the sea—it's dark.)
Nino:	*Eh, è vero.* (Yes, it's true.)
Sara:	*E sotto—ci vanno loro.* (And under—they go there.)
Luigi:	*No, ci vanno anche I granchi.* (No, also crabs go there.) [Hitting his hand against marker]

EXHIBIT 6.3

A child initiates the *cantilena.*

EXHIBIT 6.4

Other children respond in *cantilena.*

Franco: *Ci vanno I sommergibli.* (Submarines go there.)
Nino: *E anche I pescecani. E anche I pescecani.* (And also
          sharks. And also sharks.)

In her production of the *cantilena,* Sara strings together several
elements from the earlier discussion (ghosts, dark houses, ghosts
under water). Her turn is especially impressive because it involves
three separate phrases all produced in the falling and rising pitch of
the *cantilena* and all containing new elements related to the discussion with only minor repetition. Again, it is hard to appreciate the
phonetic aspects of the *cantilena* without hearing it. To preserve the
sing-song pitch, it is necessary to produce a phrase with at least four
syllables, and one has to think of something to say quickly of this
length that fits the ongoing discussion. Long turns with new information are especially difficult to produce, and difficult productions
like Sara's are appreciated by one's peers. On the other hand,
minimal participation is also valued, and rather easily produced, as
we see in Paolo's response to Sara (*Eh, è vero*). The trick here is to
add the *Eh* (or *Si* or *No*) before the *è vero* to have enough syllables

to work with. In all my attempts to participate in the children's *cantilene*, I never got past this simple but appreciated contribution. After Paolo's response, Franco, Nino, and Luigi all contribute to the *cantilena*. They either signal agreement or disagreement, refine previously mentioned information (it's under the sea), or add new information (other underwater objects like crabs, submarines, and sharks). In all of these turns the children rely on the repetition of key phrases to ensure coherence and to maintain the basic sing-song cadence and rhythm of the *cantilena*. (Adapted from Corsaro and Rizzo, 1990)

An important feature of the *cantilena* is that the routine is a consciously shared element of peer culture. That is, the children not only produce the routine but refer to it using the term *cantilena*. Additionally, the teachers and the children's parents are aware of the *cantilena*. In fact, the children's frequent chanting often irritates parents, who restrict usage of the *cantilena* in the home with the command *"Non far la cantilena!"* ("Don't do the *cantilena!*"). Interestingly, in family role play in the *scuola materna*, children in superordinate roles (mother, father, and older siblings) often use this same command when disciplining peers in subordinate roles (babies and younger children); they produce the *cantilena* in pretend quarrels. In this way the children take the adults' disapproving reactions to their peer routine and embed them into their shared peer culture in role play. We again see how many peer play routines directly (or in this case more subtly and creatively) challenge adult authority. We now turn to a more detailed look at the importance of play routines for autonomy and control in peer culture.

Autonomy and Control in Peer Culture

Earlier I noted that a major theme of peer culture revolves around children's desire to achieve autonomy from the rules and authority of adult caretakers and to gain control over their lives. This issue of control is apparent not only in children's active challenges to adult control, but also in a range of play routines in which children collectively confront curiosities, confusions, and fears from the adult world.

Challenging Adult Authority

Some argue that the many findings of how children challenge and even mock adult authority in their play suggest that this behavior may be a universal feature of children's cultures (Schwartzman, 1978). In Chapter 3 we saw that role reversal games like the boy bishops ritual existed as long ago as medieval times and that the newsies and street hustlers of turn-of-the-century American cities clearly enjoyed outwitting adults. Regarding cross-cultural studies, Brian Sutton-Smith (1976) points to "order-disorder games" that can be found in Western and non-Western societies. In these games—for example, the familiar "ring-around-the-rosy"—everyone cooperates to create order, only to destroy it by collapsing. Although some might accuse Sutton-Smith of reading too much into such games, others argue that the subtle aspects of inversion, challenge, and satire are what make these games so appealing to children.

Helen Schwartzman argues that children not only experiment with and refine aspects of the adult world in play, but also use play as an "arena for comment and criticism" (1978, p. 126). For an example, she points to some of the play of the children of the !Kung Bushmen of Southwest Africa as described by the anthropologist Lorna Marshall (1976). One of the games of !Kung children that Marshall describes is called "frogs," a reverse form of "Mother, May I?" The game begins with one child being chosen "mother for all" and the remaining children sitting in a circle. When the mother taps a child with a stick, the child pretends to sleep. While all the children are sleeping, the mother pulls hairs from her head and places them in an imaginary fire to cook. The hairs are "frogs" that have been gathered for food. When the frogs are cooked, the mother wakes her children one by one and asks each one to go and get her mortar and pestle so she can finish preparing the frogs. But each child refuses, so the angry mother goes to get the mortar and pestle herself. While she is away, the children steal the frogs and run off to hide with them. When the mother returns she pretends to be very angry and chases after the children.

> When she finds one, she strikes him/her on the head with her forefinger. This action "breaks the head" so that the child's "brains run out," and she then pretends to drink the "brains." The final part of the game frequently ends in chaos and pandemonium as the children try to dart away from mother's grasp. Soon everyone is chasing everyone else, shrieking and laughing and wacking each other on the head. (From Schwartzman's description of Marshall's report, 1978, p. 131.)

Westerners might cringe at the references to "drinking brains" and the aggressiveness of the play. On the other hand, the !Kung would see our competitive games like football or even hopscotch as similarly distasteful. In fact, Marshall points out that the !Kung do not play any competitive games (except tug-of-war) because the idea of winners and losers is not accepted in their culture, which values the group over the individual (Schwartzman, 1978, p. 130).

We explored children's secondary adjustments to adult rules in Chapter 2. Children's secondary adjustments in preschool settings contribute to a group identity and provide children with a tool for addressing personal interests and goals. Over the course of a year in a particular preschool, children's creation and participation in a wide range of secondary adjustments lead to the development of what I have termed an "underlife" in preschools (Goffman, 1961). An underlife is a set of behaviors or activities that contradict, challenge, or violate the official norms or rules of a specific social organization or institution. The underlife exists alongside and in reaction to those organizational rules of preschools that impinge upon the autonomy of the children. In this sense the underlife is an essential part of the children's group identity.

The underlife is perhaps most apparent in secondary adjustments carried out through the active cooperation of several children. These secondary adjustments normally involve using legitimate resources in devious ways to get around rules and achieve personal or private needs or wants—what Goffman calls *"working the system"* (1961, p. 210). Children frequently work the system to avoid helping at cleanup time. In preschools I have studied in the U. S. and Italy cleanup usually occurs at transition points in the day (before snacks or meals, meeting times, and so on). There is a general rule that children stop play when cleanup time is announced, and help teachers put things back in order. Children soon question the necessity and logic of cleanup time. I once overheard a child argue against putting toys away during cleanup time because "we'll just have to take 'em out all over again!"

Children often come up with several strategies to evade cleanup time: relocation (immediately moving to another area of play upon hearing the announcement of cleanup); pretending not to hear the announcement (simply ignoring the command to obey the rule for as long as possible); and using personal problem delay (claiming they cannot help clean up because of personal problems). This last strategy is particularly interesting. Children report a plethora of problems, such as feigned injury ("I hurt my foot"), pressing business ("I have to go to the bathroom"), or role play demands ("I have to finish feeding the baby").

Once in Italy, a child named Franca told one of the teachers that she could not help clean up because I was in the process of teaching her English. There was some truth to this since children often asked me how to say certain words in English, and Franca had made such a request earlier in the day. However, we clearly were not involved in this activity when cleanup time ensued. Fortunately, I was not brought into the dispute because the teacher rejected Franca's excuse out-of-hand. Nevertheless, during the course of this debate a good deal of the cleanup work was performed by other children. In fact, all of the strategies to avoid cleanup are at least partially successful for this reason. Due to organizational constraints—teachers' need to get the children to lunch, to begin a meeting, and so on—any delaying tactic is somewhat effective. It does not take long for children to learn this and to "work the system" accordingly (Corsaro, 1990, p. 20).

Children's secondary adjustments are innovative and collective responses to the adult world. Further, by sharing a communal spirit as members of peer cultures, children come to experience how being a member of a group affects both themselves as individuals and how they relate to others. Through secondary adjustments, children come to see themselves as part of a group (a peer group of students), which is in some instances aligned with other groups and in other instances opposed to other groups (teachers and adult culture). At the same time, children begin to develop an awareness of how communal values can be used to address personal interests and goals. Clear evidence of this can be seen in children's attempts to control the behavior of their peers by offering them the opportunity to share collectively in secondary adjustments. For example, on one occasion in an Italian preschool, I saw an older boy, Roberto, fail repeatedly to get a younger child, Fabrizio, to play a board game the "correct" way. Although exasperated with Fabrizio's refusal to follow directions, Roberto did not give up. He decided to abandon the game momentarily, and took a small car from his pocket. He then rolled the car toward Fabrizio, who picked it up, looked it over, and rolled it back. After playing with the car for several minutes, Roberto put it back in his pocket and suggested that they play with the board game. This time the younger child played "correctly." After a few minutes, however, Fabrizio asked to see the car again, but this time Roberto said, *"Basta così!"* ("Enough of this!") and left Fabrizio sitting alone at the table.

Confronting Confusions, Fears, and Conflicts in Fantasy Play

In Chapter 5 we explored how children's interactions with the adult world often generate disturbances or uncertainties for them. Children address some of these disturbances as they arise with parents and other adults, but they attempt to resolve many others in imaginary worlds that they create and share with peers. In these "as-if" worlds, "familiar activities may be carried out in different ways: inanimate objects may be treated as animate, one object (or gesture) may be substituted for another, and children may perform an activity usually carried out by adults" (Fein, 1981, p. 1096). This "as-if" quality does not mean, however, that there are no rules in imaginative play. Vygotsky argues that the very organization and coordination of pretend play demands attention to real-life rules and also the invention of new rules, which define and redefine the behavior of imaginary characters like monsters, fairies, and ghosts (1978, p. 95).

The study of pretend play has revealed a great deal about children's cognitive, emotional, and social development. Recently researchers have examined children's fantasy and sociodramatic play to obtain a better understanding and appreciation of children's peer cultures in their own right. Especially important is work that captures the complex improvisational nature of fantasy play and documents how children in such play address shared fears, concerns, and values (Corsaro, 1985; Göncü, 1993; Sawyer, 1995, 1997). In our previous discussion of the play of slave children in the pre–Civil War South, we saw that sociodramatic play provided an arena in which the children confronted anxieties in anticipation of the harsh worlds they would face as adults. Other researchers have noted the ubiquity and complexity of contemporary children's sociodramatic play across cultural and subcultural groups (see Corsaro, 1993; Goodwin, 1990; also see Slaughter & Dombrowski, 1989; Schwartzman, 1978 for reviews). In sociodramatic play children simultaneously (1) use, refine and expand a wide range of communicative skills, (2) collectively participate in and extend peer cultures, and (3) appropriate features of and develop an orientation to wider adult cultures.

Some play routines are only loosely connected to models from the adult world. Such routines are not well documented and in some cases seem to be acquired spontaneously in local peer cultures, while others seem to be passed along from older to younger children. Let's look at one such routine, which I refer to as *approach-avoidance play*.

Approach-avoidance play is a primarily nonverbal pretend play routine in the peer culture of preschool children in which children identify, approach, and then avoid a threatening agent or monster. The best way to get a feel for approach-avoidance play is to examine an enactment of the routine. Like many routines in peer culture, approach-avoidance is hard to appreciate outside its natural context. Furthermore, the routine is primarily nonverbal, making it even harder to capture on paper. I try to bring a videotaped enactment of the routine to life in the following case study.

The Walking Bucket

Three children from an American preschool (Beth, Brian, and Mark), who are all about five years old, are playing on a rocking boat in the outside yard of the school. Suddenly, Beth notices another boy (Steven, six years old) walking some distance from the boat, with a large trash can over his head.

"Hey, a walking bucket! See the walking bucket," shouts Beth.

"What?" says Brian. Beth, pointing to where Steven is walking, repeats, "A walking bucket. Look!" Brian and Mark turn, look, and see Steven. "Yeah!" says Brian, "Let's get off."

Brian, Mark, and Beth jump off the boat and slowly approach Steven. When they reach him, Mark and Brian push the bucket and start to lift it up.

Steven responds by lifting the bucket off his head. Brian yells, "Whoa!" and the three children pretend to be afraid of Steven and race back to the rocking boat. Steven pursues them, flailing his arms in a threatening manner. Brian, Mark, and Beth all hop onto the far side of the boat. Steven stops at the vacant side and rocks the boat by pushing down on the edge of it with his hands. Steven does not climb onto the boat, nor does he directly try to get at the other children.

Steven then returns to the dropped bucket and places it back over his head. Brian, Mark, and Beth watch from the boat, giggling and laughing.

This routine continues with Brian, Mark, Beth, and later another child, Frank, approaching Steven every time he replaces the bucket on his head. Each time he removes the bucket the children flee back to home base with Steven in pursuit. With each approach the group of children becomes more confident and aggressive. They taunt Steven (calling him a "big fat poop butt") and kick at his legs under the bucket without actually making contact. During a fourth approach, Steven flips off the bucket a bit prematurely and finds himself face-to-face with Mark. The two begin to push one another, and a teacher standing nearby intervenes, ending the play.

This example is typical of the approach-avoidance play that occurred spontaneously in the American and Italian preschools I studied. The routine is composed of three phases: *identification*. *approach*, and *avoidance*. The identification phase begins when Beth sees and refers to Steven as a walking bucket. Steven had never placed a bucket on his head before. Beth just happens to see Steven and spontaneously identifies him as a walking bucket. In approach-avoidance play children often are thrust into the role of a threatening agent in this way. Beth's playmates confirm her identification when they turn to look at Steven and Brian responds, "Yeah." Although behaviorally very simple (it involves a call for attention, shared attention, labeling, and confirmation), identification provides an interpretive frame for Steven's behavior that is in line with the shared routine of approach-avoidance. Once the identification is offered and ratified, the routine literally clicks into operation.

The approach phase begins with Brian's suggestion, "Let's get off." The three children then jump to the ground and move slowly toward Steven. Although Steven seems aware of the approach, he does not react until Mark and Brian push the bucket and attempt to lift it. Steven then lifts the bucket from his head, enabling himself to see and chase the children. The three children screech loudly in mock fear and race back to the boat. Several things are important here. It is clear that the three children are in this together. The approach is communally orchestrated, moving from Brian's proposal, to the slow advance toward Steven, to the pushing of the bucket, and finally to the feigned fear in reaction to Steven's taking the bucket from his head. A building tension occurs in the approach phase, which the children create and share.

Steven's participation to this point has been minimal. He is thrust into the role of threatening agent by the others. He is not even aware of this assignment until they push the bucket and he removes it. Steven actually begins to replace the bucket on his head, but then notices the other children running away from him toward the boat.

The children's fleeing initiates the avoidance phase. This phase can proceed only with the threatening agent's active participation. Steven flails his arms in a threatening manner as he pursues the other children back to the boat. He does not, however, move onto the boat, signaling the limits to his power as a threatening agent. The boat thus becomes a home base for the threatened children. Steven returns to the bucket and replaces it on his head. The threatening agent is now again disabled and the first cycle of the routine is complete (see Corsaro & Heise, 1990).

Before pursuing further discussion of the importance of approach-avoidance in peer culture, let's look at a more formalized version of the routine Italian preschoolers refer to as *la Strega* (the Witch).

La Strega

Cristina, Luisa, and Rosa (all about four years old) are playing in the outside yard of the preschool. Rosa points to Cristina and says, "She is the witch." Luisa then asks Cristina, "Will you be the witch?" and Cristina agrees. Cristina now closes her eyes and Luisa and Rosa move closer and closer toward her, almost touching her. As they approach Cristina repeats, *"Colore! Colore! Colore!"* ("Color! Color! Color!"). Luisa and Rosa move closer with each repetition and then

Cristina shouts: *"Viola!"* ("Violet"). Luisa and Rosa run off screeching, and Cristina, with her arms and hands outstretched in a threatening manner, chases after them. Luisa and Rosa now run in different directions, and Cristina chases after Rosa. Just as *la Strega* is about to catch her, Rosa touches a violet object (a toy on the ground which serves as home base). Cristina now turns to look for Luisa and sees that she also has found a violet object (the dress of another child). Cristina now again closes her eyes and repeats: *"Colore! Colore! Colore!"* The other two girls begin a second approach and the routine is repeated, this time with "gray" as the announced color. Rosa and Luisa again find the correctly colored objects before Cristina can capture them. At this point, Cristina suggests that Rosa be the witch and she agrees. The routine is repeated three more times with the colors yellow, green, and blue. Each time the witch chases but does not capture the fleeing children.

The *la Strega* routine highlights some additional implications of approach-avoidance play for children's peer culture. First, it allows for the personification of the feared (but fascinating) figure *la Strega* in the person of a fellow playmate. The fact that *la Strega* is now embodied in the actions of a living person is tempered by the fact that the animator is, after all, just Cristina (another child). The feared figure is now part of immediate reality, but this personification is both created and controlled by the children in their joint production of the routine.

A second thing to note is that the structure of the routine leads to both a buildup and a release of tension and excitement. In the approach phase, the witch relinquishes power by closing her eyes as the children draw near to her. The tension builds, however, as the witch repeats the word *colore,* because she decides what the color will be and when it will be announced. This announcement signals the beginning of the witch's attempt to capture the children and the avoidance phase of the routine. Although the fleeing children may seem to be afraid in the avoidance phase, the fear is clearly feigned since objects of any color can easily be found and touched. Thus, the witch seldom actually captures a fleeing child. In fact, threatened children often prolong the avoidance phase by overlooking many potential objects of the appropriate color before selecting one.

We see in the American and Italian examples that the threatened children have a great deal of control. They initiate and recycle the routine through their approach, and they have a reliable means of escape (home base) in the avoidance phase. These cross-cultural data nicely demonstrate how children cope with real fears by incorporating them into peer routines that they produce and control (see Corsaro, 1988).

Variants of approach-avoidance play have been reported in many cross-cultural studies of children's play (see Schwartzman, 1978; Sutton-Smith, 1976 for reviews). In Chapter 5 we talked about Gaingeen, a bogey described by Barlow (1985) in her study of the Murik of Papua New Guinea. In her analysis Barlow describes and analyzes a strikingly similar type of approach-avoidance play among children of the Murik in response to Gaingeen. Barlow notes that although Gaingeen is "initially terrifying and strange, early in children's experience the secret of the masked figure is revealed" and the children discover he is an adolescent boy wearing a costume (1985, p. 1). Barlow points out, however, that Gaingeen loses none of his fascination after this demystification. Rather, children incorporate Gaingeen into the routines of peer culture. For preadolescents there is a pattern in which Gaingeen himself is approached and avoided when he appears.

For the younger children Gaingeen is created by one or several children who make costumes (see Exhibit 6.5) and take on the role of Gaingeen while the other children approach and avoid.

E X H I B I T 6.5

Young children make Gaingeen costumes.

Summary

The concepts of sharing and gaining control are important to children's production of and participation in initial peer cultures. In the preschool and early elementary school years children immensely enjoy simply doing things together. However, generating shared meaning and coordinating play are challenging tasks for young children. Thus, children spend a good deal of time creating, protecting, and gaining access to basic activities and routines in their peer culture. We saw, for example, that once preschool children initiate a play activity, they tend to protect their interactive space from the intrusions of other children. Although the protection of interactive space seems uncooperative to adults, it is seen as just the opposite for the children. Given their developing cognitive and communicative skills, children have to work hard to establish shared play. Once shared play is initiated children want to keep sharing what they are already sharing, and they see others as a threat to the community they have established. What of the children seen as intruders? They wish to enter and to become part of shared play. Thus, over time, by confronting resistance to their access attempts, children acquire complex access strategies that allow them to enter and share in play. These access strategies are clear precursors to adult skills for becoming part of interaction in similar multiparty settings.

Once children establish shared play they produce a wide range of behavioral routines. None is perhaps more symbolic of childhood cultures than sharing rituals: collective activities that involve patterned, repetitive, and cooperative expressions of the shared values and concerns of peer culture. In this chapter we discussed one such activity, Italian children's production of the *cantilena*, a tonal device or sing-song chant that the children regularly produce in peer discussions and debates. Children's production of sharing routines like the *cantilena* reflects a range of concerns in the peer culture. Most important, they provide young children with a sense of excitement and emotional security.

Children attempt to gain control over their lives in a number of ways. One of the most essential is by resisting and challenging adult rules and authority. Children challenge adult rules in the family from the first year of life. Such activity becomes more widespread and sophisticated when children discover common interests in preschool settings. In these settings children produce a wide set of practices in which they both mock and evade adult authority. In fact, many of these "secondary adjustments" to adult rules are more complex (structurally and interactively) than the rules themselves.

Children attempt to deal with confusions, concerns, fears, and conflicts in their daily lives by creating and participating in various routines of their peer cultures. Young children are frequently warned of dangers by parents and other adult caretakers and, more indirectly, through their exposure to movies and fairy tales. Children, in turn, frequently incorporate a wide range of fears and dangers (from threatening agents such as monsters and witches to dangerous events like fires, floods, and becoming lost) into their peer cultures. We saw examples of such incorporation in preschool children's pretend fantasy play and their production of the approach-avoidance routine. Approach-avoidance play, a pretend play routine in which children identify, approach, and avoid a threatening agent or monster, is especially interesting because its production has been documented in several cultures which indicates its possible universality. Overall, by engaging in shared fantasy play and by producing games, routines, and rituals, children more firmly grasp and deal with social representations of evil and the unknown in the security of their peer cultures.

7

Conflict and Differentiation in the Initial Peer Culture

In Chapter 6 we focused primarily on communal aspects of children's peer cultures. We saw that children do, at times, actively oppose adult control, but that such conflict often increases the cohesion of and commitment to group identity. Peer cultures are not always, however, the picture of peace, joy, and community spirit. Young children argue, fight, push, kick, and sometimes even bite. Although physical aggression is rare, verbal conflicts and disputes are common features of children's cultures. In this chapter we will examine disputes, conflict, and social differentiation in early childhood peer culture.

Conflict and Peer Relations

Recent studies of children's friendships have documented what at first glance seems to be a contradictory fact: Conflicts frequently emerge in friendship relations. This finding seems surprising, argues Carolyn Shantz (1987), because much of the work on conflict by developmental psychologists does not carefully distinguish *social* conflict from individual acts of aggression and thus tends to focus on individual (rather than interpersonal and cultural) features of conflict. When we look closely at conflict in children's peer interaction, most especially verbal debates and arguments, we find that such conflict often serves to strengthen interpersonal alliances and to organize social groups (Goodwin, 1990). In my research in preschools in the United States and Italy, I have found that children's social relations and friendships are embodied in the everyday discursive practices—that is, the talk that goes on—in the peer cultures and in the larger communities. Let's look at talk and friendship in an Italian *scuola materna*, in an American Head Start program, and in an American upper-middle-class private preschool.

Discussion and Debate in a Scuola Materna

Italian preschool children, much like adults in their communities, frequently engage in highly stylized and dramatic discussions and debates. As we noted in Chapter 6, **discussione** is a central element of Italian everyday life. Having been exposed to and included in *discussione* by parents, teachers, and other adults in their community, preschool children generate and value this activity in their peer cultures.

In Chapter 6 we looked at an example of Italian children's use of the *cantilena* and how the *cantilena* energized and added dramatic flair to their debates. Let's return to that example and pick up the debate at its beginning.

Bad Wolves Do Not Exist

Several children (Sara, Franco, Luigi, Giovanna, and Nino, all about five years old) are sitting around a table drawing pictures. A great deal of discussion has occurred at the table before the following debate emerges. A boy (Paolo, also about five years old) has been painting at another table in the room. He overhears the dispute, goes to the table, and actively joins the discussion.

1. *Sara:*　　　Wolves do not exist.

2. *Giovanna:*　Yes, wolves exist!

3. *Sara:*　　　They don't exist—only their bones.

4. *Franco:*　　It's not true, wolves do exist!

5. *Luigi:*　　　Yes.

6. *Franco:*　　But, they do not exist only in the mountains.

[Paolo now enters scene and stands near the table where Sara and Franco are sitting.]

7. *Paolo:*　　　It's true, they exist!

[Sara waves Paolo away with her hand as she speaks.]

8. *Sara:*　　　You're not in this.

9. *Franco:*　　You're not in this. Because—

[Franco pokes his finger at Sara's chest.]

10. *Sara:*　　　You—

[Sara pushes Franco's hand away and pokes her finger in his chest.]

11. *Franco:*　　[pushes Sara's hand away] You say that I'm not in this. Wolves exist!

12. *Sara:*　　　No, it's not true.

13. *Paolo:*　　　Not even ghosts.

14. *Franco:*　　It's true.

15. *Luigi:*　　　The ghosts—

16. *Franco:*   Yah! They don't exist.

17. *Sara:*   No. No. Those, no.

18. *Franco:*   Yes. Yes, they exist. Ghosts, however, exist—

19. *Nino:*   They're in the woods.

20. *Franco:*   Eh, it's not true. Ghosts exist under the sea in houses—

21. *Luigi:*   (Inaudible)

22. *Franco:*   No.

23. *Paolo:*   In—in abandoned houses.

In this sequence several children debate the existence of supernatural phenomena (bad wolves or werewolves and ghosts), which are of much interest to young children. The debate begins with Sara's claim that wolves do not exist. Giovanna challenges Sara, claiming that wolves do indeed exist. Sara, then, gives in a bit by saying that only their bones exist. At this point several other children join the dispute, including Paolo, who was not originally involved in the main activity. Paolo comes over, paintbrush in hand, to stand next to Sara and argue, "It's true, they exist!" Third-party entry of this type is interesting, because although it was common among the Italian children, it never occurred in peer disputes I observed in American schools. In this instance, Sara tries to exclude Paolo ("You're not in this"), but Franco immediately challenges her action by throwing the same phrase back at her. In this way Franco is implicitly challenging Sara's attempt to be the boss and a violation of a basic rule in Italian children's peer cultures: Everyone has a right to be a part of any discussion. After Sara's attempted rebuttal (line 10), Franco says in essence, who are you to say I'm (or anyone) is not in this, and then goes on to argue again that wolves do exist (line 11).

Paolo, now a full participant, adds a new element arguing that ghosts do not exist. Franco first agrees with this claim (line 14), but then changes his mind (line 18). At this point there is a general discussion, with different children adding (and often arguing about) new information regarding where ghosts live if they do exist (in the woods, in abandoned houses, and finally in abandoned houses under the sea). As we saw earlier, the children take turns continuing the debate in the sing-song cadence of the *cantilena*.

Discussione is highly valued in Italian children's peer cultures for several reasons. First, it provides an arena for participation in and sharing of peer culture. The children debate things that are important to them (friendship, play activities, ghosts, werewolves, and so on) and in the process develop a shared sense of control over their social world. Second, *discussione* is a highly communal activity. It has a participant structure that has relatively easy entry requirements (for example, simple agreements, denials or repetition), but it also has the attraction of multiple opportunities for embellishment and individual creativity (for example, Paolo's introduction of ghosts). Because of its communal nature, *discussione* is not restricted to the original participants and third party entry is common. In fact, Sara's attempt to exclude Paolo was inappropriate and was responded to as such by Franco. Third, *discussione* often accompanies and, at times, even takes over teacher-directed activities like drawing, play with materials, and eating at snack and lunch times. In this way the initiation and sustaining of a discussion of their choosing gives the children a sense of power and control over their environment and caretakers. This aspect of the routine is especially powerful and satisfying for the Italian children because the general activity of *discussione* is so highly valued in adult culture.

Oppositional Talk in a Head Start Center

Head Start is a federally sponsored compensatory preschool education program for economically disadvantaged children in the United States. The program emphasizes the development of cognitive and social skills. Parents must meet income eligibility criteria in order to enroll their children in this free program. The center I observed in a large midwestern city reflected the population of its inner city location in that the overwhelming majority of the children, teachers, and employees were African Americans.

The Head Start children constructed social identities, cultivated friendships, and both maintained and transformed the social order of the peer culture through opposition and confrontation. Peer interaction and play routines often contained oppositional talk. **Oppositional talk** is playful teasing and confrontational talk that some African-American children frequently use to construct social identities, cultivate friendships, and both maintain and transform the social order of their peer cultures. "Why you following me like that for?" and "What you think you're doing, boy?" are examples of oppositional talk. Consider the following exchange, which took place while two girls were playing in the sand box.

Pam: Hey, girl, don't use that little ol' thing [scoop], use this big one.

Brenda: [Takes the bigger scoop] Ok.

Brenda: What's a matter with you girl, that's too much sugar in that cake!

Pam: No it ain't.

Brenda: I said it is, girl.

The children seldom reacted negatively to oppositional talk of this type or ran to complain to the teachers. In fact, oppositional talk and teasing were valued (much like the Italian children's *discussione*) as part of the verbal enrichment of everyday play. Particularly clever oppositions or retorts were often marked as such with appreciative laughter and comments like "good one" or "you sure told her" by the audience and, at times, by the target child. Overall, the Head Start children explored, tested out, and developed friendship skills and knowledge in the general frame of oppositional talk and teasing (see Corsaro, 1994; Corsaro & Maynard, 1996).

The children's oppositional style in peer interactions often seems aggressive to middle-class white Americans. In fact, anthropologists, folklorists, and linguists have contrasted the oppositional style of African-American speech with communicative practices of most European-Americans, who tend to minimize antagonism and direct confrontation (Abrahams, 1975; Goodwin, 1990; Heath, 1983, 1990; Kochman, 1981). Among African-Americans, opposition and conflict, according to Abrahams, "tend to be viewed as constant contrarieties, antagonisms that cannot be eliminated and in fact may be used to effect a larger sense of cultural affirmation of community through a dramatization of opposing forces" (1975, p. 63).

The oppositions and challenges among the Head Start children were normally reacted to in kind, and the overall tenor of exchanges was one of playful banter. This verbal dueling sent dual messages: (1) that a particular child could hold his or her own ground and (2) that participation in oppositional talk signified allegiance to the values and concerns of the peer culture. Ultimately what emerged among the often vying voices of the Head Start children were assertive and competitive friendship relations that led to a mutual respect and group solidarity.

Conflict and Friendship in an American Upper-Middle-Class Preschool

In the private upper-middle-class preschool, emphasis was on individual expression and recognition of the uniqueness and rights of others. The teachers' interactions and style of discourse reflected a great deal of patience and respect for the children's individual needs. Although the teachers encouraged children to attempt to solve their own problems and disputes through talk and reflection, they also were open and comforting to children who came to them with complaints about the behavior of peers. The teachers' language style and suggestions for how to handle conflict affected the nature of peer and friendship relations in the preschool.

I observed a classroom of younger children (three-and-a-half to four-year-olds) and another of older children (four-and-a-half to five-year-olds) in the private preschool. The younger children used the word *friend* to attempt to gain access to play, to protect shared activities from intruders, to build solidarity and mutual trust in the play group, and to attempt to control the activity of playmates. Conflict frequently developed regarding the nature of play. In such instances, the children often used friendship in attempts to get their way. Consider the following example: Helen, Eric, and several other children are playing with toy dinosaurs in a sand box. Eric hops his dinosaur close to Helen's and then flips it around so that its tail hits against Helen's toy. "Stop that!" says Helen. Eric repeats the action, and Helen says: "I won't be your Buddy!" Eric says, "Ok," and begins to bury his dinosaur in the sand.

The "denial of friendship" strategy that Helen uses here was often effective at this preschool. The children took such threats very seriously, often giving in immediately or becoming upset and going to a teacher for comfort. The use of the strategy was, however, somewhat of a double-edged sword. Children on the receiving end in one instance could quickly turn things around and issue threats of their own in the next instance.

In the classroom of older children, several overlapping small groups or cliques of close friends developed over the course of the school term. There were also boys and girls who played with a number of peers but did not belong to any particular friendship group. The interaction in the friendship groups was similar to the social relations of close friendships described in Thomas Rizzo's (1989) study of middle-class American first-grade children. Rizzo found that when the first-graders noticed shortcomings or problems in their friends' behavior, they insisted that their friends must make the necessary changes to set things right. This insistence often led to disagreements and disputes.

In the friendship groups of the older children I observed, such disputes were intense and, at times, persisted over the course of an entire day or even several days. In one instance a girl, Shirley, became very upset when her best friend, Megan, refused to allow her to enter a game Megan was playing with two other girls in their friendship group (Mary and Veronica). Mary and Veronica were pretending to be pet ponies under the direction of their owner, Megan. After Megan said Shirley could not play, Shirley began to cry and threatened Megan, saying they would not be "best buddies" anymore. She also said Megan would not be invited to her birthday party. Megan would not give in, however, so Shirley went off to complain to a teacher. The teacher suggested that Shirley "talk it over" with Megan or play with someone else. Shirley returned to plead her case, but to no avail. In the end, the two girls got into a shoving match and both began to cry. At that point, we all went back inside the school, and a teacher sat the two girls down and talked to them about the problem. After the talk, Megan and Shirley sat alone, still sobbing, in their cubbies until lunch time. Later in the day after lunch and naptime, however, I saw the two girls sitting together and holding hands while watching a circus video.

In his work with first-grade children, Rizzo described numerous friendship disputes of this type. He argues that such disputes not only helped the children obtain a better understanding of what they could expect from each other as friends, but also brought about intrapersonal reflection, resulting in the children's development of unique insight into their own actions and roles as friends.

The Contextual Nature of Conflict and Community

Overall, these comparative studies capture the complex relation of conflict and friendship in peer cultures. We see that peer relations and friendships are, in many ways, a reflection of the values and practices of the local and more general communities and cultures in which they emerge. The comparative analysis demonstrates the importance of viewing friendship as a collective and cultural process. In this view, culture is not simply a force or variable that affects how children come to be or have friends. Rather friendship processes are seen as deeply embedded in children's collective, interpretive reproduction of their cultures.

Social Differentiation in Initial Peer Cultures

Although social participation and friendship are central processes in the peer cultures of young children, differentiation in peer relations begins in early childhood and increases dramatically as children move into preadolescence. Social differentiation in young children's peer cultures are related primarily to gender and status. We shall discuss each in turn.

Gender Differentiation

The first sign of social differentiation in young children's peer relations is increasing gender separation. Gender segregation begins in preschool and becomes so dramatic in elementary school that "it is meaningful to speak of separate girls' and boys' worlds" (Thorne, 1986, p. 167). In one of the first ethnographies of preschool children, the anthropologist Sigurd Berentzen observed peer interaction and culture among five-to-seven-year-old children in a Norwegian preschool in 1967. Berentzen found that the children constructed their peer cultures primarily around gender contrast. Both boys and girls followed the self-imposed rule that "girls/boys don't play with boys/girls" with few exceptions (1984, p. 158). Girls and boys also organized their activities around different concerns. The boys valued competition and toughness, while the girls were mostly concerned with affiliation or establishing best friends.

Later studies in American, British, and Australian preschools and elementary schools reported similar findings (Best, 1983; Cahill, 1986; Davies, 1989; Paley, 1984; Thorne, 1993; Walkerdine, 1990). Vivian Paley's (1984) *Boys & Girls: Superheroes in the Doll Corner,* which is based on observations in her kindergarten classroom, nicely captures the play themes of boys and girls. As boys in the guise of Darth Vader and Luke Skywalker (predecessors of today's Power Rangers) lay claim on the block area and roam the outside play yard, girls gather in the doll corner to devise "dramatic plots that eliminate boys and bring in more sisters and princesses" (1984, xi). When the boys come around the doll house to put out a fire, capture robbers, or have some dinner (even superheroes eat!), the girls resist this intrusion in their space. The boys are just as protective of their play, scoffing at the girls' attempts to build castles, houses, or zoos in the block area. Bothered by such conflicts and the gender polarity it symbolized, Paley at first encouraged compromise, primarily through attempts at the partial domestication of the boys in order to make them more acceptable to the girls. In the end, however, Paley decided that indeed the robbers should stay out of the doll house, not because boys behave badly, but because the story lines of the fantasy play of the boys and girls do not mesh. As a reflective teacher she learned from the children that the "integrity of fantasy must be preserved" (1984, p. 90).

Is gender differentiation among young children always this dramatic? Is it universal? As Thorne (1993) has pointed out, in much of the work there is a tendency to exaggerate gender differences and ignore similarities. Boys and girls do play and work together in educational settings, especially in more structured and group projects. Also, although instances of boys and girls playing together in free play are rare, they do occur and merit careful analysis. Features of group composition and setting are important. In a review of cross-cultural studies of children's worlds, Whiting and Edwards found strong support for the emergence of gender segregation at about age six, but noted that segregation "seems to be a feature of same-age, not the mixed-age, social interaction" (1988, p. 80).

In my research in the United States and Italy I have found, in line with the general findings noted above, much more gender segregation among older children (five-to-six-year-olds) as compared to younger children (three-to-five-year-olds). However, gender segregation and different activity preferences by gender were greater for American upper-middle-class children than for African-American or Italian children, regardless of age. These findings may be related to the communal orientation and age composition of the programs. In line with the communal orientation of Italian preschools, the curriculum of the *scuola materna* I studied often involved small groups of four or five children (mixed by age and gender) working on different aspects of elaborate group projects that lasted over several weeks (see Corsaro & Emiliani, 1992; Edwards, Gandini, & Forman, 1993 for a discussion of the communal orientation). Also, the Italian preschool was mixed age in composition, with a nearly equal number of three-, four-, and five-year-olds. There was also a communal orientation in the Head Start center, and the African-American girls were, on the whole, more assertive and independent in their relations with each other and with boys than were the upper-middle-class white girls I studied (also see Goodwin, 1990; Schofield, 1982).

What do these qualified findings on gender segregation suggest regarding the formation of gender identity among young children? Traditional developmental theories with their emphasis on biological factors, reinforcement contingencies, or stages of cognitive development fall short in that they all focus on gender development as a process of individual change or adjustment to societal roles. The focus is on outcomes or developmental paths, rather than on children's active construction and involvement in their social worlds. Recently a number of theorists have linked gender directly to social action and collective practices (Connell, 1983, 1987; Davies, 1989; Thorne, 1993; Walkerdine, 1986; Willis, 1990).

Perhaps the best example of this general theoretical approach as applied to preschool children and gender can be seen in the work of Davies (1989; also see Fernie, Davies, Kantor, & McMurray, 1993). Her work stresses children's active role in their construction of gender identities and is a clear break from traditional functionalist notions of socialization and gender. Davies argues that masculinity and femininity are not inherent properties of individuals, but rather are structural properties of society. Social actors are constrained but not determined by these properties. Through our use of discursive practices (how we speak and act) we contribute to reproduction and change in society. Therefore, "as children learn the discursive practices of their society, they learn to position themselves correctly as male or female, since that is what is required of them to have a recognizable identity within the existing social order" (Davies, 1989, p. 13). The rigidity of such positioning, however, can often be problematic and constraining, and children soon realize that minor refinements and even genuinely different positionings are possible and desirable.

Children often run into what they see as problems in positioning themselves regarding gender in spontaneous productions of role play. For example, I once observed a role-play event where a wife (a girl) and a husband (a boy) cared for two pet kitties (two boys). In the play the husband helped the wife clean by moving furniture and vacuuming. For his efforts, he was praised as a "strong and handy man" by his wife. The kitties then urinated on the floor and were shooed from the house by the angry husband and wife.

After several repetitions of this general routine, one of the boys tired of being disciplined and bossed around as a kitty, abandoned the role, and proposed that there be two husbands. This proposal was embraced by the other husband, and the two boys danced around shouting happily: "Two husbands! Two husbands!" The wife, however, was dismayed by this turn of events and rejected the proposal saying, "I can't marry 'em, two husbands." The problem was solved (at least long enough for the role play to continue) with the wife becoming a kitty and the husbands "marrying themselves" (Corsaro, 1985, p. 102–104). The switch in position from kitty to husband allows one of the boys to escape the subordinate role and allows for the future possibility of praise as a strong husband, all the while keeping traditional gender roles intact (boys are husbands and girls are wives). The girl, however, is threatened by the prospect of two husbands and moves to a subordinate role, seemingly unappreciative of the benefits of having two strong, handy men around. Perhaps she is aware that both benefits and costs would be doubled!

Davies and her colleagues provide similar examples that demonstrate the creativity and flexibility of preschool children "in their reinvention and maintenance of the rigid structure" of traditional gender roles (Fernie, Davies, Kantor, & McMurray, 1993, p. 103). However, children sometimes go beyond reinvention and maintenance to bend and even break the traditional gender frame in their role-play activities. An excellent example of the former is what I have termed "animal family role play." In this play, which I observed in both the United States and Italy, children pretend to be animals with assigned family roles (usually mothers and children, with girls in the mother role and both girls and boys as children). The children produce typical human family routines but with some important differences. First, the children are both more aggressive and more mobile in their play. In contrast to human family play, which normally is confined to a playhouse area and is relatively subdued, animal family play normally occurs outdoors, with family members (wolves, tigers, and lions were favorites) moving from a cave or den to roam around the yard screeching and scratching at each other and at other children in the area. Second, the care and discipline of baby animals was more physical but less restrictive than in human family role play. Babies often were playfully swatted for their misbehavior, but also were allowed to roam away from the den to play for lengthy periods without supervision. Finally, animal family play was less rigidly structured than human family play. Mothers performed family chores like cleaning, cooking, and even shopping, but also go off to play with other kids (usually running and chasing games with other girls) who do not have defined roles in the animal family.

Fernie, Davies, Kantor, & McMurray (1993) present the positioning strategies of a young girl, Lisa, as an example of the breaking of nontraditional gender frames. Over the course of the year, Lisa aligned herself with a high-status, core group of five boys in the preschool, boys who frequently engaged in superhero role play. In both peer play and teacher-directed activity, Lisa embraced the male superhero role of Batman, rather than the feminine alternative, Batgirl. Furthermore, it was clear that Lisa did not take the role just to gain entry to the boys' core group; she assumed the role even when the boys were not present. In one instance, Lisa persuaded one of the youngest girls in the class to come to her Batman house, wear a cape, and hold a stick for a gun. Happy with her new recruit, Lisa put her hands on her hips and announced, "We're bad. Stay out. This is our house." (Fernie, Davies, Kantor, & McMurray, 1993, p. 102).

In these last two examples we see children resisting dichotomized gender roles and displaying an openness to multiple positioning or ways of being male or female. These examples also suggest some possibilities of breaking down strict gender segregation among preschool children in free-play activities. As Davies notes, encouraging "home corner behavior" among boys and more "macho" type play among girls is seldom successful (1989, p. 133; also see Paley, 1984). Children are confused by the purpose of such pressures and see them as arbitrarily restrictive of their play. Instead, Davies recommends encouraging a wide range of positionings in play. As a result, children are free to develop new positionings and to "find ways of thinking about and describing their own and other's behaviour independently of what we currently think of as 'masculine' and 'feminine'" (1989, p. 133–34).

Status Differentiation

Earlier we saw that young children's resistance to adult rules leads them to develop a sense of "we-ness" or a group identity, which is a central feature of peer cultures. Emerging after and existing alongside this dynamic of affiliation, however, is another more contentious, competitive one (Fernie, Kantor, & Whaley, 1995). This competitive dynamic leads to the emergence of subgroups and status hierarchies within subgroups of peers, especially during kindergarten and the early elementary grades.

Formation of status hierarchies. A number of researchers have examined processes of status differentiation in peer groups. One group of researchers has identified dominance hierarchies in which higher ranked children consistently win out over those at lower ranks in aggressive conflicts (LaFrenier & Charlesworth, 1983; Strayer & Strayer, 1976). Such findings must be evaluated with caution, however, given their strict focus on aggression and given certain ecological features of the settings and groups studied (Connolly & Smith, 1978). Group size is important, because the larger the group, the more opportunities children have to avoid the aggressive behavior of some children and seek affiliation with others. More important, differentiation within groups of children is highly complex and cannot be understood by focusing only on physical dominance. Children frequently compete with and attempt to control one another using a wide range of interpersonal and communicative skills, and status hierarchies are often fluid and constantly changing. Such fluidity and complexity is increased when competition itself (through physical contests, verbal dueling, and narrative skills) is valued more than actually winning (see Goodwin, 1990).

Some researchers have found clear status hierarchies among preschool and elementary school boys (Berentzen, 1984; Best, 1983). Berentzen reports that the Norwegian preschool boys he studied constantly engaged in competition, made note of rankings, and acted in accordance to them (1984, pp. 107–108). In Best's study, elementary school boys often negotiated rank in advance of activities. Such ranking was based on perceived toughness and resulted in a designated chain of command (first, second, third captains). The boys referred to rank in structuring play and settling disputes (1983:75).

Resistance of status hierarchies. Although Berentzen and Best found clear patterns of ranking among the boys, girls in these studies resisted explicit rankings and relied on more subtle methods for controlling one another. I, however, found no pattern of clear and stable status hierarchies among either boys or girls in my observations of American and Italian preschool children. Age may be a factor in the difference in these findings, especially given that most of the children in Berentzen's study were between the ages of six and seven years old. In general, I found frequent competitive behavior among underdeveloped or highly fluid status hierarchies. This pattern was apparent in our earlier discussion of conflict in the peer relations of these children. The findings are also very similar to those of Goodwin (1990), whose research with preadolescent African-American children we shall discuss in Chapter 8.

The lack of stable rankings in my studies relates to the children's preoccupation with *process over structure* in peer relations. That is, the American and Italian children were most interested in debating and negotiating where they stood with one another rather than in establishing and maintaining rankings. Attempts to be leader or boss usually were quickly challenged and were often thwarted. The older girls in the Italian preschool, for example, frequently debated about who should or should not be *"il capo"* (the boss or leader). In instances where a leader was agreed upon, the chosen girl would offer up plans of action and things would go fine for awhile. Then minor violations of the leader's instructions would occur. The leader would soon become upset, but the other girls would appease her and promise to obey. Soon thereafter, however, the violations would grow more serious, and the leader's rules would be mocked with laughter and derision. The leader would then stomp off, refusing to play anymore. In most cases, the other girls would run after her, promising to straighten up if given one more chance. The leader would usually return, only to have the whole thing happen all over again!

I found similar resistance to girls' attempt to be the boss in my American data (also see Maynard, 1985, 1986; Rizzo, 1989). In one such instance three girls (Ruth, Shirley, and Vickie, all about five-and-a-half years old) are looking through department store catalogs and selecting items to cut out and paste on paper to make a collage. The girls are concentrating on what they call "girls' stuff" and refer to some of the other items as "yucky boys' stuff." After they have been playing for ten minutes or so, another girl, Peggy, comes over and stands near Shirley.

Shirley points to a picture of a couch in a catalog. "We don't want that couch, that's dumb." "All we want is the pretty stuff," says Ruth.

Peggy now announces, "If you are going to come to my birthday, you have to obey my orders."

"Oh, we don't care," responds Ruth. Ignoring Ruth, Peggy continues, "And every girl in the whole school is invited. . . . Shirley, every girl."

Vickie now says, "Every girl, Shirley called every girl?"

"I'm going to put a sign up," continues Peggy, "that says, 'No boys allowed!'" "Oh good, good, good," says Vickie. "I hate boys."

Peggy now adds further information about her party, noting, "And the girls can't do whatever they do—they gotta obey my rules."

Shirley quickly rejects these restrictions, declaring: "Then we're not coming."

"Yeah, but the point is," adds Ruth, "we're cutting out all these for, for presents for your birthday, but we'll forget about it. We're not coming!"

Although the other girls seem to take Peggy's proposal about her birthday party seriously in this example, they probably do not believe that a birthday party only for girls would ever take place. It was a common practice in the preschool for all of the members of class to be invited to birthday parties. Here Peggy's aim seems to be to insert herself into the ongoing activity, and to take charge of it with the negative references to boys. The other girls seem open to the notion of excluding boys but are quick to reject Peggy's attempt to set proposed rules that would put her in charge of their behavior. In this example, all of the girls except Ruth were part of a friendship clique composed of six of the older girls in the class. There was a clear resistance in this group to any girls setting themselves up as leader or boss (see Corsaro, 1994, pp. 18-20). Berentzen found a similar pattern for the Norwegian preschool girls he studied, noting that their "cultural premises and criteria of rank lead to their constantly denying each other's rank" (1984, p. 108).

Mary Martini's study of mixed-age-and-gender play groups of Polynesian children of the Marquesas Islands adds further insight into complex processes of status negotiations among young children. Polynesian children learn early in life that there are different rules for interacting with those of higher status (parents and other adults) and with those of equal status (peers in the same age range). Children are required to be restrained and compliant when dealing with adults, but peer relations are based on reciprocity (Martini, 1994). This reciprocity is based on both "a continual willingness to share what one has with others" and by status rivalry (Howard, 1974, p. 206; Martini, 1994, p. 77). For example, Martini discovered a complex dominance hierarchy of (usually) older children (six- and seven-year-olds) in the roles of noisy and quiet leaders, three- to five-year-olds in the role of initiate members, and toddlers as peripheral members of the group. The use of the term *dominance hierarchy* can be misleading here, because the children work together in the specialized roles to coordinate group activity:

> Noisy leaders introduce activities, direct group play, and keep players on track. Quiet leaders invent new play, monitor the bossiness of noisy leaders, and care for peripheral toddlers. Initiate members follow the leaders and support each other as they go through the process of hazing. They also care for peripheral toddlers and generally hold the group together from the inside. Peripheral toddlers are interested observers. Their incompetence highlights the skills of the older children. Older children gain status by helping and teaching dependent toddlers. (Martini, 1994, p. 98)

This coordination of roles, argues Martini, "leads to [the] children generally avoiding danger, caring for their own needs, settling disputes efficiently, and distributing goods fairly" (1994, p. 99).

Martini's research and other comparative studies remind us of the Western bias that is evident in much of the research on children (also see Harkness & Super, 1992; Nsamenang, 1992b; Schildkrout, 1975; Weisner & Gallimore, 1977; Whiting & Edwards, 1988). In the mixed-age-and-gender groups of children in many non-Western societies, attempts to control other children are most often *prosocial* rather than *egoistic*. That is, the goal is to maintain group cohesiveness rather than to attain individual desires (see Whiting & Edwards, 1988, p. 182). Martini contrasts this preference for prosocial versus egoistic control to peer interactions among middle-class American children who learn to value goal-directedness and individual achievement early in life. Such values clearly affect the nature of their peer relations as they move from preschool settings into kindergarten and the early grades.

Core groups and rejected, neglected, and controversial children. A number of researchers have noted the emergence of higher status or core groups in the peer cultures of preschool, kindergarten, and elementary school children (Best, 1983; Fernie, Kantor, & Whaley, 1995; Paley, 1992; Thorne, 1993). Members of these core groups often work together to resist the entry of new members. Here the resistance goes beyond the tendency to protect interactive space, an idea we discussed in Chapter 6. The protection of interactive space involves children's attempts to maintain control over specific play events that they have worked very hard to create. When stable core groups emerge in peer cultures, children are most often rejected simply because they are not members of the group; the rejection often has nothing to do with the protection of interactive space. The actual process of restricting membership often serves to solidify the core group. Most children do not accept rejection from core groups without a struggle. They may eventually gain acceptance by adopting core group values and play preferences, or they may work with other rejected children to develop their own core groups (Fernie, Kantor, & Whaley, 1995).

Some children may play at the periphery of these core groups yet remain active participants in peer culture. Other children, however, are continually rejected; still others make little effort to enter peer play. Many clinical psychologists and educators argue that isolation from the peer group can have serious long-term effects on emotional development. Three types of low-status children have been identified in the research literature: rejected, neglected, and controversial children (see Ramsey, 1991, pp. 91–93).

Rejected children usually fall into two main groups: *aggressive-rejected children,* whose aggressive behavior leads others to resist their inclusion in play; and *withdrawn-rejected children,* who withdraw when they fail in their attempts to gain access to play groups (Asher & Coie, 1990; Hatch, 1986; Ramsey, 1991). Neglected children are not consistently rejected, but they fail to become active participants in peer culture. They are often loners or "the quiet children who are content in their roles as minor players in the social arena" (Ramsey, 1991, p. 86). Controversial children are what some might call "characters." As Ramsey notes, these active, enthusiastic, and humorous children "have a major impact on the social life of the classroom, but their peers do not agree about what that affect is" (1991, p. 87; also see Coie and Dodge, 1988). As a result controversial children are seldom fully integrated into peer cultures.

I have encountered at least one such controversial child (it was usually a boy) in each of the several preschool classrooms I have studied. Their humor and enthusiasm can be infectious, but at the same time their peers often come to see them as overbearing. In one of the American classrooms I studied, a boy (Daniel) spent a lot of time telling jokes and riddles and concocting very elaborate play plots. Consider the following example of Daniel's riddle.

The head teacher, Mary, is in the playhouse with several children, pretending to have dinner. Daniel is one of the children and he says, "Mary, I want to tell you a riddle."

"Ok," replies Mary.

Daniel asks, "How can a man fall into the ocean and not get his hair wet?"

"I don't know," says Mary. "Maybe he had a hat on."

"No," yells Daniel. "He was bald-headed!"

All the children and Mary laugh, but Daniel laughs the loudest and continually repeats the word "bald-headed." Daniel then leaves the playhouse and runs around the school calling out to different children: "You're bald-headed!" Some children protest, saying they are not bald-headed, while others laugh gleefully and join Daniel in the name calling. Eventually, the teachers respond to the ongoing disruption and put an end to the "bald-headed" episode.

Reactions to Daniel's complex plots were also mixed. He would sometimes gain the initial cooperation of several children and would propose complex lines of action as if he were a movie director. On one occasion he had me and several children pretend to be the audience for a proposed puppet show. He gave each of us two wooden blocks (one a bar of candy and the other a flashlight to find our seats) and instructed us to "sit down and get ready for the show!" Then he and another boy, Tony, went behind a bookcase and began banging away with hammers, ostensibly building the set for the show. After about ten minutes of banging he reappeared and said the show was about to begin. Then there was more banging and the audience began to dwindle. Meanwhile, I sat and waited patiently with Sue, Sheila, and Christopher. Finally, Daniel and Tony pushed two chairs up behind the bookcase, climbed onto the chairs, and called for our attention. We thought the show was about to begin, but Daniel announced that Tony "messed every thing up" by not letting him use the good hammer, and that "the puppet show was canceled." Tony denied this accusation and begin pushing Daniel, and the two fell from the chairs. Tony hurt his leg and begin to cry, and a teacher ran over to help. I remained seated, but the other children got up to leave, with Sheila dropping her candy and flashlight to the floor and declaring: "What a gyp!"

"You Can't Say, You Can't Play": sharing and exclusion among peers. In her book, *You Can't Say, You Can't Play,* Vivian Paley presents her viewpoint regarding children's attempts to exclude peers from play. Rather than taking the view that children's attempts to exclude peers derive from a need to protect interactive space, she views such attempts as examples of rejection and considers them hurtful. In her book, Paley describes how she first proposes the general rule "You Can't Say, You Can't Play," discusses it with her kindergarten class and with first-through-fifth-graders in her school, and then institutes the rule. (The meaning of the rule, of course, is, You can't tell another child that he or she can't join in and play.) As Paley explains, most of the children are against the rule, protesting that they want to play with their friends or that some kids don't play right. Other children, especially those frequently rejected, generally support the rule, saying it hurts their feelings to be left out. In the midst of all this discussion Paley realizes that an essential part of her curriculum (placing disruptive children in "time out") is a violation of the rule, and she terminates the "time out" procedure. Eventually, the "You Can't Say, You Can't Play" rule is established and, despite some rough spots, it works pretty well. There is less exclusion and the kids are generally nicer to one another.

In Paley's study, the teacher (Paley), most of the students, and the rule itself (at least on its surface) were clearly middle-class American. The children frequently complained about their peers being mean and hurting their feelings. The teacher was responsive to such complaints, and she developed a rule to address exclusion and meanness. When talking over the rule with the children after its institution, Paley traces its origin from another cultural context, the book of Leviticus from the Old Testament. She supplies the appropriate quotation: "The stranger that sojourneth with you shall be unto you as the homeborn among you. . . ." (1992, p. 102). The quotation seems to bring about a recognition on her part. "You see, lately, I've come to understand," she says, "that although we all begin school as strangers, some children never learn to feel at home, to feel they really belong." "They are not made welcome enough," she concludes (1992, p. 103). Thus, Paley hopes that the institution of the rule will bring about a more humane and communal classroom.

Paley, however, overlooks the importance of the predominately white, middle-class cultural context in which she attempts to articulate the rule. In this and other middle-class American schools there is, as we saw earlier, an emphasis on individual expression and a recognition of the uniqueness and rights of others. In such a cultural context the rule seems restrictive to the individual rights of the majority of the children, and, therefore, it is resisted. Paley also fails to consider why that very cultural context creates the *need* for such a rule. Let's return to the work of Martini and to my research in the Italian *scuola materna* and in an American Head Start center. In these groups of children there was a great deal of conflict, opposition, and debate in peer interaction and culture. Yet, a general group ethos existed in which the children competed individually to collaborate collectively (Corsaro & Maynard, 1996). In these groups the continual exclusion of particular children was rare, children seldom complained to teachers about hurt feelings, and "time out" was not a routine part of the curriculum. To the eyes and ears of many middle-class Americans, however, these groups of children seem threatening. Their debates and competitions seem too rough and intense and the teachers seem a bit authoritarian. Viewed in this way, a rule may seem necessary for maintaining fairness. In evaluating these different responses to the practice of excluding children from play, we must remove our cultural blinders and remember that peer cultures are affected by and contribute to the reproduction of and changes in adult cultures within which they are embedded.

What then of Paley's rule? I think it is a good one. But it may take more than the proscription "You can't say, you can't play" to create a group ethos that echos young Franco's attitude when he reprimanded Sara's attempt to exclude Paolo in the *discussione*: "Who are you to say that I or anyone is not in this!"

Summary

Conflict and social differentiation are central elements of peer culture. Developmental psychologists have long stressed the importance of conflict for creating disequilibriums and providing clues for the elaboration of new cognitive structures and skills. More recently, psychologists, anthropologists, and sociologists have argued that conflicts are not merely cognitive, but are relational in that they naturally emerge in children's interactions with adults and peers. In our comparative analysis of conflict, discussion, and friendship processes in three culturally different preschools, we saw how these processes constitute and bring about changes in peer cultures. We saw, for example, that Italian children frequently engaged in *discussione*, highly stylized and dramatic public debates in peer interaction. Such debates are highly communal activities in which the children address concerns that are important to them and, in the process, develop a shared sense of control over their social world. African-American children produced a similar communal activity, oppositional talk. In this activity the children playfully tease and challenge one another in peer play. The verbal dueling that makes up oppositional talk sends a dual message: (1) that a particular child can hold his or her own ground, and (2) that participation oppositional talk signifies allegiance to the values and concerns of the peer culture. In contrast to the Italian and African-American children, we saw that American upper-middle-class preschool children took conflicts much more seriously. Their disputes were much more emotionally intense and were often related to attempts to control the behavior of other children they saw as friends. Overall, these comparative research findings demonstrate that conflict contributes to the social organization of peer groups, the reaffirmation of cultural values, and the individual development and display of self.

Conflict also contributes to the structural complexity of and differentiation in peer cultures. Processes of differentiation by gender and status emerge in the peer cultures of young children. Although a general tendency toward increased differentiation by gender and status in peer cultures may be universal, cross-cultural comparative research cautions us against assuming that these processes work themselves out in the same fashion. We must especially guard against the general acceptance of patterns discovered in the peer relations of white, middle-class children in the United States as models for understanding children's cultures. We will continue to take comparative studies into account in Chapter 8, where we examine peer cultures and identity formation as children move from early childhood to preadolescence.

8

Preadolescent Peer Cultures

When does childhood end? That is a hard question to answer. Defining the boundaries of childhood (and deciding on the range and limits of our consideration of the sociology of childhood) is a difficult task. Childhood is a social construction that is clearly related to, but not determined by, physical maturation, cultural beliefs about age, and institutional age grading.

For purposes of this book, childhood will include preadolescence, which is generally defined as the period from seven to thirteen years of age. We will not be able to discuss the transition to adolescence or adolescent peer culture. In the field of sociology, however, adolescence has received much more attention than childhood, and there have been some excellent recent studies that look specifically at the transition to adolescence (see Corsaro & Eder, 1990; Eder, 1995; Thorne, 1993). We will include adolescence in our discussion of the social problems of children and youth in Chapters 9 through 11.

In Chapters 6 and 7 we identified two basic themes in children's peer cultures: (1) **communal sharing**, the strong desire for sharing and social participation, and (2) **control**, children's persistent attempts to actively gain control over their lives. In this chapter we will discuss how these themes are produced and extended in the peer cultures of preadolescent children. We will be especially concerned with how the extensions of these patterns are related to children's development of unique social selves or identities as they make the transition from childhood to preadolescent peer cultures.

Peer Cultures in Preadolescence

Most of our knowledge of the peer cultures of preadolescent children is the result of research in Western societies. However, we know from the research discussed in Chapters 5 through 7 that children's groups are much less age-segregated in non-Western societies. Children who are seven to ten years of age in these societies spend much of their lives in mixed-age groups caring for and playing with younger siblings and other younger children in their local communities. These preadolescents have much less time for peer play in general, as they take on a range of tasks to help support their families. Furthermore, as we will see below, research across racial, ethnic, and social class groups in the United States challenges some of the well-documented patterns in the peer cultures of white, middle- and upper-class children. Therefore, we must be careful to keep these differences in mind as we explore the basic themes of sharing and control in the peer cultures of preadolescent children.

Friendship Processes in Preadolescent Peer Cultures

As we saw in Chapter 6, preschool children immensely enjoy simply being and doing things together. They often signal recognition of their ability to carry out joint actions with verbal references to friendship such as "We're friends, right?" (Corsaro, 1985; Parker & Gottman, 1989). However, generating shared meaning and coordinating play are often difficult tasks for young children. Thus, preschoolers spend a great deal of time creating and protecting the shared play and peer routines that provide them with a sense of excitement and emotional security.

Things are different for preadolescents. Children seven to ten years of age easily generate and sustain peer activities. However, they now collectively produce a set of stratified groups, and issues of acceptance, popularity, and group solidarity become very important. We will explore the importance and complexity of this increasing differentiation in peer relations by examining social participation and friendship processes, the nature and structure of differentiated friendship groups, and friendship, differentiation, and gender in preadolescence.

Social Participation and Friendships

In preadolescence the primarily nonverbal play routines of early childhood (for example, approach-avoidance and other play routines) are gradually replaced by verbal activities that involve planning and reflective evaluation. For example, Rizzo reports that first-grade children appeared to have an internalized concept of friendship that serves multiple functions in peer relations. Specifically, in his year-long ethnography of first graders, Rizzo found that the children "attempted to determine the existence of friendship by comparing the internal concept with specific features of interactions with frequent playmates, to act in accordance with this concept when with friends, and to object when their friends failed to live up to their expectations" (1989, p. 105). In short, the children had the beginnings of a reflective awareness of what a friend should be, and they realized that they did not have to wait until they found themselves playing with a peer to have a friend. They could try to control who their friends would be!

Many times, however, the children found that their friendship bids (asking to be one's friend or being nice to someone) were often not accepted, and were at times actively rejected. Having a better awareness of what being a friend involves did not ensure that they could develop close friendships. In fact, in Rizzo's study the most enduring friendships were the result of what could best be termed "local circumstances" of play and peer relations. Children became involved in types of play they enjoyed and, like the preschoolers we discussed earlier, they verbally marked and agreed that they were friends. However, unlike the younger children, the first graders would maintain these patterns of shared play with certain children over time and come to mark the relationship as special—by considering themselves to be best friends.

Best friends, then, often tried both to protect their friendships from the possible intrusions of others and to expand their friendship group. It is not surprising that these two processes came into conflict in a variety of ways. First, even though best friends wanted to expand their groups beyond their two-person dyad, they were very sensitive to the possible disruption of the fragile, dyadic best friend relationship. Therefore, they often displayed jealousy when their best friend played with others without them, and they quarreled with their best friend about the general nature of his or her play with others.

Rizzo and others see these disputes and conflicts as serving many positive functions, which I will address in the next section. Here I want to discuss another process in peer relations that develops shortly after best friendships are formed: the increasing differentiation of friendship groups.

Social Differentiation and Friendships

Preadolescent children's alliances are often linked to changes of positions in friendship groups, providing the children with opportunities to test a series of social identities. Children's social identities "are thus oriented towards alliances with other children in activities that also separate the children" (Evaldsson, 1993, p. 258). For example, in Rizzo's study best friends often tried to expand their group by constructing "clubs," with membership offered to other kids they liked. The children would sometimes give names to these clubs, but the clubs seldom had any real purpose except to provide a way of expanding the friendship group. Some children were not offered membership, and others were rejected, resulting in the beginning of the development of stratified groups.

In Rizzo's study these groups were rather loosely bound and often broke down and then reformed. In Ann-Carita Evaldsson's study of the play of Swedish seven- to ten-year-olds in after-school centers, the children formed more stable friendship groups that were centered around different activities in the two centers. In one center the children highly valued possession of things, skills in acquiring these possessions, and competence in disputes and discussions about these valued objects. In this center the children frequently engaged in physical games, especially marbles, but competence in debating who was good at these games, in disputing issues of fair play, and in discussing who had the best possessions (marbles) was valued as much as competence in actually playing marbles. In the second center the children's identities and friendship processes were more relational and emotional. Instead of centering around physical activities, skills, and talk about such, the children in the second center were more concerned with appearances, romances, and involvements in secret activities. These values were displayed "in intimate alliances, where comparisons, guessing, teasing and joint laughter support social differentiation" (Evaldsson, 1993, p. 259).

We will return to Evaldsson's study to look more closely at the nature of these play activities and games in the next section, because they nicely illustrate how children address ambiguities, concerns, fears, and conflicts in peer culture. What is of particular interest here, however, is that gender was not a central factor in the differentiation of friendship groups at the two centers she studied. This finding is quite different from the findings of studies of friendship processes among American white, middle- and upper-class preadolescents.

Social Differentiation, Friendships, and Gender

As we saw earlier, many studies have documented increasing gender differentiation in children's peer interactions beginning at around five or six years of age and reaching a peak in the early elementary school years (Adler, Kless, & Adler, 1992; Berentzen, 1984; Gottman, 1986; Oswald, Krappman, Chowdhuri, & von Salisch, 1987; Thorne, 1993). Although there is extensive sex segregation in peer relations in this period, it is rarely complete; most studies show consistent mixed sex grouping and cross-sex interaction (usually on the order of 10 to 20 percent) even in the preadolescent period (Thorne, 1993). What is more important for our understanding of peer cultures is not simply the gender segregation that surely occurs in the preadolescent period, but the nature of interactive patterns and interpersonal processes within the segregated groups. Here there is a growing debate about whether or not girls and boys have different peer cultures.

Thorne argues that a familiar story line runs through the literature on children and gender. "The story opens," notes Thorne, "by emphasizing patterns of mutual avoidance between boys and girls and then asserts that this daily separation results in, and is perpetuated by, deep and dichotomous gender differences" (1993, p. 89). These differences are seen as both affecting and being affected by the structure and nature of activities in gender segregated groups. For example, several studies have found that boys interact in larger groups (Lever, 1976), engage in more aggressive and competitive play (Adler, Kless, & Adler, 1992; Best, 1983), and frequently organize their activities and relations around organized sports (Adler, Kless, & Adler, 1992; Eder & Parker, 1987; Fine, 1987; Lever, 1978; Thorne, 1993; Thorne & Luria, 1986).

In a recent article, Adler, Kless, & Adler (1992) discuss how the nature of these different activities contribute to popularity within the peer cultures of preadolescent boys and girls. They defined popular children as those who "are liked by the greatest number of their peers, who are the most influential in setting group opinions, and who have the greatest impact on determining the boundaries of membership in the most exclusive social group" (1992, p. 172).

Adler, Kless, and Adler found that "boys and girls constructed idealized images of masculinity and femininity on which they modeled their behavior" (1992, p. 169). These images were reflected in a set of **focal concerns**, which affected popularity in boys' and girls' cultures. Focal concerns are a specific set of values, interests, and problems central to the peer culture. Boys' focal concerns revolved around a cult of masculinity or being tough, around physical contests, autonomy and self-reliance, and around a culture of coolness or detachment. Girls' focal concerns, in contrast, centered around the valuing of compliance and conformity, a culture of romantic love, an ideology of domesticity that favored intimacy and emotional expression, and an orientation to ascriptive norms related to appearance and material possessions. These findings are generally in line with claims by the psychologist Carol Gilligan (1982). Gilligan argues that girls have a **"different voice"** in that they value relationships and caring, as opposed to boys' concerns with individual rights and abstract notions of justice. Girls are so concerned with maintaining personal relationships that they strive to avoid conflict and negotiate problems indirectly for fear of seeming uncooperative.

Gilligan's work has led to the general acceptance of the "two cultures" view of children's gender socialization, differences in men's and women's styles of talk, and the nature of social relationships across gender groups more generally (Barnes & Vangelisti, 1995; Gilligan, 1982; Hare-Mustin & Maracek, 1988; Maltz & Borker, 1982; Tannen, 1990). However, we should not be too quick to accept this view of children's gender relations. It has recently been called into question for several reasons.

First, most studies have been of white, middle- and upper-class American children. African-American and Latino boys and girls are much less separated in their play than white, middle-class children. Also, the nature of peer activities, concerns, and values of African-American and Latina girls are much different from white, middle- and upper-class American girls (Goodwin, 1990; Schofield, 1982; Thorne, 1993). Goodwin, for example, found that African-American and Latina girls engage in highly complex physical games and play in which competition and verbal conflict are recurrent and highly valued (1990; in press). The important point here is not simply that studies upon which the two cultures view is based have limited generalizability. Rather, the issue is that findings and interpretations in line with the separate culture view implies that there is something about the *very nature of being male or female* which leads to these differing values and social relations by gender. The implication is, therefore, that the pattern should be universal. There is little support for such a claim.

It is important to note that the issue runs deeper than possible class and cultural differences in gender relations among children. There is also the problem of interpreting data *only* in line with the two cultures view, which stresses very clear cut, almost dichotomous, sexual differences and perspectives. In many of the studies exceptions to the general pattern are pushed aside and seldom pursued. Rarely, if ever, is there a search for negative cases. How might things be done differently? How might we go about identifying and interpreting exceptions to the separate cultures view? Thorne has argued for the importance of grounding observations in a wider range of social contexts (focusing on the less visible and peripheral as well as on the most conspicuous and dominant groups and settings). We need to study both the core groups of the leaders and the more peripheral groups of less popular children. Goodwin has championed the intensive microanalysis of naturally occurring events—how children actually go about playing games like jump rope and discussing friendships and gossiping in their everyday lives. Goodwin's point is especially well-taken. Even with the recent increase in ethnographic studies of peer relations, there is still a common reliance on reports of children's activities rather than on direct study of the activities themselves. In the next section we will focus on what preadolescents do in a range of social settings. We will return to discuss gender relations, and we will explore more generally how children's activities help them to gain control over their lives and further develop a sense of self and identity.

Autonomy and Identity in Preadolescent Peer Cultures

Everyday activities in peer cultures enable preadolescents to negotiate and explore a wide range of norms regarding friendship processes, personal appearance, self-presentation, heterosexual relations, personal aspirations, and relations with adult authority figures. By participating in organized and informal games, verbal play routines, and collaborative storytelling, preadolescents explore developing norms and expectations about themselves and their place in peer and adult culture without the risk of direct confrontation and embarrassment. Let's explore these activities, looking at how they relate to friendship relations, conflicts and disputes, and the challenging of adult control and authority.

Verbal Routines, Games, and Heterosexual Relations

Like preschool children, preadolescents often engage in play routines that involve communal sharing. However, preadolescents with increased language and cognitive skills have more control over when and how such routines might occur. Thus, in addition to more loosely structured play routines, preadolescents often participate in formal games both spontaneously and in organized settings. Children of this age also talk about their play and games in a reflective way, and they can appreciate the subtle and symbolic aspects of play routines both during and after their enactments. Finally, preadolescent children often address concerns about appearance, self-presentation, and heterosexual relations within play routines and games. In this sense they use the "as-if" or pretend frame of play and games as a secure base for addressing sensitive and potentially embarrassing concerns, desires, and ambiguities.

Routines, verbal play, and humor. Preadolescent children often mark allegiance to friendship bonds through participation in sharing routines. These routines are similar to the general celebration of simply playing together that we saw among preschool children. Here, though, the very nature of participation in the routines forces children to think about their relation to one another and their place as individuals in a group.

Consider the Israeli sharing routine *"Xibùdim,"* documented by the anthropologist Tamar Katriel (1987). Katriel conducted naturalistic observations of the sharing routine and also interviewed twenty preadolescents (ages nine to twelve) and ten younger children (ages five to seven). *Xibùdim* usually occurred on the way home from school:

> A group of five children approaches the *falafel* [snack or treat] stand. One exclaims "I'm buying." Another counters, *"Bexibùdim! Bexibùdim!"* in a melodious chant. He gets a *falafel* portion, holds it in his hands, and all take a bite in turn, with a gay clamor. After the third one has eaten, the buyer mutters, *"Hey, beraxmanut"* (with pity) and offers it to the last child. He then eats his falafel, walking along with his friends. (Katriel, 1987, p. 309)

As we can see, this routine has a definite structure: (1) the *opening* or announcement of an intention to buy a treat by a particular child; (2) the *acknowledgment* by other children, usually involving the exclamation *"Bexibùdim! Bexibùdim!"* uttered in a melodious chant; (3) the *purchase* of the treat by the proposer; (4) the *offering* and sharing of the treat, with each accompanying child taking a small bite; and (5) the optional *recycling* of a second round of sharing. The routine involves delicate negotiation in that, as Katriel has noted, the bite size has to be regulated so that everybody gets a share and about half the treat is left for the owner. (This is illustrated by the owner's request for pity before offering the last bite.) According to Katriel, the sharing of treats in *xibùdim* "can be viewed as a ritualized gesture that functions to express and regulate social relationships within the peer group" (1987, p. 307). A key element here is the concept of the individual's respect for others in her or his group of friends; *xibùdim* is derived from the verb *lexabed*, whose literal meaning is "to respect." In an interview, an eleven-year-old girl explained her insistence on getting a bit of her friend's treat in this way: "It's not that I will die if I don't get a bite of the popsicle, that I will die a day earlier or something, but it is simply . . . respect, as the word says." (1987, p. 307). This statement, along with the main features of the routine, support Katriel's insightful interpretation of the routine as a "symbolic sacrifice in which one's self-interest and primordial greed are controlled and subordinated to an idea of sociality shaped by particular cultural values, such as equality and generalized reciprocity" (1987, p. 318). Finally, on a more concrete level, sharing routines such as *xibùdim* are fun! Their production "serves to reassert the very existence of children's peer group culture" as a "celebration of childhood" (Katriel, 1987, p. 318).

Routines like *xibùdim* also are interesting because they simultaneously assert individual rights and creativity and collective solidarity. Many other activities in preadolescents' peer cultures possess this characteristic, especially those related to verbal games and humor. For example, preadolescents produce and embellish a wide range of **children's lore**—games, jokes, chants, rhymes, riddles, songs, and other verbal routines that are created and transmitted by children over time and across societies. Such lore has been well documented by child folklorists (Gomme, 1964; McDowell, 1979; Opie & Opie, 1959, 1969). These activities are rich with laughter, which serves as a communicative marker. It both signals that the activity at hand is not serious and "also signifies support; others with you" (Frønes, 1995, p. 223).

We saw examples of children's lore in our earlier discussion of humor among preschool children, as well as in the Italian children's chanting routine or *cantilena*. However, the humor and verbal play rituals of preadolescents are often more complex, reflective, and portable than those of preschoolers. Merely saying the words "pee-pee" or "poo-poo" can generate laughter anywhere or anytime among preschoolers. However, this joke provides little opportunity for reflective awareness or embellishment, and its expression in play and games often disrupts the activity at hand. Preadolescent children collect jokes and riddles and practice and embellish their presentations, often embedding the joking and laughter in other peer activities. They try out jokes on older siblings and parents and discover that this audience also can be the source of new additions to their developing repertoires. These jokes and riddles often have a two-step, set-up-and-punch-line structure, which demands a certain level of cognitive decentering (the punch line or solution must be inferred from the set up) and language skills (questions must be asked, words phrased or voiced in a certain way, and so on).

My daughter is constantly trying out new jokes on me. Here is an example of one she told when she was about six years old: "What do you call a train filled with bubble gum?" "I don't know." "A Chew-Chew Train!" From an adult point of view, the jokes get better as the child ages. When she was eight my daughter's jokes contained elements of indirectness, involving a play on words or some other type of deception in the setup. She learned many of these from other kids but also several from her uncle. Here are two examples:

1. "If there are twenty sick sheep [sounds like "twenty-six sheep"] and one dies, how many are left?" "Twenty-five." "No, nineteen. I said twenty *sick* sheep!"

2. "If a plane crashed right on the border between Canada and the United States, where would they bury the survivors?" "I don't know, probably in their hometowns." "No silly, they don't bury survivors!"

Like the preschool children who laugh over and over again at the mere mention of certain bodily functions, preadolescents like to repeat their jokes again and again and laugh uproariously at the punch line. They are often unconcerned when the joke's recipient gets the right answer and laugh just as loud at his or her statement of the punch line. Adults, on the other hand, tire of these types of jokes pretty quickly and would rather not hear them even a second time. However, such adult reactions often make repeating the jokes more fun for the children and give them a sense of control over their elders. My daughter would preface many of her jokes (especially several she had heard from her uncle) by saying, "Daddy, pretend you didn't hear the one about—." She did this so often that at one point I threatened to strangle my brother for telling her the jokes. Not fully appreciative of my teasing, she said "Daddy, you're not really going to strangle Uncle Joe, are you?"

Games, secrets, self, and interpersonal relations. Preadolescent children like to play games. They play a variety of games in a wide range of informal and formal settings. Although there has been a great deal of work documenting such games and how children's participation influences their cognitive, emotional, and social development, studies of children *actually playing games* are rare. Several recent studies have addressed this neglect.

One example is Fine's 1987 study of Little League baseball teams. This work is important because it shows how preadolescent boys' participation in organized sports over an extended period of time provides them with a number of interactive settings and occasions for the production and maintenance of a local peer culture. During a Little League season the boys do much more than learn and practice baseball skills and develop a competitive ethos. Interwoven within the culture of baseball is a local peer culture in which the boys develop a strong sense of male bonding and address a wide range of concerns about identity and their perceptions and relations with girls. The boys also use the activities of baseball practice and games as a backdrop for producing, sharing, and acquiring the language, jokes, and lore of preadolescent cultures.

Perhaps some of the best work on **children's games as situated activities** is that of Goodwin (1985, 1990) and Evaldsson (1993). By situated activities these researchers mean games that are produced in real settings with real children who often have long interactional histories. Research that is based on verbal reports of children's participation in games or that relies on analysis of the form and structure of games abstracted from the actual performances miss this "situated" aspect. Such research is bloodless, so to speak. It surely tells us something about how children spend their time and about the developmental implications of participating in games with various physical, cognitive, language, and emotional demands. But if one really wants to capture the rich social world of children's lives and peer cultures it is necessary to enter their play, to be willing to get your pants dirty and shoes muddy.

This is just what Goodwin and Evaldsson have done. Goodwin has studied the play and games of African-American and Latino children in the United States for many years. She has observed, audiovisually recorded, and analyzed these children participating in a wide range of play and games (dramatic role play, team sports, jump rope, hopscotch, racing, pitching pennies, and more) in their neighborhoods and in nearby playgrounds. Goodwin has found that the children's play and games are marked by complex verbal negotiations, disputes, and conflicts through which the children display and develop social identities and organize their peer cultures. We will return to look at Goodwin's work in detail in the next section, where we consider the importance of conflict and disputes in children's peer culture. Here we want to look more carefully at Evaldsson's recent study of children's participation in games in Swedish after-school programs.

Evaldsson studied two different programs for six- to ten-year-old children over an eight-month period. She found that the children repeated games day after day. The children in the Panda center preferred to play and trade marbles, while the children at the Bumblebee center often engaged in jump rope. Marbles is a highly complex game. Piaget (1932) analyzed in some depth the game's contributions to children's negotiation strategies and their moral development. Evaldsson, on the other hand, focused on how children relied on repeated performances of the game to create a locally shared peer culture and to display and evaluate selves and identities in that culture.

Marbles involves skills in playing the game—that is, aiming and shooting marbles at a hole or at another player's marbles, quickly anticipating the flow of play, and shouting various restrictions regarding shooting. Evaluating the value of marbles from a competition and trading standpoint is also important. Although the children in the study played marbles in dyads, there was always an audience of nonplayers who observed and often participated in arranging matches, evaluating the play, and negotiating marble trading. Evaldsson found that boys primarily played the games, with girls more actively involved in evaluating the play and trading.

The games and trades had natural histories in that they occurred over the school term, and during this period of time the children came to assess each other in terms of these various skills. In her documentation of the history of marble play as a complex series of situated activities, Evaldsson found that the children's selves were intimately related to status, which was linked to the possession and negotiated value of marbles as things. In other words, as the children increased and decreased their status in relation to their possession of the valued objects, they used talk to negotiate the value of the objects (Evaldsson, 1993, p. 133). The whole process was made even more complex by shifting alliances of children in judgments and negotiations during both the playing and trading of marbles. Thus we see the developing notion of identity or self embedded in the collectively produced peer culture.

Jump rope, like marbles, is rule-governed and participants are expected to have a particular orientation to one another during play (Evaldsson, 1993; Goodwin, 1985). Although there is a good bit of variation, the general pattern in jump rope is for two children to hold opposite ends of a rope and turn it for a third child who jumps when the rope hits the ground. The child who jumps is normally entitled to continue until she misses. When this occurs the jumper exchanges places with one of the turners, who now has the opportunity to jump. Legitimate misses are the fault of the jumper and not the turner. Therefore, misses are sometimes negotiated to assign fault, and these negotiations can become very heated and complex. Jump rope is competitive because successful jumpers earn high status and often obtain the valued position of "first jumper" in initial rounds of play. However, a most interesting fact of jump rope is that *children must cooperate to compete.* There is a built-in motivation to turn the rope fairly for jumpers because if one turns too fast or not in synchrony with the beat, there is a chance that when the jumper next becomes a turner she or he will do the same for the previous offender (Evaldsson, 1993; Goodwin, 1985).

We can clearly see from the above description that jump rope is much more complex than some previous studies, like those of Lever (1978), suggest. Lever argued that girls' games like jump rope or hopscotch are eventless turn-taking games with much less complex structures than boys' competitive sports games. Such a misperception is the result of not observing, recording, and carefully analyzing the play of the games themselves. However, the complexity and significance of the games is even more apparent when their production and place in peer culture is examined over long periods of time.

Let's consider a typical game of jump rope in Evaldsson's study. She found that in the Bumblebee after-school center, both boys and girls engaged in jump rope activities on a regular basis. The most frequent game was "Cradle of Love." This variant of jump rope can be played a number of ways, but the most common variety at the Bumblebee was this one: A jumper jumps as turners and members of an audience call out the letters of the alphabet. If the jumper misses on a particular letter, others call out the name of another child or of some media character, who then becomes the potential (or pretend) love interest of the jumper. For example, if Amy misses at the letter "P," someone may call out "Paul!" Then Amy jumps to the rhyme, "Paul do you love me. Tell me truly aye or nay." Then the speed of turning is increased and the rhyme continues: "Yes-No Yes-No Yes-No," with the romantic link confirmed or denied according to when a miss occurs. If a jumper succeeds in moving through the entire alphabet, she can propose the name of the love interest without the constraint of the initial letter. However, in this case other children quickly offer up potential names for the jumper to evaluate.

We can see that repetitions of this game among boys and girls who spend a lot of time together take on characteristics that have as much to do with their developing relationships toward the opposite sex as they do with their competitive skill in jumping. Let's look at a more extended example from Evaldsson's work.

Cradle of Love

Sara has just successfully jumped through the alphabet. She gets to pick a name, and two children suggest Dag ("Dan" in Swedish), who is one of the most popular boys with girls in first grade. Sara seems a bit embarrassed and quietly says no. Then the children suggest comic book characters like Batman and Superman and Sara responds no to all these suggestions. The children then return to offering names of children in the group.

| *Ania:* | Leif? |
| *Sara:* | No. |

Paul:	Paul?
Fred:	Someone in your class?
Paul:	Axel?
Ania:	Paul?
Fred:	Paul?
Sara:	Nope.
Axel:	Per-Ola?
Paul:	We've already had Per-Ola.
Sara:	Dag (very quietly). I'll take Dag then. Yes, Dag then.
Mona:	Dag in our class?
Sara:	Nope.
Ania:	Dag sitting over there in the green cap?
Paul:	Is that him?
Sara:	Tuuurn!
Paul:	Him (pointing).
Fred:	Wowww! Wooowie!
All:	Dag Do You Love Me
	Tell Me Truly Aye or Nay (turning faster now)
	Yes-No Yes-No Yes-No Yes-No (turning stops)
	Yeeeessss!
Flera:	Yeesss ho ho ho (laughing)
Fred:	Dag! (Calling to Dag)
Flera:	Ha ha ho ho ho ho (laughing)
Rick:	Dag well that doesn't necessarily mean Dag.
Fred:	But she said Dag.
Ania:	Congrats, Dag!

Source: Adapted from Evaldsson, 1993, pp. 117–119

Evaldsson suggests that Sara was probably too shy to reveal her true preference for Dag when the name was first suggested. Also, because there was more than one Dag in the group, the matter was somewhat ambiguous. However, Sara clears up the ambiguity later and takes the game seriously when she chooses the boy she is fond of in real life. Now this ordinary, everyday game of jump rope is intensified or transformed as the "pretend" versus "real" frame is blurred. This transformation is nicely signaled with the children's laughing, shouts of "Woowie" and the teasing of Dag and Sara. In this way, in the midst of the jump rope game, love becomes a public topic that can engage nearly all the children at that center. Sara takes a chance by addressing her real concerns, feelings, and uncertainties about boys, but she is "protected" by the safety of the play frame, which in this case she dares to stretch.

In addition to participating in organized games, preadolescent children also create their own cultural artifacts to organize and share their activities. For example, children at this age often separate themselves from others through the sharing of secrets. Sharing secrets involves activities ranging from verbal whispering to the writing and passing of notes, the establishment of secret clubs, and the production of complex texts and artifacts. The whispering talk and control of space marks the fact that members of a secret club are part of an exclusive group.

The children in Evaldsson's study produced a number of artifacts related to secrets in their peer culture. These included "love lists" and "fortune tellers." Both boys and girls constructed love lists upon which they wrote the names of best friends in order of preference. These lists were then shared with selected friends and often became the topic of discussions, teasing, and sometimes disputes. Children created fortune tellers by folding a sheet of paper into four parts, then folding the corners into the center, and finally folding the paper into four parts again. The folded paper was then arranged to fit two fingers from each hand for opening and closing (Evaldsson, 1993, p. 196. See Exhibit 8.1).

After constructing the fortune teller, children painted the different parts various colors and wrote messages in the corners that were concealed by the folds. They often talked together as they decided what messages to write. They then played with the fortune tellers in dyads, with other children observing. In play the owner of the fortune teller asks the other player to choose a number and then counts it out, opening and closing the folds. Then the owner asks for a color and upon hearing the response folds back the corner of that color and reads the message aloud. Most messages either teased or insulted the recipient, saying for example that he or she looked like a monkey or was in love with a particular child. The children were fascinated with the magic quality of fortune tellers and greatly appreciated that these artifacts were of their own creation. The creation of and play with fortune tellers is not restricted to Sweden, of course, as they also have been documented among American children (Knapp and Knapp, 1976). Many readers may have constructed them in their youth. They are similar, of course, to toys like the Magic Eight Ball and decoder rings.

An important point about both love lists and fortune tellers is that they are durable creations of peer culture. They not only conceal private informa-

EXHIBIT 8.1

Making a "Fortune Teller"

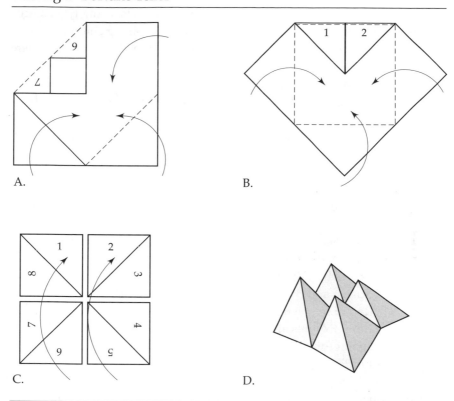

Source: Evaldsson, 1993, p. 197. Used with author's permission.

tion and secrets but make them last longer and allow for their transformation outside the situation of actual use. This transformation often generates a traceable history of their use, which can make them subjects of teasing, debates, and conflicts among peers.

Disputes, Conflict, Friendships, and Gender

Many activities that bring preadolescent children together and build friendships are often the source of disputes and conflicts. Rizzo, for example, found that as first graders developed best friendships they set higher expectations for their friends' behaviors. These expectations often led to disagreements and arguments. In fact, it is a common lament of many kindergarten, first, and second grade teachers that so-called "best friends" seem to be fighting all the time! We have to be careful, however, not to accept the adult perspective regarding conflict among young children too readily—most especially the middle-class American adult perspective. Middle-class American adults are often uncomfortable with disputes and conflicts among children. As we saw in our earlier discussion of the peer cultures of preschool children, there is wide variation in the nature and evaluation of conflict and argumentation across cultures and across subcultural groups within American society. Furthermore, recent research documents the positive aspects of conflict and disputes in children's everyday lives. Let's look at some of this research. We will first examine verbal conflicts and disputes in peer relations, and then behavioral routines involving cross-gender conflict.

Verbal disputes and conflict in peer relations. What are some of the causes of conflict and disputes among preadolescents? How are conflicts important in their daily activities and peer cultures? The chief cause may be the increased differentiation in friendship groups in preadolescence. However, conflict, especially arguments and teasing, also can bring children together and help organize their activities. In this sense cooperation and competition are not mutually exclusive and often coexist within the same activities (Goodwin, 1990, p. 84). Recent research on peer conflict among elementary school children shows how disputes are a basic means for constructing social order, cultivating, testing, and maintaining friendships, and developing and displaying social identity (Davies, 1982; Fine, 1987; Goodwin, 1990; Katriel, 1985; Maynard, 1985; Rizzo, 1992).

Goodwin's work on preadolescent children's play and games in neighborhood settings clearly demonstrates the important role of conflict in the organization of peer activities. For example, Goodwin found that the African-American children she studied organized their talk to *build and highlight opposition*. Boys engaged in arguments and ritual insults as way of dramatizing their play and to construct and display character. Conflicts and disputes seldom reached clear resolution as disagreements between individual children often expanded into group debates. In short, conflict was enjoyed, even relished, and the children actually cooperated to embellish and extend rounds of arguments and insults. Furthermore, the children never complained to adults about peer teasing and insults, rarely excluded peers from play, and did not produce rigid status hierarchies.

Let's take a closer look at Goodwin's work on conflict among preadolescent African-American and Latina girls to capture the tenor of her work. The research is especially important because the everyday lives of these children are seldom carefully studied, but are often misunderstood in American social science.

An especially impressive example of research on children's dispute routines is Goodwin's (1980, 1990) analysis of gossip disputes among black female preadolescents. Unlike the direct competitive disputes of males (Goodwin, 1990; Labov, 1972), black females frequently engage in gossip disputes during which absent parties are evaluated. The airing of such grievances frequently culminates into *he-said-she-said confrontations*. A **he-said-she-said confrontation** can be defined as a type of gossip routine that is brought about when one party to a dispute gossips about the other party in his or her absence. The he-said-she-said confrontation comes about when the absent party challenges his or her antagonist at a later point in time. Consider the following example.

> In the midst of play, Annette confronts Benita saying: "And Arthur said that you said that I was showing off just because I had that blouse on." (Goodwin, 1990, p. 195)

Annette is speaking to Benita in the *present* about what Arthur told her in the *recent past* that Benita said about Annette in the *more remote past*. This complex temporal structure is crucial to he-said-she-said exchanges because the accusation locates the statement made by the defendant about the speaker as having been made in the speaker's absence. Such "talking behind one's back" is considered a serious offense in the peer culture. In her analysis Goodwin specifies the complex linguistic structures that the children use in such confrontations to order a field of events, to negotiate identities, and to construct social order. The gossip routine is important because it is inappropriate to insult, command, or accuse others openly in the girls' peer culture.

Goodwin's analysis is noteworthy for two other reasons. First, it demonstrates that conflict routinely occurs in the girls' peer interactions even though it may take a more indirect form than that of the boys. These findings dispute the work of Gilligan and others we discussed earlier, which maintains that girls are concerned with maintaining relationships and thus avoid confrontations. Second, the complexity of these speech activities clearly refutes claims that working- and lower-class African-American children rely on a dialect that is "nonlogical" (Bereiter and Engleman, 1966). Researchers who have made such claims have not bothered to study the children's language as it is produced in natural settings.

Goodwin has also recently carried out comparative studies of disputes and conflicts in preadolescent girls' playing of hopscotch. On the surface hopscotch seems to be a simple turn-taking game, demanding a fair amount of physical coordination. One person jumps at a time through a grid of squares usually numbered from one to nine. The object is to be the first player to advance a token (rock or bean bag) from the lowest to the highest square and back again. At the start a player tosses her token from below square 1 into a square and, without changing feet, jumps from one end of the grid and back again on one foot, avoiding squares where other tokens have been tossed. Where there are two unoccupied squares next to each other, the jumper's feet should land in the two adjacent blocks. If a player falls down, steps on a line, or outside the correct square, she loses her turn.

Hopscotch can involve a great deal of negotiation about the rules. In the hopscotch play of the African-American and Latina girls that Goodwin studied, nonjumpers intensely scrutinized the body movements of jumpers and were quick to call out infractions and enforce the rules. Consider the following example.

Lucianda takes her turn, jumping twice in square two and possibly putting her foot on the line of square one. Joy sees the violation and yells, "You out."

Lucianda shakes her head no, "No I'm not!"

"You hit the line," counters Joy. And now Crystal comes over in support of Joy and says, "Yes you did. You hit the line. You hit the line" as she points to the line.

Lucianda leans towards Crystal. "I ain't hit no line!"

"Yes you did," shouts Alisha, who has now come over to the group. Crystal supports Alisha, smiling and shaking her head as she points to the spot of the violation, "You did. You s—"

"No I didn't," interrupts Lucianda.

"Yes you did," counters Alisha again.

"Didn't she go like this?" Crystal asks the others. And then looking at Lucianda she says, "You did like this" as she steps on the line in an imitation of Lucianda's jump. "You did like that."

Joy now walks up to the grid and rubs her foot across the line, "Yeah, you hit that line." Then she taps the line twice with her foot and says "Right there, honey!"

Finally, another nonjumper, Vanessa, comes over and says to Lucianda, "You out now!" (Adapted from Goodwin, in press, pp. 18–19)

In this example we see that the girls negotiate and enforce the rules with a great deal of teasing and dramatic flare. In fact, in many cases the stylized disputes and arguments over misses or what were labeled "as attempts to cheat" became more important than the actual play of hopscotch. Rather than simply following the rules or ignoring them, the girls work and play with them, often purposely highlighting opposition (Goodwin, in press, p. 22).

Things were quite different in the hopscotch play of the middle-class white girls Goodwin observed. Instead of closely observing and evaluating the play, the children paid less attention to misses and mitigated their responses to them.

Linsey, Liz, Kendrick and Kathleen are playing. Linsey throws her stone and hits a line. Linsey then begins jumping. "Oh! Good job Linsey! You got it all the way on the 7," says Liz.

Kendrick clearly sees that Linsey has hit a line with her foot. She shakes her head, "That's—I think that's sort of on the line though." "Uh," says Liz to Linsey, "your foot's in the wrong spot."

"Sorry," says Kendrick, "that was a good try."

Later Linsey is jumping again and she makes it through several squares. "You did it!" shouts Cathleen. "Yes!" repeats Linsey. She then hits a line as she nears the end of her turn.

"Whoa," says Cathleen softly. Kendrick then laughing a bit says encouragingly, "You accidently jumped on that. But that's okay." (Adapted from Goodwin, in press, p. 21).

Some feminist scholars see the mitigated nature of children's speech of this type as positive, arguing that it demonstrates concern for affiliation and promotes relational solidarity (Barnes & Vangelisti, 1995). Goodwin, however, notes that group solidarity can be achieved in a variety of ways. Furthermore, she points to a "lack of accountability for one's action" in the mitigated language style of the middle-class white girls in the above example. She argues that interpersonal conflict is often the heart of social life. In fact, conflicts seldom disrupted play in her data; rather, they added spice and flair. In this view, conflict and cooperation are not opposites but overlapping processes that are embedded in the larger ethos of playfulness. Disputes, teasing, and conflict can add a creative tension that increases its enjoyment (Goodwin, in press, p. 24). We can make one final point on the relation between conflict and cooperation in children's play: when children who have spent most of their time in different sociocultural groups come together for play, they often misinterpret each other's styles. Middle-class white girls, for example, often find the teasing, oppositional style of Latina and African-American girls to be threatening, bossy, and mean, while African-American and Latina girls see the mitigated and polite style of middle-class white girls as patronizing (Corsaro & Rosier, 1992; Schofield, 1982). These findings show the value of research on differences in interpersonal interaction and play styles across sociocultural groups. The identification of sources of misinterpretations can be a first step in improving cross-cultural relations.

Borderwork in cross-gender relations. The relation between teasing, conflict, and tension in peer relations is probably nowhere more apparent than in cross-gender relations among preadolescents. Girls and boys are often apart at this age, but for certain activities they do work and play together with little obvious attention paid to gender. For example, a number of researchers have found that children often play in mixed gender groups in neighborhoods, most especially if the play groups are also mixed in age (Ellis, Rogoff, & Cromer, 1981; Goodwin, 1990; Thorne, 1993; and Whiting & Edwards, 1988). Others have found consistent cross-gender interaction in schools, but primarily in settings that are not controlled by peer groups such as in classroooms and in extra-curricular activities (Lockheed, 1985; Thorne, 1993). However, it is in peer-dominated and highly public settings in schools—like cafeterias and playgrounds—that gender separation is most complete. In fact, many activities and routines of preadolescent children's peer cultures in these settings seem to be all about gender. In these activities and routines, girls and boys try to make sense of and deal with ambiguities and concerns related to gender differences and relations. Many of these activities involve conflict, disputes, and teasing. Thorne has captured the complexity of such activities with her discussion and analysis of *borderwork*.

Borderwork refers to activities that mark and strengthen boundaries between groups. When gender boundaries are activated, "other social definitions get squeezed out by heightened awareness of gender as a dichotomy and of 'the girls' and 'the boys' as opposite and even antagonistic sides" (Thorne, 1993, p. 66). In her work in elementary schools Thorne identified several types of borderwork. The first type is *contests* between groups of girls and boys. Among the groups Thorne studied, contests were initiated by both children and teachers. Sometimes teachers pitted boys and girls against each other in math and spelling competitions. On one occasion a teacher named the two teams "Beastly Boys" and "Gossipy Girls," thereby supporting such contests and gender stereotypes (Thorne, 1993, p. 67). Boys and girls would at times play cooperatively in sports games on the playground, but these games were often transformed into competitive boy-girl competitions full of taunts, teasing, and insults usually aimed at the girls.

Another type of borderwork, *chasing*, is also competitive, but this activity is more symbolic in its affirmation of boundaries between girls and boys. Cross-gender chasing is very similar in structure to the approach-avoidance routines of preschool children that we discussed in Chapter 6. In fact, I observed several instances of cross-gender approach-avoidance play in my work with preschoolers. Among preadolescents chasing routines usually begin when a child from one gender group taunts the members of the other group. These taunts lead to chases that are often accompanied by threats that are seldom carried out. For example, boys may taunt and tease girls, leading the girls to run after the boys and threaten to catch and kiss them. These routines are generally referred to as "chase-and-kiss," "kiss-chase," and "kissers and chasers" (Parrott, 1979; Richert, 1990; Sluckin, 1981; Thorne, 1993). In her work, Thorne found that the chases had a long history, with children talking about them for days afterward with friends and even parents (1993, p. 69). Children talk about cross-gender chases because this type of borderwork gives rise to lots of tension. Children are experimenting with their growing concerns and desires regarding the opposite sex. In fact, like approach-avoidance play among preschoolers, chasing routines include the children's marking and acceptance of safety or free zones where children find relief from mounting tensions of the chase. Among the preadolescents, however, safety zones are more than geographical spaces to which children flee to escape threatening agents. For preadolescents, the areas serve as both physical and psychological havens where the children reflect on and talk about the meaning of their experiences. In this way, the preadolescents have more direct control over the meaning of the play and collectively create shared histories of the events.

Thorne found that episodes of chasing sometimes entwined with *rituals of pollution* in playground activities. Rituals of pollution are play routines or rituals in which specific individuals or groups are treated as contaminated (as in "having cooties"). Pollution games have been observed in many parts of the world (Opie & Opie, 1969; Samuelson, 1980). Thorne found that variants of "cootie games" were very much a part of cross-gender conflict and teasing in that while "girls and boys may transfer cooties to one another, and girls may give cooties to girls, boys do not generally give cooties to boys" (1993, p. 74). Thus, girls are central to pollution games that contribute to boys' power and control over them. In fact, boys sometimes treat objects associated with girls as polluting and threatening to their status in all boy groups.

Like pollution games, the final type of borderwork, *invasions,* has much to do with power and dominance of boys over girls. Thorne found a pattern, which has been observed repeatedly in similar studies of preadolescent children's activities on playgrounds. The boys in Thorne's study would, individually or in groups, deliberately disrupt the activities of groups of girls (Thorne, 1993, p. 76; also see Grant, 1984; Oswald, Krappman, Chowdhuri, & von Salisch, 1987). Boys ran under girls' jump ropes, kicked their markers from hopscotch grids, and taunted and teased the girls in attempts to disrupt their play. Although boys much more frequently invaded girls' space, there were some interesting exceptions to this pattern. First, while some boys specialized in disruptive behavior, the majority of the boys were not drawn to the activity. Thorne suggests that the frequent disrupters may have acted like bullies in their behaviors with peers more generally. Second, Thorne described a small number of fifth- and sixth-grade girls who organized themselves into what she called troupes and roamed the play-ground in search of action. These girls would often chase boys. The leaders of these troupes were often tall, well-developed girls who somewhat intimidated the boys.

These exceptions are important because they draw our attention to the complexity of interpreting the importance of borderwork. Borderwork, like the jump rope activities among the Swedish preadolescents in Evaldsson's study, is play, but in the play children address issues that are of serious concern. In this way the key feature of these types of play is ambiguity and tension. However, this tension is what makes the activities so appealing to children.

Thorne rightly points out that a good deal of borderwork tips the balance of power to boys, because they are frequently the aggressors, control more space, and seem not to suffer from any negative implications that might be associated with engaging in such rituals. Furthermore, borderwork often supports gender stereotypes and exaggerates gender differences. As a result, girls are clearly more apt to be adversely affected by the negative elements of borderwork than boys. However, Thorne argues that borderwork does create a space where preadolescent girls and boys can come together to experiment and to reflect on how to relate to one another. The trick is how to encourage changes in or set limits to some types of borderwork to preserve that space and the delicate play frame while evening the balance of power, which more often than not now tilts in the boys' direction.

Challenging Adult Authority and Norms

Preadolescents, like preschoolers, see adults as having ultimate power over their everyday lives. Possessed of increased autonomy on the one hand and a lack of adult status on the other, preadolescents continually find themselves at odds with adults. Their challenges to adult authority are at once more subtle and more direct than those of preschoolers, and these challenges are shared and evaluated more reflectively in their peer cultures.

Consider some findings from an innovative study of the hallway behavior of elementary school children by Don Ratcliff (1994). Ratcliff found that the children most frequently moved about hallways in phalanxes. He defined a *phalanx* as two or more people side by side, usually facing the same direction and moving at least temporarily toward some presumed destination. Members of phalanxes normally engage in communication as they move.

The general rule in the elementary school was for children to move as quietly as possible in the halls in files. As a result, moving in phalanxes in hallways was valued in the peer culture, because it gave children control of their interactive space, enabled them to talk and be with friends, and allowed them to challenge the authority of teachers all at the same time. Ratcliff found that "kids like phalanxes." Some children noted that they felt happy, cool, bad, excited, and "as good as anybody else when they were in the phalanx" (1994). In interviews with teachers, Ratcliff found that some teachers saw phalanxes as disruptive but seldom enforced the rule against them. One teacher admitted talking to other teachers in hallway phalanxes and therefore, saw it as hypocritical to forbid them. The children were probably well aware of the teachers' double bind in this situation, and this may have made the behavior even more meaningful and enjoyable for them.

Most preadolescents enjoy getting the upper hand with teachers and parents. They often mock adult rules and imitate and exaggerate adults' communicative styles in rule enforcement. For example, Parker (1991) talks about middle school basketball players who complained about their coaches' strict adherence to practice drills. During a practice drill the players were expected to practice only fundamental basketball moves. As they gathered before practice, the boys would violate this philosophy by dribbling through their legs, throwing passes behind their backs, and taking thirty-foot jump shots. Preadolescents also enjoy creating dramas in which they recall past events involving teachers and parents disciplining them for misbehavior. In these narratives, children often act out the roles of adult authority figures, taking care to precisely capture and mock their voices, expressions, and gestures (Eder, 1988; Fine, 1987; Davies, 1982). Often, certain children become widely known and popular in peer culture for their ability to impersonate, mock, and make fun of adults.

Unlike preschoolers, who sometimes balk at adult authority and rules but eventually give in, preadolescents are much more likely to stand their ground against adult rules. Preadolescents are especially sensitive to what they see as adult hypocrisy and injustice and band together to demand their rights. In Chapter 3 we saw an example of such resistance in our earlier discussion of the newsboys' strike in turn-of-the-century America. Several researchers of contemporary preadolescent peer cultures report similar findings (Davies, 1982; Evaldsson, 1993; Thorne, 1993). For some preadolescents the challenging of adult authority goes beyond talking back, arguing, or pointing out injustices. In fact, actively defying adult authority, challenging adult rules, and receiving disciplinary action often comes to be valued among preadolescents. Thus, earning a reputation as a troublemaker can result in higher status in the peer group (Adler, Kless, & Adler, 1992). Although challenging adult authority and being in trouble was more highly valued among males, Adler, Kless, and Adler also found that girls who participated in taboo activities or who belonged to a wild or fast crowd were highly popular in their peer culture (1992, p. 179).

Summary

In this chapter we examined the peer cultures of preadolescent children and defined preadolescence as the period from seven to thirteen years of age. Given the lack of research on preadolescent culture in non-Western societies, and because children in these societies often take on adult responsibilities in preadolescence, our discussion focused primarily on Western societies. We were, however, careful to consider racial, ethnic, and social class differences in our review.

We first considered the relation between friendship, social differentiation, and gender. Preadolescents, compared to preschool children, have developed more stable concepts of friendship, and they strive to make their interactions with peers fit their developing conceptions of how best friends should behave with one another. One result of these attempts to link cognitive concepts and behavior is increasing social differentiation in the peer culture. As preadolescents forge social alliances and secure friendship relations with peers they also separate themselves from others. These processes of separation are most apparent in gender differentiation in peer interaction, which reaches its peak in preadolescence. Many theorists argue that gender differentiation affects and is affected by deep, dichotomous, and universal gender differences (that is, by the very nature of being male or female). According to this view women have a different voice in that they value relationships and caring for others, while men are concerned about individual rights and notions of justice. These differences have been found among preadolescents, where studies show that girls' concerns center around the valuing of compliance and conformity, romantic love, and an ideology of domesticity, while boys' concerns revolve around a cult of masculinity, around physical contests, autonomy, and self-reliance. Other theorists challenge this separate culture view of peer relations. They argue that the examination of naturally occurring peer interaction in a wide range of social settings and groups reveals a good deal of gender mixing in preadolescent peer relations. Further, these studies of children's situated activities (activities produced in diverse settings by children who have long interactional histories) document a greater complexity in gender relations in preadolescence, which challenges the separate culture view.

Studies of situated activities also provide important information on preadolescent children's lore (games, jokes, riddles, songs, and verbal and behavioral routines) and how children in the process of engaging in these activities address issues related to self, identity, and autonomy from adult control. Our discussion of situated activities focused most specifically on children's games, verbal dispute routines, and cross-gender play and rituals. Evaldsson and Goodwin's studies of the actual play of jump rope and hop-scotch within children's peer cultures over time revealed that these games were much more complex than earlier studies, which focused only on the rules and structures of the games, had claimed. Evaldsson found that the pre-adolescents not only developed certain physical, communicative, and cogni-tive skills in playing jump rope, but that they also used the game as an arena for addressing personal concerns, feelings, and uncertainties regarding gen-der relations. Goodwin's research demonstrated the importance of cultural variation in the play of games. She found that African-American and Latina girls took the rules of hopscotch very seriously, engaged in highly complex and dramatic debates about rule enforcement, and teased each other regard-ing poor performances. This style of play contrasted with that of the middle-class white girls, who often overlooked rule violations and mitigated their responses to their peers' miscues. These findings, along with those from Goodwin's documentation of the complex linguistic structure and impor-tance of conflict rituals like the he-said-she-said dispute routine, show how conflict and cooperation are often overlapping processes that are embedded in the larger ethos of playfulness. Goodwin's work also demonstrates the importance of comparative work for documenting differences in preadoles-cent peer cultures across sociocultural groups.

How conflict can sometimes contribute to the social organization of pre-adolescent peer relations and can generate creative tension in preadoles-cent peer relations also was evident in Thorne's work on borderwork. Borderwork refers to activities that mark and strengthen boundaries be-tween groups. In her study of cross-gender relations among preadolescents, Thorne identified three types of borderwork (contests, chases, and invasions) that heightened the awareness of gender and gender differences. Contests were initiated by children and teachers that transformed classroom les-sons and peer games into competitions of boys against girls. Chases, like contests, were competitive, but they were more symbolic in their affirma-tion of boundaries between boys and girls. In chases boys often taunt and tease girls in line with the aggressive nature of boys' peer culture, while the girls threaten the boys with kissing or affection, resulting in "chase-and-kiss" games. Chases are often intertwined with rituals of pollution, where specific groups are treated as contaminated (as in "having cooties"). It is girls who are normally seen as contaminated in cross-gender chases, and in this way the borderwork often contributes to boys' power over girls. The final type of borderwork, invasions, also has much to do with power and dominance of boys over girls. Thorne found that some boys invade girls' space and purposely disrupt their play and taunt and tease them. Despite some exceptions, Thorne concluded that girls are clearly more apt to be adversely affected by the negative elements of borderwork than boys. She argued that there were creative elements in borderwork and suggested that adults might be able to encourage changes and limits to some types of borderwork, which preserve the creative elements while evening the balance of power between girls and boys.

Overall, preadolescence is a time when children struggle to gain stable identities, and their peer cultures provide both a sense of autonomy from adults and an arena for dealing with uncertainties of an increasingly complex world. The many positive features of their peer cultures (for example, verbal routines, games, and enduring friendships) allow preadolescents to hold on to their childhoods a little longer, while simultaneously preparing themselves for the transition to adolescence. A crucial factor in preadolescent peer culture is children's ability to reflect on and evaluate the meaning of their changing worlds in talk with each other and with adults. In this sense, preadolescents become aware of themselves as individual actors in the collective production of their peer cultures. They also come to recognize how their peer cultures affect and are affected by the more general adult world.

PART FOUR

Children, Social Problems, and the Future of Childhood

"If this year's Halloween follows form, a few children will return home with something more than an upset tummy: in recent years, several children have died and hundreds have narrowly escaped injury from razor blades, sewing needles and shards of glass purposefully put into their goodies by adults" (*Newsweek*, 1975, p. 28 as quoted in Best, 1990, p. 132).

Although the incidence of what has been called "Halloween sadism" cannot be accurately measured, Joel Best investigated the phenomenon by reviewing newspaper accounts of such incidents. He found little support for the *Newsweek* claim. Over a twenty-four-year period in four major American newspapers, Best found stories about seventy-eight alleged incidents. Injuries were reported in only twenty of these cases and only two of these involved deaths. The first case was a report in which a five-year-old died after eating heroin that he had found in his uncle's home, not in his candy. In the second case, a boy did die after eating Halloween candy laced with cyanide; however, investigators determined that his father and not an anonymous stranger had contaminated the candy. From his analysis, Best concluded that Halloween sadism is an **urban legend**, a contemporary, orally transmitted tale that depicts a clash between modern life and more traditional lifestyles and beliefs (Best, 1990, pp. 134-137; Brunvand, 1981). Many urban legends involve threats to or concerns about young children.

On Wednesday, March 20, 1996, at 9:30 a.m. local time in Dunblane, Scotland, "a heavily armed psychopath went berserk in the local elementary school, fatally shooting 16 youngsters and their teacher and wounding 12 others" (*Newsweek*, 1996, p. 13). The children, all kindergartners, were happily playing in physical education class in the school gym when the man, a former scout leader and suspected pedophile, went on his shooting rampage. No one disputed *Newsweek's* account of this event. Nor could anyone really answer the simple question "Why?" which was placed over the Dunblane kindergarten's class picture on the cover of the magazine's March 25, 1996, issue.

"Svay Pak, Cambodia—She giggled for a moment, a 13-year-old girl named Sriy, all sparkling eyes and white teeth, her laughter washing over the grunts from a pornographic video playing a few feet away. Then the brothel owner strutted over.

The owner, a hearty woman in her late 20's, who paid good money to buy Sriy, cheerfully and explicitly recommended her anatomical features and said that the $10 fee was not so great because 'she only just lost her virginity'" (Kristof, 1996, p. 2).

Sriy, one of tens of thousands of children working in Asia as sex slaves, had lost her virginity two years earlier, when she was forced into prostitution. She serviced up to ten customers a night. Sriy had first been sold by her stepfather to another brothel before she was sold to this one. She has to continue to work "until the debt is deemed to be repaid. Or until she gets AIDS" (1996, p. 2). Ironically, girls like Sriy are most desired by brothel owners because customers desire younger girls and boys who are regarded as more likely to be AIDS-free.

In these three distinct but related scenarios, children are victims of adults. The first represents a malaise of dispair in modern industrialized society regarding our inability to fully protect our children from unthinkable harm. This fear, that some unfathomable evil could reach out and strike our children at any time—via poisoned candy at Halloween, Satanic witchcraft in daycare centers, or a mad pedophile with a cache of powerful handguns in a kindergarten—is very seldom borne out. Sometimes, however, the unthinkable does occur, as it did in Dunblane, in Oklahoma City, and in Union, South Carolina where Susan Smith strapped her two young sons into their car seats and sent them to their deaths at the bottom of a lake. The occurrence of these events, along with dramatic and widespread news coverage, frightens and worries us. We debate and argue, sometimes rationally and sometimes not, about how best to protect our children. In these debates, our fears and our need to extinguish them often cause us to push children into the background. In these moments, often without our awareness, we make kids themselves the problem. If only there were some way to better protect them. If only we could keep them with us and away from the evils of modern society. If only they were more careful. If only they were grown up and not kids anymore. By their very dependence on us, and because of our nagging doubts about whether we can adequately protect them in a rapidly changing world, children become the social problem.

The Dunblane massacre and the Oklahoma City bombing were horrible and tragic events, but such occurrences are rare. Unfortunately our fear that our children may fall victim to such random evil often draws our attention away from the persistent and growing social problems of the world's children. What are the social problems of children? Consider the child who is sexually molested and impregnated by her mother's boyfriend and becomes a child-mother at age fourteen in New York City; the child who is forced into prostitution like Sriy at age 11; the ten-year-old who works twelve hours for thirty cents a day in a metal factory in central India; the nine-year-old who tries to avoid land mines in war-torn Mozambique; the children who find themselves ducking bullets from a drive-by shooting on the way to school in inner city Chicago; the children in rural Mississippi who have responsibility for four younger siblings and the care of the house; the children in São Paulo, Brazil, who must sell candy to survive and who are constantly fearful of being kidnapped and executed. Consider the children, some only infants, who are in danger of being physically, sexually, or psychologically abused in poor, middle-class, and even wealthy families anywhere in the world.

These are the everyday and very real social problems of children. Unlike the Dunblane massacre or the Oklahoma City bombing, these problems rarely make newspaper headlines. When they do, they, too, upset us and make us uneasy. However, they do not make us afraid. We try to push these problems out of our consciousness. These are someone else's children, someone else's responsibility. Why do their parents not take better care of them? Why are their families, neighborhoods, and cultures so violent, cruel, and indifferent? Why are there not better laws to protect these children? Why are possible solutions to these problems so expensive?

In this part of our examination of the sociology of childhood, we will consider children as social problems, and also the social problems of children. Chapter 9 examines children as social problems, looking first at growing levels of anxiety about children's well being and safety in rapidly changing industrialized societies. We then will explore the reverse of this phenomenon, the tendency in modern societies to blame some children, most especially the economically disadvantaged, for their very vulnerability. Chapter 10 looks directly at the nature and extent of social problems of children. We'll examine disturbing global trends in poverty, family instability, and violence, all of which have contributed to a dramatic decline in the quality of life of many of the world's children. Finally, in Chapter 11, we'll revisit and summarize some of the main themes in the book and discuss the future of childhood by focusing on some major challenges facing the world's children. And we'll consider the wide range of things we all can do right now to enrich children's lives.

9

Children as Social Problems

This chapter contemplates children as social problems. Many middle- and upper-class parents in industrialized societies are experiencing a growing unease about their children's everyday safety and security. We'll examine how this concern about children's wellbeing plays itself out differently for working-class and poor children whose social needs and problems often entail substantial economic costs to society. We'll discuss how certain political responses to these costs downplay social and economic circumstances and, instead, point to personal responsibility of parents and children as the main (if not the only) solution to the social problems of poor children. In the process, poor children themselves often come to be blamed for their own victimization.

The Bogeyman Syndrome and the Power of Rhetoric

In the introduction to this part of the book I mentioned the widespread fear of Halloween sadism in the United States. Although few cases of such sadism have been reported since the late 1980s, parents still remain frightened. In many communities children are allowed to "trick-or-treat" only in the immediate neighborhood or inside lighted and protected shopping malls. Very few children roam the streets far from home, free to demand candy from adults and perhaps play tricks on them, as in the past. In short, Halloween has, to a large extent, fallen victim to the **bogeyman syndrome**, the general fear of the victimization of children in contemporary industrialized societies, most especially the United States (Louv, 1990, pp. 28–41).

The Social Construction of Children as Social Problems
How did the bogeyman syndrome come about? Sociologist Joel Best, who as we saw earlier investigated and found little evidence for Halloween sadism, points to two important factors: (1) the sentimentalization of children, which evolved gradually in the eighteenth and nineteenth centuries and (2)

claims-making processes that occur in the definition and construction of social problems in modern societies. Let's look at each of these factors in turn.

In her historical study of the changing social value of children, sociologist Viviana Zelizer (1985) noted how a new definition of childhood became well established in response to children's decreasing contributions to family economy in industrialized society at the turn of the century. Schooling became compulsory and many child protection laws, especially laws restricting child labor, were established. These changes brought about a sentimentalized vision of childhood in which children were to be nurtured and protected.

Best has argued that this sentimentalization of childhood had a major effect on the definition of the social problems of children. He maintains that the social problems of children, like all social problems, are to a large extent subjective in nature. By this he means that there is little objective agreement on the nature of social problems. Rather, social problems are defined or constructed as a result of claims-making processes or *rhetoric*. In this instance, *rhetoric* refers to the persuasive communication various social groups employ to try to convince others of the existence and degree of various social problems like poverty, crime, or child abuse.

In her historical study, Zelizer showed how the nature of this rhetorical process was evident in the widespread concern that was expressed over children's accidental deaths in New York in the first three decades of the twentieth century. Of primary concern were child deaths in public places, especially city streets. Many public and private organizations and groups banned together to promote safety campaigns and laws to reduce accidents that resulted in child injuries and deaths. These campaigns were successful in that accidental deaths for children began to decline in the late 1920s and 1930s, even though automobile fatalities rose steadily overall during this period. Zelizer, however, argued that safety campaigns alone could not explain this decrease. These campaigns were only one aspect of a trend that promoted the domestication of children—their movement from the streets and their increased isolation from the adult world (Zelizer, 1985, pp. 49–55). Children now spent more time in the home, school, and in playgrounds. Thus, we see that one cost of protection for children is their loss of control over their lives and of freedom to carve out their own spaces. This is a point we will return to below.

Best extends Zelizer's view of the power of rhetoric in instances where adult groups seek to protect children, in his analysis of the concern over child abduction by strangers in the 1980s. Several notorious cases of children being abducted and killed by strangers in the late 1970s led to much concern and debate about the prevalence of such occurrences. Perhaps the most well-known case, the kidnapping and murder of Adam Walsh, was depicted in a television movie, *Adam,* in 1983. Adam's father, John Walsh, testified before Congressional committees about the problem and was one of the leaders of a movement to increase public attention to the problem. Walsh and others pointed to shortcomings in the procedures of criminal justice organizations, including the FBI, regarding recordkeeping on missing children. Walsh pointed out that the FBI kept better records of missing automobiles than it did of missing children.

The fact that the statistics on missing children were poor was a major element in the nature of the rhetoric of claims regarding this problem. Missing children crusaders used inclusive statistics that captured the extent of the problem with very broad strokes. For example, a frequently repeated claim was that 1.8 million children were reported missing in the United States each year (Best, 1990, p. 46). This figure was an extrapolation from available records in various states and cities and included runaways, which in fact made up the majority of the cases. Still, the claimsmakers argued that 50,000 of these 1.8 million cases were stranger abductions, with children returned in 10 percent of the cases, murdered in another 10 percent, and the remaining 40,000 unaccounted for. Best argued that the claims-making rhetoric started with a large inclusive figure of 1.8 million and then used the smaller, but still shocking 50,000 figure to typify the problem. While hardly typical of missing children, prominent cases were given great attention by the media on news programs, and mass-produced pictures of missing children began turning up on billboards, milk cartons, utility bills, and even "junk mail" ads.

The missing child crusaders' success in dramatizing what they saw as a serious problem resulted in what Best termed a "backlash of counterclaims." Investigative reporters from several newspapers disputed the 50,000 abducted children claim, pointing to the fact that the FBI investigated only 67 cases of child abduction in 1984. Others joined in the backlash pointing to what they saw as growing hysteria, and some pediatricians and child psychologists argued that fears of abduction might harm more children than kidnapping (Best, 1990, pp. 48–51).

Not surprisingly, according to Best, critics of the missing children crusaders tended to distort the original claims in their counterclaims. They sometimes argued that the abduction figures were padded—that the numbers cited included runaways—when this was never the case. However, instead of pointing out such distortions, the advocates of missing children first seemed to back off statistics altogether (arguing that one abducted child is one too many), and then to redefine the whole category of stranger abduction. One example of such redefinition was the inclusion of sexual molestation cases where the victims (often preadolescent girls) have been moved from one location to another in the commission of the crime, but not kidnapped. The goal of this numbers game is, according to Best, to maintain the focus on the original typified example of the problem, here, stranger abduction (1990, p. 52).

Similar controversies and rhetorical claims-making processes have run their course in recent years in other areas of social problems related to children. Many of these have involved charges of sexual abuse in child care centers and even in whole communities. Some even involved bizarre claims of satanic ritual and witchcraft as part of the rhetorical strategy. In most cases the charges have not led to convictions. For example, in the MacMartin case in California, several preschool teachers were imprisoned for a number of years before and during a trial in which they were found not guilty. In the "Cleveland case" in Great Britain, more than two hundred children were suspected victims of familial sexual abuse and were removed from their homes. They were later returned and the charges judged to be spurious (Jenkins, 1992).

Losing Sight of the Everyday Social Problems of Children

Two questions must be considered regarding the rhetoric of claimsmaking that is applied to child victims. These two questions are addressed only in passing by those, like Best, who take a constructivist view of social problems. First, why do the typified, but often distorted, examples (child abduction and murder, satanic rituals, and so on) have so much appeal in claims-making processes when they are such rare events? As one investigative report in the *Denver Post* put it, the number of such abductions was "fewer than the number of preschoolers who choke to death on food each year" (as quoted in Best, 1990, p. 48). (Of course there is something hollow about this argument. Child abductions by strangers are more frightening than accidental deaths, even if they are less likely to actually occur.) Still, why do these sensationalized events command our attention?

Second, why do those who engage in such rhetoric seem to lose sight of the real character of social problems that affect children's everyday lives? Typified cases—those that are highlighted because they are thought to embody the essential characteristics of such incidents—draw all the attention, while typical social problems of children—those that occur on an everyday basis—get lost in the rhetoric. For example, at one point in his analysis Best argues that the missing-child movement could have responded to its critics by retypifying the problem and shifting their focus to the plight of runaways. But they did not. Why? Surely, runaways constitute the majority of missing children, their numbers are very high, many have been maltreated in their families, and most live in very threatening circumstances. Why do their problems seem less appealing? Finally, how can we debate the improper categorization of girls who have been sexually molested as stranger abduction victims without acknowledging that such molestations are so destructive of the lives of many children?

To answer the first set of questions we need to return to the image of the bogeyman. Although social constructionists like Best (1990, 1995) and Jenkins (1992) focus primarily on how fears connected to the vulnerability of children play themselves out in public discourse, they do offer some speculations about the underlying causes of the bogeyman syndrome. Their "displacement or substitution" model holds that "a contemporary 'politics of anxiety' about an uncertain future leads people to displace their vague and free-floating worries onto more manageable concerns, with clear representations of innocent victims threatened by deviant individuals rather then by unfathomable systemic changes" (Stephens, 1993, p. 249).

Jenkins pushes the argument a bit further, arguing that this sort of displacement can be used to push through restrictive laws on sexual behavior or religious cults, increase censorship, and impose harsher criminal penalties and parole procedures that would be difficult to legitimize under the United States Constitution (1992, p. 20; Stephens, p. 249). For example, recent incidents like the child sex murders of Polly Klaas and Megan Kanka have led to more restrictive laws regarding child sex offenders. Although more than half of the states now require convicted sex offenders to register with government authorities after they leave prison, the tragic case of Megan Kanka prompted the New Jersey legislature to pass Megan's Law. Megan's Law requires community notification that past offenders are living in their midst. The constitutionality of the law is being challenged in court, and all sorts of questions are being raised about possible side effects, such as vigilantism against past sex offenders who claim they have reformed and paid their debt to society. However, the images of young Polly Klaas and Megan Kanka are compelling. As columnist Anna Quindlen observed, "it is easy to imagine embracing any measure that gives even the illusion that we can make the world a less dangerous place for the little loves of our lives" (1994, p. 11). Even though the constitutionality of New Jersey's Megan's Law is still being challenged in the courts, a federal version of the law was overwhelmingly passed in Congress and quickly signed into law by President Clinton in May 1996.

It is clear that the media plays an important role in the bogeyman syndrome and the displacement model (Louv, 1990, p. 31). A recent cover of the *New Yorker* (1995) depicted three young children in a playroom surrounded by toys. The children were all white and the large collection of toys suggested an upper-middle-class home. One boy was cutting paper dolls out of the newspaper with the word DRUGS running across the freshly cut dolls. The same child wore a party hat made from newspaper with the word RAPE clearly visible. His playmates, a boy and girl, wore similar hats. The headline running across the top of the girl's hat read "Terrorist Bombers," while the large, block initials "O.J." could be seen on the boy's hat. Only the artist of the magazine cover, A. Spiegelman, knows precisely what she or he was trying to depict. However, three points seem clear. First, children are threatened by many dangers that seem to be beyond the control of even the most caring adults. The United States is a heterogeneous and rapidly changing society. As we saw in Chapter 4, we spend less time with our kids because of increasing job demands and rely on day care centers, after-school programs, and other institutional settings to care for our kids. Second, these dangers, however remote, are magnified and sensationalized by the press and media. Third, and perhaps most importantly, these dangers are no longer confined to children of the lower classes and the poor. These three ideas combine to create a sense of unease, a lack of control in an ever-changing and more threatening social environment—the bogeyman syndrome.

What of the second question? Why do those who engage in rhetorical claims-making processes seem to lose sight of the real social problems that affect children's everyday lives? Here the answer is related to *what children* we are talking about. For example, as tragic as the murders of Polly Klaas and Megan Kanka were, they were no more deplorable than the violence perpetuated by and on primarily poor, minority children in the United States every day. In 1989 the homicide rate for black, male ten-to-fourteen-year-olds was 7.3 per 100,000 (4 per 100,000 for black females of this age group). The rate was a startling 92.7 for black, male fifteen-to-nineteen-year-olds (12 per 100,000 for black females). Keep in mind that the overall homicide rate for the United States was around 10 per 100,000, which also was the rate for white, male fifteen-to-nineteen-year olds (the rate for white, fifteen-to-nineteen-year old females was 3 per 100,000). To gain a more concrete understanding of these statistics, consider that there were 3,020 teenagers murdered in the United States in 1990–91 (a rate of nearly 17 per 100,000), compared to 17 teenagers murdered in France in the same period (a rate of .4 per 100,000).

These statistics, as well as reports of drug-related killings and drive-by shootings, do of course make the newspapers. However, we seem to have become hardened to such stories. Further, there has been no groundswell of support for tougher penalties for those who sell guns to youth, or for promotion of crime prevention programs and youth organizations that offer alternatives and protection to youth in impoverished environments. This lack of attention to the violence and other very real problems in the lives of children who live in poverty alerts us to the specific applicability of concepts like the bogeyman syndrome and the priceless and sentimentalized child. These concepts apply to middle-class children in mainstream society. Indeed Zelizer points out that "the sacred child is thus a private luxury; children in need of public support are treated unsentimentally, assisted only if the investment is justified in economic terms" (1985, p. 216). Best, Louv and others also caution that we must be careful that the needed debunking of the excessive fears of child victimization not draw our attention away from the very real, everyday social problems of many of the world's children (Best, 1990, p. 188; Louv, 1990, p. 32; Stephens, 1993, p. 251).

Blaming the Victim

Before turning to an examination of various social problems in Chapter 10, it is useful to consider a second way children are seen as social problems. **Blaming the victim** refers to the tendency to hold children personally responsible for the complex social and economic forces and problems that so dramatically affect their lives. At first glance it might seem odd that children, who, we all agree, deserve our attention, protection, and support, come to be blamed for many of the social problems that affect their lives. However, we know from our earlier discussion of socialization theories, which view children as incomplete and immature, that children are also seen as in need of instruction, training, and discipline. For this reason, children often are treated as an out-group—as separate from and inferior to adults.

Children as an Out-Group

Because of their immaturity and dependency on adults, children have limited rights and, as noted child authority Penelope Leach points out, they are often treated as an **out-group**. By this Leach means that children are not seen as adults in the making, or as junior selves, but as inferior and not worthy of the same respect as adults (1994, p. 204). As we've discussed in earlier chapters, this tendency leads us to overlook children's perspectives and the autonomy and creativity of their peer cultures. When it comes to viewing children as social problems, this tendency to separate children from ourselves and fail to take their viewpoints into account has many unfortunate consequences, as we shall see.

The Scandinavian countries are the most noted in the world for their recognition of children's rights. In 1981 Norway established a **Children's Ombudsperson**, an office that houses a person or representative children can go to with complaints when they feel their rights are violated or when decisions are made that greatly affect their lives and their views are not taken into account. Consider a few of the housing cooperative rules that a group of children sent to their Ombudsperson in 1989:

- Children are not allowed to scribble on walls.
- Children are not allowed to make noise in the corridors.

- Children are not allowed to hang around inside the building outside other apartments.

- Children must not leave belongings outside; such belongings will be placed in the rubbish containers. (Leach, 1994, p. 210)

These rules exist in a country that is one of the most enlightened in the world when it comes to children's rights! However, it should be pointed out that in the United States and many other countries, there are housing developments where children are forbidden to live altogether. In commenting on these rules Leach points out that children should not, of course, be allowed to write on the walls or make lots of noise in the corridors. The point is that *"nobody* should be allowed to do so and therefore that notices—and enforcement of regulations—should either address all age groups or none" (Leach, 1994, p. 210). Furthermore, some of the rules clearly discriminate against children. The children are not to hang about talking in the halls, but as Leach points out, surely nobody would break up a group of adults talking about last night's game (or complaining about their kids, for that matter). And how about property rights? Would it be acceptable to place in the rubbish containers items of value that adults have left lying around?

One characteristic of rules like these above and of thoughts about children in general is that there is often a tendency to accentuate the negative. The implication is that because some children behave badly, they all do. For example, I recently read an op–ed piece in my local newspaper in which an economist referred generically to children as "brats." He introduced his article with a personal story about one particular child who had misbehaved in a department store. However, the article was about children in general (their costs to society, and so on) and soon the word *brats* was substituted for *children*. Of course, some children might legitimately be classified as brats, and most children behave badly now and then. However, this tendency to generalize and regard all children negatively can have dire consequences for children, especially when it surfaces in various political ideologies and agendas.

Personal Responsibility and Blaming the Victim

When I was a teenager in the 1960s, the memorable phrase, "Ask not what your country can do for you, ask what you can do for your country," from John Kennedy's inaugural address, still had some meaning. Lyndon Johnson initiated the war on poverty and the federal government was seen as the leader in fighting social problems. Then things changed. The question Ronald Reagan asked in his first presidential campaign was, "Are you better off today than you were four years ago?" The phrasing here was intentional. He did not ask is the *country* or is your *community* better off today. By this time people no longer viewed the federal government as a leader in solving social problems; rather, it was seen as the cause of the problems. The prevailing attitude was that the government should stay out of people's personal affairs, and people should take care of themselves. More recently this view has translated into a crusade about morals and personal responsibility.

The debate over whether problems like unemployment, poverty, crime, divorce, and teen pregnancy are primarily the result of individual values and behavior (the conservative position) or socioeconomic structural factors (the liberal view) is long and ongoing. Since the mid 1980s the conservative view has had more influence. This fact has profound implications for children and youth, because more and more of them are living in poverty, are from divorced families, are victims of crime, are teen mothers, or are the children of teen mothers. We will discuss these social problems of children at length in the next chapter. Here, let's examine how the current ideology of personal responsibility plays itself out when it comes to children living in poverty. We'll look especially at teen mothers.

When politicians look for ways to cut a growing budget deficit, welfare spending is an obvious target. Setting aside the fact that the real value of the welfare benefit package (cash assistance plus food stamps) for a family of four fell 26 percent between 1972 and 1992 (see McLanahan, 1994), removing welfare mothers from the chain of distribution is an appealing budget-cutting strategy for those who argue personal responsibility. Their argument is that welfare actually creates poverty by encouraging poor women to have more children and gain increased benefits (Murray, 1984). Although it is true that welfare may induce some women to have more children, there is little evidence to support Murray's view that this is a widespread pattern or that welfare increases dependency (Bianchi, 1993; Lehman & Danziger, 1995). In fact, in 1992 nearly 73 percent of families who received Aid For Dependent Children (AFDC) had two or fewer children and the average AFDC family size has decreased from 4.0 to 2.9 persons from 1969 to 1992 (The Twentieth Fund, 1995; U.S. Congress, House Committee on Ways and Means, 1994). Further, although most welfare recipients move on and off assistance over a period of several years, 30 percent of welfare recipients leave welfare permanently in less than two years, and 50 percent leave welfare permanently in less than four years (Bane & Elwood, 1994; The Twentieth Fund, 1995). In some ways these facts are unimportant to the personal responsibility argument, because underlying them is the belief that poor women should not have children at all. However, to voice this out loud takes the argument a step too far even for most conservatives (see Jenks & Edin, 1995). After all, many of us (liberal or conservative) would not be around if our parents had made fertility decisions on the basis of their income. And many Americans do not believe in making children suffer for their parents' decisions. As a result, the personal responsibility approach to welfare has become more focused on *out-of-wedlock births of teenage mothers.*

The teen pregnancy debate. As we will see in the next chapter, the dramatic increase in the rate of out-of-wedlock births among American teens from 1960 to the early 1990s is a highly complex problem that can be linked to several interrelated factors. However, the debate about its causes has often centered around one main issue: More and more teenagers are engaging in promiscuous sexual behavior. President Clinton referred to the problem as an "epidemic of illegitimacy"; conservatives like Charles Murray maintain that this factor drives a whole range of social problems, from poverty and welfare to crime and drugs (Kramer, 1995). This line of thinking led Clinton to propose welfare programs that require teen mothers to sign personal responsibility contracts to stay in their families and stay in school or look for work if they are to receive welfare benefits. Murray goes much further, saying welfare to teen mothers should be cut off altogether.

Framing the teen pregnancy debate as primarily a matter of personal responsibility is quite appealing. Highly complex socioeconomic conditions that have dramatic effects on peoples' lives can be explained by the much more concrete and understandable failure of individual teenagers to control their sexual impulses (Luker, 1991). As we will discuss more in the next chapter, although the risk of teen pregnancy is universal, some youth are much more at risk than others. The families, communities, schools, and other institutions are just not working for many young girls who become teen parents. They see little hope in their futures and often drift into sexual relations, pregnancy, and parenthood. Let's put this structural argument aside now, though, and pursue further the conservative focus on the individual behavior of teen girls.

Let's assume for the sake of argument that all teens start off on equal footing when it comes to making decisions about sexuality. Some teen girls become pregnant and have children out of wedlock, others do not. Many of the girls who do will need to turn to the government for welfare support for themselves and their children. Such support is not only costly, the argument goes, it also rewards the irresponsible behavior, behavior that should be punished, or at least shamed. We can do as Clinton suggests and administer a little shaming in a positive way by having girls sign a personal responsibility contract before they can get support, or we can go the tough love route and follow Murray's proposal to cut welfare support off altogether for teenage girls.

Before we act on these proposals, however, it is useful to consider some of their underlying assumptions and how they compare to the real lives of the children they most affect. First, these proposals assume that all (or the overwhelming majority of) teen births are the result of *teens* acting irresponsibly. Thus, adolescent females and males need to learn to take responsibility for their actions. If they can't act responsibly (or if their parents can't keep them in line) the government should not be expected to bail them out. Second, the proposals assume that all females (even very young girls) are ultimately responsible for their sexuality, resulting pregnancies, and births.

The first assumption, that teen births result from teenagers acting irresponsibly, seems credible. Teenage mothers are giving birth to out-of-wedlock babies. But are the *fathers* of these babies also teenagers? A national survey of about 10,000 teen mothers conducted from 1989 to 1991 found that half of the fathers of babies born to mothers between the ages of fifteen and seventeen were twenty years old or older, and 20 percent of the fathers were six or more years older than the teenage girls they impregnated (Landry & Forrest, 1995; Steinhauer, 1995). Several state surveys report similar results. For example, a 1993 California study found that nearly 65 percent of infants born to mothers between the ages of ten and nineteen were fathered by men of post–high-school age. This finding did not vary significantly by race or ethnicity; the proportion of infants fathered by adults was only slightly higher for Hispanic and non-Hispanic white mothers than it was for black mothers. Even more troublesome was the finding that the younger the mother, the greater the age gap. With high school girls, fathers were, on average, 4.2 years older than their partners, and with mothers in junior high school, the fathers were on average 6.7 years older. Furthermore, 13 percent of the adult fathers were at least twenty-five years of age (Males and Chew, 1996). Similar findings were reported in Washington state, where the average age of fathers of infants born to twelve-to-seventeen-year-old girls was twenty-four (Males, 1994; Steinhauer, 1995).

Although some of the cases involve seventeen-to-nineteen-year-old girls bearing the children of men a few years older, the number of girls sixteen and younger who are being impregnated by adults is shocking. Clearly the assumption that the teenage pregnancy problem is simply *kids* having sex is wrong. In many states laws of consent prohibit people over the age of eighteen from having sex with those under sixteen, and in California the age of consent is eighteen. In spite of this, many blame young girls not only for bearing the children of these unions, but also for a whole range of other social problems. What we have here, based on the very laws of our society, is a classic case of blaming the victim. What's to be done? Columnist Ellen Goodman recently suggested that it may be time to dust off the

statutory rape laws and return the word *jailbait* to American society's vocabulary. After all, she argues, "a 13-year-old girl is by no means on a level
playing field with an 18-year-old boy. Nor is a 15-year-old on a par with a 26-
year-old" (Goodman, 1995). Reviving statutory rape laws surely makes more
sense than placing the blame for adult misbehavior squarely on the shoulders of children. Some might object that most of these men would be hard to
track down, that they have few resources, or that the legal system is already
clogged with minor crimes. Others might argue that these girls (or their parents) should be wary of older men and should reject their sexual advances.
These arguments again miss the point: These "older men" are adults. *It is
their responsibility to control their sexual urges and not prey on young girls.*

Finally, this issue has to do with gender as well as age. The second assumption underlying recent proposals to control teen out-of-wedlock births
is that females are ultimately responsible for their sexuality. Some, like
Murray, even argue that it is the female's duty, in civilized cultures, to keep
the natural sexual urges of males in check. The very idea is wrongheaded,
but such an argument is clearly absurd when we are talking about young
girls and adult men. It is even more ludicrous when we consider that significant numbers of teen mothers are the *victims of sexual molestation, rape, and
sexual assault.* In the studies we discussed above, 70 to 75 percent of the
youngest teen mothers (those fourteen and under) report they were molested, coerced into having sex (or raped), or sexually assaulted during their
childhoods (Males, 1994; Steinhauer, 1995). In the study in Washington state,
the mean age of the male offenders was 27.4 years (Klein, 1996). In some of
these cases the offenders were stepparents or boyfriends of mothers or older
sisters. As is often the case in sexual abuse, the girls are often frightened, have
emotional attachments with their offenders, or blame themselves for their
situation. The latter response is hardly surprising in a society that assumes
most teen mothers are morally irresponsible.

One recent proposal to help teen mothers advocates government run, pri-
vately funded "second chance homes" where pregnant teens "could be protected from predators, given something like the structure and support of a
permanent home, taught motherhood and morality" (Klein, 1996). Conservatives like this idea; liberals say it sounds like orphanages. Speaking for conservatives again, Charles Murray says, "I'd like to see it given a try. At the
very least, it might have a deterrent effect. Of course I'd also like to see some
city try a complete suspension of benefits, so we could compare the results"
(as quoted in Klein, 1996, p. 39). Under Murray's plan both teenage mothers
and their children are punished without any real accounting of the charge of
personal irresponsibility. With both of the solutions, all pregnant girls are

lumped together to be held personally accountable for their pregnancy—whether they have been personally irresponsible or not.

Blaming the victim clearly is not the answer to the problem of teenage pregnancy. Although it is true that all teenage girls become pregnant because they have had sex, the reasons and circumstances that led to their sexual activity are many and varied. The politics of shame ignores this complexity and does a great disservice to teen mothers and their children.

Summary

As we saw in this chapter, children are often viewed as social problems. One example of this tendency is captured in the notion of the bogeyman syndrome, which illustrates the general fear of the victimization of children in contemporary industrialized societies, especially in the United States. The bogeyman syndrome can be seen in the widespread belief in certain urban legends concerning threats to children's safety (like Halloween sadism) as well as in the disproportional concerns about relatively rare crimes (such as child abduction and sexual abuse in day care centers). The bogeyman syndrome developed for two main reasons: (1) an increasingly sentimentalized view of children and (2) the *rhetoric* various social groups employ to convince others of the existence of social problems. Such rhetoric is often constructed in a variety of ways. For example, the problems of economically secure children are often differently constructed than are those of the economically disadvantaged. Middle- and upper-class parents take care of their children's basic needs and are thus much less dependent on federal and state welfare programs than are the parents of poor children. However, they are quick to organize and lobby their communities and the federal government when they believe the general welfare and safety of their children is threatened. This is evidenced by the recent, swift passage of a federal version of New Jersey's Megan's Law, which requires states to notify law enforcement officials and the community when a convicted sex offender moves into a neighborhood.

Parents of poor children have a much more difficult time getting their case heard; they must struggle to meet the basic needs of their children and often come to rely on government support. As a result, the economic costs of the social problems of these children are much more visible. The political rhetoric that occurs in response to the social problems of poor children often involves an inverse conceptualization: The victims come to be blamed for their social problems. In this rhetoric, children often are seen as an out-group whose rights and needs are less important than those of adults. In fact, in some cases the needs of certain groups of most especially poor children are seen as inconvenient, burdensome, and even threatening to the moral order. Much of the rhetoric in the recent debate regarding the problem of teen pregnancy is a prime example of blaming the victim. Some argue, for example, that the problem of teen out-of-wedlock births is so acute and so threatening to society that all teen mothers and their children should be denied government assistance. Others take a less extreme view but still hold that a lack of personal responsibility on the part of teenagers is the main cause of the problem. The fact that children of many of these teens are fathered by adults and that a large proportion of teen mothers grew up and live in impoverished environments and that a significant number of teen mothers are victims of incest, rape, or sexual assault is often overlooked.

Although entry into the arena of public debate about children's social problems may be more difficult for economically disadvantaged children in the United States and around the world, these children, their parents, and their advocates are speaking up more and more. Indeed the extent and severity of the social problems of the world's children seem overwhelming. It is for just this reason that advocates for children have a responsibility to speak out. In the next chapter I shall continue this debate by addressing the social problems of children.

The Social Problems of Children

To explore and discuss the social problems of children in detail would take us beyond the scope of this book. Instead, in this chapter we'll examine the general state of the world's children, identify positive trends and setbacks in our attempts to improve the quality of children's lives, and consider some real-life examples, which put a human face on the difficult challenges many children encounter every day of their lives. We'll explore three broad categories: poverty and the general quality of children's lives, the breakdown and reorganization of traditional family structures, and violence and the loss of childhood.

Poverty and the Quality of Children's Lives

In her book *Putting Children First*, Penelope Leach (1994) presents a wise quote from David Rogers, the then president of the Robert Wood Johnson Foundation: "Human misery is generally the result of, or accompanied by, a great untidy basketful of intertwined and interconnected circumstances and happenings." Leach then goes on to add that it "is not poverty alone that fills those baskets, but poverty is the thread that tangles them up" (Leach, 1994, p. 191). Of all the factors that contribute to the social problems of children, poverty is the most pervasive and the most insidious. Poverty clearly steals the childhoods and often the very lives of many children in the developing world. However, in recent years the proportion of children living in poverty in industrialized societies has increased dramatically, especially in the United States. Let's examine the effects of poverty on children's lives in developing countries and in the industrialized world.

Problems and Progress in Developing Countries

Most of us have a familiar and painful image of child poverty in the developing world. Starving children are affected by droughts or famine, or suffer from diseases that are well in check in developed countries. However, although problems of malnutrition, lack of vaccinations, and poor health care still plague many children in poor countries, improvements have been made in recent years. For example, the first United Nations World Summit for Children in 1990 set a number of goals for improving the quality of life of children in the developing world. These included a one-third reduction in child deaths; a halving of child malnutrition; immunization levels of 90 percent; control of the major childhood diseases; the eradication of polio; the elimination of micronutrient deficiencies; a halving of maternal mortality rates; primary school education for at least 80 percent of children; the provision of clean water and safe sanitation to all communities; and the universal ratification of the new Convention on the Rights of the Child (UNICEF, 1995a). The means used to measure progress in these areas are far from perfect, and several setbacks have occurred because of wars, new diseases like AIDS, and major debt problems in the developing world. Still, UNICEF reports that more than 100 of the developing nations (including more than 90 percent of the developing world's children) are making significant practical progress toward meeting these goals. Malnutrition has been reduced, immunization levels are generally being maintained or increased, deaths from measles are down by 80 percent, and the incidence of many other diseases has been reduced significantly. In addition, progress in primary education has resumed and the Convention on the Rights of the Child has been widely and rapidly ratified. In human terms this progress means that approximately 2.5 million fewer children will die in 1996 than died in 1990, and millions will be spared insidious impediments to their development due to malnutrition. It also means that at least three quarters of a million fewer children each year will be disabled, blinded, crippled, or born mentally retarded (UNICEF, 1995a). These are significant achievements that deserve high praise. They demonstrate that hard work and commitment to goals can pay off. More important, such progress makes it possible to counter charges that efforts such as these fail in the developing world and that organizations like the United Nations are ineffective.

Yet, most of the children of the developing world are still greatly affected by poverty and the related problems it breeds. In fact, in some countries initial progress has been followed by continuing setbacks. These setbacks are all the more frustrating and threatening for children because they are occurring at a moment in history when traditional values, family organization, and economic structures are rapidly changing in the developing world. Let's consider two cases from South America and Africa.

Poverty and street children in Brazil. Many countries in Central and South America have experienced mass urbanization and its many related social problems. The country most well known for the plight of its street children is Brazil. The problems of Brazil's street children, however, must be placed in context. Deteriorating economic conditions persist; however, recent attempts have been made within the country to recognize and address the problem. Although there have always been wide disparities in the distribution of wealth in Brazil, the country experienced strong economic growth between 1960 and 1980. Annual growth rates of 10 percent during this period led to profound economic and social changes and to the development of a modern and diversified economic structure. Unfortunately, this period was followed by a severe recession in the 1980s, when the gross national product (GNP) dropped over 6 percent, the average minimum salary declined 33 percent, and inflation soared to a level of 50 percent per month. These changes were accompanied by rapid population growth: from 119 to 144 million in the ten years from 1980 to 1990, with approximately 40 percent of the population under seventeen years of age. Furthermore, since the early 1960s Brazil has become highly urbanized. By 1990 the population of São Paulo and Rio de Janeiro exceeded, respectively, 17 million and 11 million and fourteen other cities had more than 1 million inhabitants (Rizzini, et al., 199, pp. 56–57). It is not surprising that these factors combined to worsen severely the situation of the poor, most especially children.

Most studies of economic growth and the physical quality of life have ignored children or treated them as faceless variables (Bradshaw, 1993). International reaction to the deplorable condition of Brazil's street children has drawn some direct attention to children, but think of what it took to get this attention. Children were being killed—*executed*—often because of the fact that they were poor! A study cited in Rizzini et al. (1994) found that 457 children were murdered on the streets of Rio, São Paulo, and Recife in one six-month period in 1989. "Most of the victims (390) were males and most (336) between 15 and 17; only 11 had police records, and 13, at the most, were suspected of drug trafficking. The overwhelming majority had known addresses and lived with their parents. None was known to have ever carried weapons" (Rizzini et al., 1994, p. 66). Rizzini et al. go on to note that:

> These crimes, which resembled executions, are believed to have been committed by hired gunmen. Police are investigating drug traffickers and gangsters who are the prime suspects; individuals who take justice into their own hands ("vigilantes," "death or extermination squads"); and a third group, the military and civil police and private security guards. Few of these cases have been resolved. It is worth emphasizing that the victims are commonly perceived as *a social evil which should be suppressed* [italics added]. (1994, p. 66)

The last line of this quote is especially chilling. Even if *all* of the victims were small-time drug traffickers or petty thieves, did they deserve to be summarily executed? And why has not this "common perception" of

a social evil resulted in the summary execution of suspected *adult* drug traffickers and thieves? It is clear that young children—even those whose primary reason for being on the streets is *the poverty of their families*—are easy
prey for such vigilantism. Fifty-four percent of Brazilian children live in
households in which the monthly per capita income is half the minimum
wage or less (Rizzini et al., 1994, p. 65).

As depressing and bleak as the situation of Brazil's street children is,
negative reactions to the problem and cries of outrage (both internationally
and domestically) have resulted in many new programs, policies, and in
much-needed legislation. Much of this action has been spurred by **nongovernmental organizations** (NGOs), organizations that have no government
affiliation and that promote change and address various social and economic
problems at the community or grass-roots level. As Rizzini et al. note, imple-
menting these laws "to make a real difference in the everyday lives of *all* children in Brazil is the challenge that lies ahead" (1994, p. 98).

Progress and setbacks in Kenya. More and more, children in many of the countries of Sub-Saharan Africa find themselves on urban streets in a struggle for
the economic survival of their families. The causes of their poverty are similar to those in countries of South America. The main culprit is the severe recession of the 1980s and the resulting debt crisis. Kenya is a good example of
what is happening in many parts of Africa. After gaining political independence in 1963, and continuing until 1980, Kenya's national economy was one
of the strongest in Africa. The annual total gross nation product growth av-
eraged 9.7 percent, with inflation and unemployment remaining relatively
low (Bradshaw, Buchman, & Mbatia, 1994). However, economic growth then
slowed and reached a point of nearly zero growth in the early 1990s. Inflation also increased dramatically to a rate of more than 40 percent, resulting
in severe hardships for many citizens.

This economic downturn led the International Monetary Fund, the World
Bank, and other global financial organizations to demand increasing debt
and austerity programs (Bradshaw, 1993; Bradshaw, Noonan, Gash, &
Sershen, 1993). In Kenya, as in most developing countries, a very large percentage of the population are children: 59 percent of the population is under
age twenty, and more than 27 percent are under five years of age (Bradshaw,
Buchman, & Mbatia, 1995). These children's lives were altered dramatically
by these changes as nutrition, health, education, and other social service programs were cut back. One effect of child impoverishment has been the large
increase in street children working as beggars, parking boys, or as laborers
in small business establishments. These children have, for the most part,
abandoned their education and are often exploited by adults. Although most

of the street children are boys, girls are often employed as housemaids, where they work for long hours doing housework and caring for young children. There also has been an alarming increase in child prostitution, with many young boys and girls contracting sexually transmitted diseases, including HIV. One recent estimate was that 20 percent of children with AIDS are in the five-to-fourteen age range, an increase that is tied directly to street prostitution. This statistic is made even bleaker by the fact that 8 to 9 percent of the general population in Kenya is HIV-positive and many more persons are expected to become so. This means that if children do not contact the virus and die before their parents, many of them will become AIDS orphans (Bradshaw, Buchman, & Mbatia, 1995).

Although the problems of Kenya's children seem overwhelming, there are possible long-term solutions to their problems. The brightest rays of hope may come from NGOs like those in Brazil, which have sprung up in local communities and can make a real difference in children's lives. Support of these organizations, especially by foreign donors and the international financial community as well as government reform, could bring about real change.

Poverty and Child Labor in Developing Countries
One area where growing recognition of the plight of children in developing countries may be affecting change is in the area of child labor exploitation. Child labor in the developing world is a complex issue. One reason for the routine exploitation of children's labor is the contradictions that exist between legislation and enforcement of child labor laws in many parts of the world. As Qvortrup notes, many countries "turn a blind eye" to the reality of extensive, full-time child labor despite child labor laws. Furthermore, because much of children's work is illegal, "they are rendered vulnerable to exploitation over conditions, hours, pay and safety standards—factors which for adult workers are regulated by their unions" (Qvortrup, 1991, p. 31). Two possible solutions to these problems are: (1) international condemnation of the problem along with carefully developed economic actions against offending countries, and (2) creative activism by NGOs within offending countries.

Exploitative child labor exists throughout the developing world, but it is most appalling in South Asia, where, in countries like India and Pakistan, children are often sold into indentured servitude or kidnapped to work on farms and in factories, mills, and sweatshops. Carpet factories especially value young children "because they can squat easily, and their nimble fingers can make the smallest, tightest knots" (*Chicago Tribune,*

1995). Recent international outrage has led a German-Indian export-import association to form the Rugmark Foundation, which certifies carpets that are made in childfree factories. Because of the Indian government's general indifference to the problem, however, two bills under consideration in the United States would ban all Indian carpets. One supporter of the bill, Iowa senator Tom Harkin, asked, "Can we really afford the price that children pay to make these products? (*Time*, 1996).

Although condemnation and legislation from outside the offending countries is important, social movements and activism within the countries is most effective. A number of NGOs in India and Pakistan have organized child workers, lobbied their governments, and promoted mass demonstrations and rallies against the exploitation of child workers. Some groups and organizations go further and raid factories in search of children. Such raids have resulted in the rescue of many ill-treated child workers. One child, Iqbal Masih, was not so lucky.

The Abraham Lincoln of Child Workers

Not long ago, at age ten, Iqbal Masih sneaked away from a Pakistani carpet factory, where he had worked since he was four years old. (He was sold into indentured servitude by his parents for less than $16.) A labor organizer told Iqbal that he did not have to return to work because of new child labor laws. But Iqbal went back anyway to tell other child workers. Over the next two years, Iqbal roamed the Pakistan countryside, entering factories and bringing the message of freedom to his peers (*Chicago Tribune*, 1995, p. 6). His activism drew international attention, and Reebok International brought him to Boston, where he was presented with a human rights award from Reebok. In a seven-minute acceptance speech, Iqbal said he wanted to become a lawyer "'so he could be the Abraham Lincoln of his people'" (*Chicago Tribune*, 1995, p. 6). With the promise of a four-year scholarship from Brandeis University, Iqbal began to attend school in India as he continued his labor activism. However, he received repeated death threats, and on Easter Sunday, 1995, Iqbal was shot to death while riding his bicycle with friends near his grand-mother's house in the small village of Muritke, Pakistan. It is believed that he was killed by vengeful members of the carpet industry. In his short and tragic life, Iqbal Masih had accomplished much. "He was so brave . . . you can't imagine," said Ehsan Ullah Kahn, the labor organizer who first told Iqbal he did not have to return to his oppressive bosses. "He also has managed to free thousands of children" (*Chicago Tribune*, 1995, p. 6).

Child Poverty in Industrialized Countries

In the wealthy nations of the world, children are not shot on the streets for being poor, nor are they allowed to be sold into indentured servitude. The overwhelming majority of children in Western industrialized societies live in relative comfort with high aspirations and bright futures. However, many poor children do live in the modern industrialized world, and a significant number live in impoverished and dangerous environments. Children's poverty varies across wealthy nations. The richest nation in the world, the United States, has the one of the highest poverty rates. Worse, despite a growing awareness of the problem, the proportion of children living in poverty is on the rise in the United States and in several other Western countries and is much higher than it was twenty years ago. Let's examine this problem by considering recent trends in child poverty in the United States, looking at divergent poverty rates among children and the elderly, and comparing American child poverty to that in other industrialized countries.

Trends in child poverty in the United States. There are a number of ways of measuring poverty. In the United States the official poverty rate provided by the Census Bureau reflects an **absolute measure of poverty** that is supposed to represent the dollar amount a family needs to achieve a "minimally adequate" standard of living (Bianchi, 1993). The absolute rate is misleading for several reasons. First, it is based on pretax rather than after-tax income and does not take into account access to resources such as food stamps and medical coverage. Poverty measures that take tax and income transfer resources into account are used to figure what is normally referred to as the **posttax and transfer poverty rate**. Second, many argue that poverty is a relative concept and that what is considered "minimally adequate" varies as average living standards increase or decrease (Bianchi, 1993, p. 94; Hernandez, 1994, p. 13). Those who believe in the importance of using **relative measures of poverty** normally set the poverty rate between 40 and 50 percent of the median income of all families in a particular community or country at a given time. For a variety of reasons, different reports of child poverty in the United States and other countries are based on different poverty measures. This leads to a great deal of confusion and distortion in political debates about the extent and causes of child poverty. In our discussion we will always be clear about the particular measure being used and why it is most relevant given a particular comparison.

In terms of absolute measures of poverty, the proportion of children who lived in poverty in the United States in the late 1930s was very high (nearly 70 per cent) but declined dramatically in the 1940s and 1950s as the country emerged from the Great Depression and enjoyed an economic boom after World War II. The rate continued to drop in the 1960s, reaching a low of 14 percent in 1969. Child poverty increased in the 1970s and early 1980s as economic growth slowed and the country suffered through several recessions. After reaching a high of 22.3 percent in 1983, the child poverty rate dropped to 19.5 percent by 1988 as a result of sustained economic growth. This reduction, however, was much less than was expected and was in no way comparable to the major drop in child poverty during the economic boom of the 1950s. Further, with the recession that began in late 1990, the proportion of children in poverty began to increase again and reached a level of 21.8 percent in 1991 (see Bianchi, 1993). These patterns of child poverty are not confined to the highly segregated inner-city neighborhoods of large metropolitan areas. Poverty rates are similar if not higher among non-metropolitan children (Lichter & Eggebeen, 1992). Overall, as Bianchi notes, recent patterns indicate that "poor macroeconomic growth continues to move more children into poverty, but good macroeconomic performance seems less able to do the opposite" (1993, p. 95).

Why might this be the case? There are a number of interrelated reasons. Most often cited as the main cause are the dramatic structural changes in American families since the 1950s. A major increase in the divorce rate and in the number of nonmarital births (especially to young, poor women) has moved many women and children into poverty (Hernandez, 1994; Sidel, 1992). The problem is increased by the fact that the fathers of many of these children have not taken seriously the responsibility of providing for their offspring, nor have state governments, until recently, passed and enforced child support laws to ensure that fathers meet their responsibilities. Some have argued that the federal government needs to become involved in the efficient collection of the $34 billion a year in unpaid child support from deadbeat dads (Skocpol & Wilson, 1994).

We will return to discuss the effects of changes in family structure on children's economic, social, and psychological well-being below. Here, we need to look at another important factor in child poverty: the way social welfare policies in the United States affect children and the elderly.

Social welfare policy and divergent poverty rates of children and the elderly. Although Americans advocate strict equality in the distribution of political and judicial rights, they are wary about supporting attempts to ensure economic equality that involve government redistribution (Burtless, 1994, p. 83). Unlike most Western European countries, the United States is a highly market-oriented society and designs its social welfare programs accordingly. This fact is nowhere more evident than in the disparity between the poverty rate of children compared to that of the elderly.

As many progressives like to point out, the great society programs (the expansion of Social Security and the institution of Medicare and Medicaid) in the 1960s substantially reduced poverty among the elderly (Carville, 1996). In calculating this change, using a posttax and transfer poverty rate—a measure that takes tax and income transfer resources into account—is crucial. Using such a measure the poverty rate for persons sixty-five years and older in 1960 was around 30 percent while by 1994 it was reduced to 12 percent. The major reason for this reduction was government programs that support the elderly. Similar government programs for children are much less generous. To estimate the difference let's look at how government programs affected rates of poverty among the elderly and children in the United States in 1986. For the elderly (persons sixty-five and older) the poverty rate before taking government programs and tax credits into account was 46.5 percent. After taking the programs and tax credits into account the poverty rate was 10.9 percent, a reduction of 33.2 percent. Things were quite different for children seventeen and under in 1986. The poverty rate was reduced from 22.3 percent to 20.4 percent when taking government programs and tax credits into account, a reduction of only 1.9 percent (Hewlett, 1993, p. 16; Smeeding, 1991). Overall, we see that the rate of reduction in poverty was nearly nineteen times more for the elderly when compared to children and that the overall poverty rate for children was nearly double that of the elderly. These differences in the poverty rates for the elderly and children have persisted since 1986. In fact, social welfare policies and a number of other factors have contributed to a general trend in which the quality of the lives of the elderly and children have moved in different directions—up for the elderly and down for children (Preston, 1984; Sgritta, 1994). Do we care more for our elderly than we do for our children? Does it make sense to invest more in the elderly than in children?

Most Americans, young and old, would answer "no" to both questions. Yet, we currently treat our elderly much better than our children. The reasons for this are complicated. Let's return to the nature of social welfare policy in the United States. The two largest social welfare programs for the elderly, Social Security and Medicare, are **social insurance programs**. These programs are financed by payroll taxes and are paid by those currently employed and their employers and the benefits are provided to the retired, dependents of deceased workers, and insured unemployed (Burtless, 1994, p. 54). Social insurance programs differ from other types of social welfare programs in that they are not **means-tested** or restricted to only the poor. Means-tested programs distribute money and other types of resources to the poor and near poor (Burtless, 1994, p. 53). In theory social insurance programs pay for themselves: People who work pay taxes, and these payroll taxes cover their Social Security and Medicare costs in their retirement years. However, right away there is a problem with such thinking. Many people have entered into retirement (and therefore been entitled to Medicare) after paying very little into the system. Further, due to advances in medical technology and the success of the programs themselves, the elderly are living longer and longer. Thus, these programs become more and more expensive as the number of people covered increases. This economic problem is accelerated by the growing costs of medical care; new technologies like heart transplants keep people alive longer but are very expensive.

Calculated in terms of 1990 dollars, Medicare spending increased from $35.5 billion in 1975 to $120.4 billion in 1992 (an increase of 220 percent or an average of nearly 13 percent a year; see Burtless, 1994, p. 57). There has been a similar percentage increase in Medicaid, a program that, contrary to what most people think, is primarily for the elderly and disabled and not for poor children. In fact, half of the people in nursing homes in the United States are covered by Medicaid (Carville, 1996, p. 74). Overall, these two programs, along with Social Security, were implemented at a cost of $455 billion in 1992. This accounted for nearly 65 per cent of total social welfare spending in the United States for that year (Burtless, 1994, p. 57). Such large investment in the elderly reflects our society's appreciation of their past productivity. It also indicates the political power of the elderly who are well organized and who tend to vote in high numbers. For example, nearly 69 percent of all eligible elderly voted in the 1988 presidential election—the highest of any other age group.

However, at some point our society must question such large and expanding investment in the elderly, most especially when America's investment in *children* pales in comparison to that given the elderly. For example, in 1992, programs that directly affect the lives of poor preschool children, such as Aid for Families with Dependent Children (AFDC, $22.9 billion) and Head Start ($2.6 billion) were meager in comparison to those for the elderly. Further, contrary to popular belief, AFDC payments increased an average of only .05 percent per year from 1975 to 1992 (from $22.7 billion to $22.9 billion in 1990 dollars, Burtless, 1994, p. 57). Yet, many would argue that even this increase and level of welfare spending is too much. Such attitudes are understandable in a country where most social welfare programs related to medical care, nutrition, and housing are means-tested. Because only the truly impoverished are covered by most of these welfare programs, many working people who can barely make ends meet and cannot afford health insurance come to resent those who receive basic benefits without working.

Variations in Child Poverty and Quality of Life in Industrialized Countries

Most other countries in the industrialized world do not make such sharp distinctions between entitlement programs like old age pensions and other types of social welfare. In these countries basic nutrition, medical care, family leave, child care, and preschool education are provided at a base level for all citizens. In short, other industrialized countries have attempted to deal with the very real demands of increasing social welfare costs of the elderly while at that same time maintaining investments in their children (Sgritta, 1994). These countries are less market-oriented than the United States, and their citizens are willing to pay higher rates of taxation for the social benefits they receive.

This difference leads to a number of interesting patterns regarding the quality of life among children. Lee Rainwater and Timothy Smeeding (1995) looked at both overall child poverty rates and the general economic well-being of children in the United States and seventeen other industrialized nations. The authors used a relative measure of poverty (children under eighteen living in households with income below half of the national median) that was adjusted for family size and age of head of the household. The survey studied the period from 1982 to 1991. Overall, they found that the market-oriented and relatively low tax rate system in the United States resulted in a high level of income inequality compared to the rest of the industrialized world. As we can see in Exhibit 10.1, the United States has a much higher overall rate of child poverty (21.5 percent) than any other of the countries studied. The poverty rates were all under 10 per cent in Western Europe (with the exception of 12 percent in Ireland) and they were under 5 percent in eight of the countries, with the least child poverty in Finland and Sweden. In the other industrialized countries that were studied, the rates were generally higher than those in Western Europe (11.1 in Israel, 13.5 in Canada, and 14.0 in Australia), but such rates were still well below the rate in the United States.

Child poverty rates, however, do not tell the whole story. Rainwater and Smeeding also looked at the economic well-being of children across income levels of households in the eighteen countries. Here they found that in the United States, high-income children are better off than their counterparts in other industrialized nations, while *our poor children are much worse off than low-income children in almost all other industrialized nations.* For example, American children whose families are in the upper 20 percent of the income distribution have much higher standards of living (as measured by real spendable income) than do similarly situated children in the other countries studied. In fact, only Switzerland and Canada were within 20 percent of the United States standard (Rainwater & Smeeding, 1995, p. 8). At the middle-income level, Danish children are slightly better off than American children, while children in most of the other countries enjoy a standard of economic well-being similar to that in the United States (the exceptions being the United Kingdom, Israel, and Ireland). For children at the lower end of the distribution (the bottom 20 percent of incomes), Rainwater and Smeeding

EXHIBIT 10.1

Child Poverty in Eighteen Countries

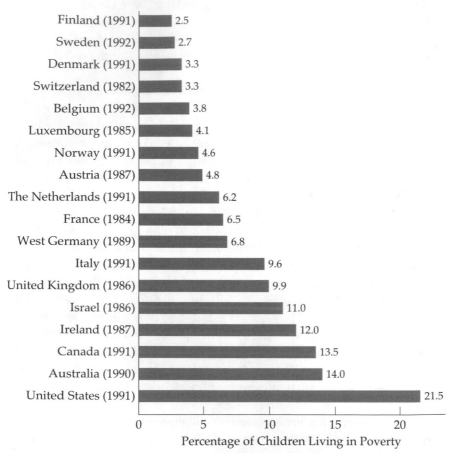

NOTE: Numbers in parentheses indicate the year of the report.

Source: Adapted from Rainwater and Smeeding, 1995, p. 11.

found "a very different and surprising picture" (1995, p. 8). They observed that in six countries (Switzerland, Sweden, Finland, Denmark, Belgium, and Norway) low-income children have real standards of living *at least 50 percent higher than in the United States!* In four other countries (Germany, Luxembourg, Netherlands and Austria) low-income children were at least 30 percent better off than in the United States. And only in Israel and Ireland "do low-income children have a lower real standard of living than do children in the United States" (1995, p. 9). We must also remember that although most of the countries studied provide paid maternal or family leave, some form of government-supported child care, and early education programs, the United

States provides either no such services or has very limited programs, such as Head Start. Therefore, the economic challenges that poor families and their children face are much greater in the United States than in any other country in the industrialized world. Overall, these data indicate a much greater level of commitment for the well-being of *all* children in other countries of the industrialized world as compared to the United States.

The Human Face of Poverty: The Story of Nicholas

Given growing concern about the budget deficit, opposition to higher taxes, skepticism about welfare policy, and the political power of the elderly, it is unlikely that the United States will face up to its growing problem of child poverty anytime soon. However, some things can be done right away, and we will consider several important first steps in the next chapter. For now, we close this section with an inspiring case study of an inner-city Chicago boy who is doing his best to make the most of his childhood in very difficult circumstances.

Growing Up Fast: The Story of Nicholas

In 1993, *The New York Times* published an important series of articles entitled "Children of the Shadows," which captured the lives of ten children growing up poor in American cities. The first article, written by Isabel Wilkerson (1993), told the inspiring story of Nicholas, an African-American ten-year-old living with his family in the dangerous Englewood section of Chicago. The economic circumstances of Nicholas and his family can be expressed quite simply—they are very poor. However, his family structure and those of his mother and other adults who care for him are very complex. Wilkerson describes a scene in which the boy is called from his fourth-grade classroom and asked to explain why no one has picked up his younger sister, Ishtar, from her morning kindergarten class. Nicholas has a hard time explaining "that his mother, a welfare recipient rearing five young children, was in college trying to be-come a nurse and so was not home during the day, that Ishtar's father was separated from his mother and in a drug-and-alcohol haze most of the time, that [the] grandmother he used to live with was at work, and that, besides, he could not possibly account for the man who was supposed to take his sister home—his mother's com-panion, the father of her youngest child" (Wilkerson, 1993, p. 1). In the end, Nicholas simply says that his stepfather was supposed to pick up Ishtar, and he then gives the principal the phone number of his aunt.

Nicholas's mother, Angela, fits many of the stereotyped descriptions of welfare recipients. She is black, a tenth-grade dropout who bore her first child, Nicholas, at age sixteen and then had four more children with three different men. Angela also went through a very difficult period in which she was addicted to crack cocaine. Her mother cared for her children; Angela went through treatment and has stayed away from drugs ever since. She has been on and off welfare and has worked a long succession of jobs, from picking okra in Louisiana to waiting tables in downtown Chicago. She, like most of us, has made mistakes—the two biggest being her teenage pregnancy and her drug addiction. When the poor make mistakes, however, they seldom get a second chance and the recovery process is long and hard.

Angela and her mother are deeply religious and attend services in a tiny storefront church, Faith Temple, several times a week. The deep spirituality of many inner-city African-Americans is often overlooked in the stereotypes. It is this spirituality, an Ethiopian-derived Christianity, that has kept Angela striving for her goal—a nursing degree that could pull her family out of poverty and into the working class. Spirituality also sustains her family against many of the dangers—crack houses, drive-by shootings, robberies—of their inner-city environment. (Eighty people were murdered in Angela's neighborhood in 1992; as Wilkerson points out, this is more than the number of murders in Omaha and Pittsburgh combined for that year) (1993, p. 16).

Every morning before her children go to school, Angela shakes an aerosol can containing a special religious oil and tells them to close their eyes tight as "she sprays them long and furious so they will come back to her, alive and safe, at day's end" (Wilkerson, 1993, p. 16). She has faith in the oil, but she also recites the rules to her children each morning: No playing on the way to and from school, and if you hear shooting—run! "Why do I say run?" the mother asks each day. "Because a bullet don't have no eyes," Nicholas and his brother, Willie, shout in reply. Once Willie almost got shot on the way home from school as he straggled along behind his brother—a sixth-grade boy pulled out a gun and started shooting. Willie heard the shots and ran, unhurt, to catch up with his brother. So far the rules and the oil have worked.

In many ways Nicholas is a typical ten-year-old. He gets only average grades, and he slides down banisters, shirttail out, hoping to become a fireman. But he has many of the responsibilities of a man. He must look after his younger siblings, often getting their breakfast each morning and washing clothes at night since the children have so few things to wear. "I know my baby's running out of hands," Angela says low one night as Nicholas works on the laundry. She worries about him, and Nicholas, in turn, worries about her and about his siblings. He worries much too much for a young boy. He was worried the morning his mother had an early test and he had to take the little ones to day care before going to school himself. At the day care center, his youngest brother, John-John, began to cry as Nicholas walked away. "Nicholas bent down and hugged him and kissed him. Everything, Nicholas assured him, was going to be O.K." (Wilkerson, 1993, p. 16).

Changing Family Structures and Children's Lives

In Chapter 4 we discussed recent structural changes in families in industrialized and developing societies and how such changes affect the lives of children. Here we want to consider these changes in the family as social problems of children; that is, we want to estimate how the various changes may or may not negatively affect children's lives and the nature of their childhoods. We concentrate on Western industrialized societies, because there has been a good deal of social research on how children in these societies are affected by changes in family structure, as well as much political debate and some policy formation related to these changes. Three types of structural changes in the family are seen as the most potentially harmful to children: (1) the increase in the number of families where both parents are working, (2) the dramatic rise in divorce, and (3) the growing number of nonmarital births. The last two changes are, of course, directly related to the growing number of single-parent families. We discuss each of these structural changes in turn.

Work, Families, and Childhood

In looking at work, families, and childhood in the United States, we will first consider the possible effects on children of the dramatic increase in the number of women in the workforce who have children. We then discuss what the United States and other industrialized countries are doing to support working families and their children.

Working mothers and young children. In 1995 more than two-thirds of women with preschool children were working outside the home in the United States. There has been a similar increase in working mothers in most industrialized countries. The major result of this structural change in families for children is that they spend more and more time in nonparental care.

A series of studies in the 1980s raised questions about the effects of infant child care on the security of children's attachments. In these studies, secure attachment was measured by children's response to their mother's return after a brief separation in what has been called the **strange situation experiment**. In this experiment infants are brought by their mothers to a playroom setting in a laboratory. They are engaged in play with some toys by the mother, and are then left alone with a female researcher. The infant's response to her mother's brief absence and to her return are seen as indicators of the child's attachment to the mother. Attached children are expected to show anxiety during the mother's absence and relief upon her return. The reunion behavior turned out to be most important in the original use of the strange situation experiment by Ainsworth, Blehar, Waters, and Wall (1978), who found that children who either ignored, avoided, or actively resisted their mothers upon reunion had problems with emotional security later in life. None of the children in the original study had attended infant day care, but later studies found that "infants of full-time working mothers were 1.6 (Belsky & Rovine, 1988) or 1.2 (Clarke-Stewart, 1989) times more likely to be classified as insecure in their relationship with the mother" (Clerkx & Van Ijzendoorn, 1992, p. 72).

These results, though alarming, were questioned on many grounds, most especially that of whether the child's behavior upon reunion could be considered a valid measure of secure attachment. It was pointed out, for example, that it was hardly surprising that a child who had a great deal of experience in daycare might ignore her mother and continue to play with toys after the mother returned following a brief absence. In fact, many would see this behavior as quite normal and indicative of security and independence on the part of the child (Clarke-Stewart, 1989; Eyer, 1993). Finally, the most recent research on this issue sponsored by the National Institute of Child Health and Human Development found that "the sense of trust felt by fifteen-month-old-children in their mothers was not affected by whether the children were in day care, by how many hours they spent there, by the age they entered day care, by the quality or type of care, or by how many times care arrangements were changed" (Chira, 1996, p. 1). *The thing that did affect infant's trust was a mother's sensitivity and responsiveness.* For mothers who are lacking in these skills, the troubled mother-infant bond can be increased by poor-quality child care.

Providing quality child care and early educational programs is the most important way we can support families in our contemporary global economy. Before turning to this issue, however, let us step back and take a look at the whole way the child attachment debate played itself out in the

United States. When the first cautionary reports about infant child care were published (most especially those by Belsky, 1988, 1989; Belsky & Rovine, 1988), they were quickly picked up by conservative commentators and politicians. Conservative columnists like Joan Beck and Mona Charen used Belsky's work to condemn all day care (not just infant day care) in broad critiques that accused working women of putting their jobs and careers ahead of their children. These commentators also were critical of government-supported child care; they considered it an intrusion into family life and went so far as to suggest that liberal behavioral scientists were actually suppressing findings that did not fit their ideological views. Liberal commentators, politicians, and some researchers responded to such overstatements and also cautioned that most women worked because they had to and that raising women's guilt about leaving their infants in the care of others is more harmful than such care itself. However, these responses often seemed to imply that there was no good alternative other than infant care for the children of working parents during the first few months of children's lives. Putting the scientific basis of concerns of attachment aside, we surely can think of better alternatives that support families with young children. Let's look at family leave, child care, and early education policies in the United States as compared to Western Europe.

Social policy regarding maternity and family leave. Debates about infant attachment and, in fact, most debates about the harmful effects of nonparental care for young children in the United States, are counterproductive in two respects. First, the real issue regarding infant care centers not around day care but around reasonable government policy regarding maternity and family leave. Until 1993 the United States was the only industrialized country in the world, except South Africa, with no formal policy for maternity leave. The Family and Medical Leave Law, which was passed in the initial months of the Clinton administration, mandates employers of fifty or more employees provide up to twelve weeks of *unpaid*, job-protected leave to employees for certain family and medical reasons. Reasons for the leave include: the birth of the employee's child, or its placement as an adopted or foster child; the care of the employee's spouse, son or daughter, or parent, who has a serious health condition; or a serious health condition that makes the employee unable to perform their job. The length of the leave (up to the maximum twelve weeks) is at the discretion of the employee. Although the Family and Medical Leave Law was clearly a step in the right direction, especially because of its guarantee of job protection, the fact that the leave is unpaid is a major shortcoming. Most working-class and low-income families (especially single-parent families) cannot afford to take more than a week or so off of work because of the lost income.

Other industrialized countries are far ahead of the United States on this issue. All West European countries provide maternity leave at 50 to 100 percent of earnings (most from 90 to 100 percent)—from six weeks to one year. Most countries also provide additional family leave time (normally during the child's first year) at some percentage of earnings or at a flat fee.

A brief look a three representative West European countries is instructive. Sweden has a highly complex and generous system of maternity and family leave. Families (mothers or fathers or some combination) are entitled to 360 days of leave at 90 percent of earnings, and another 90 days at a low flat fee. The leave can be taken full- or part-time, from birth to the child's eighth birthday. Fathers are also entitled to 10 days of paternity leave at full pay upon the birth of a child. Additional leaves are provided for parents of children under twelve for illness and for visits to children's schools. In Italy, whose policies fall in the middle range of European countries, 12 weeks of maternity leave at full pay is mandated, and up to 6 months of additional family leave (for the father or mother) is provided at 30 percent of earnings. Finally, Greece, on the low end of the European scale, provides 12 weeks of maternity leave for mothers at 50 percent of earnings.

Given these policies, one can see that debates of child attachment and infant care rarely arise in Western Europe. There is clear recognition that families need support in a child's first year. Most European policies first went into effect in the mid to late 1980s and usually do not take the form of simple government mandates to employers. Rather, the government (through general income or related taxes), employers, and employees all contribute in some way to the cost of such programs.

Social policy regarding child care and early childhood education. Debates about child care in the United States seldom address the importance of distinguishing between nonparental child care and early education programs, nor do they properly focus on how to provide *high quality* services in these areas. In the United States all prekindergarten children are lumped together irrespective of age in debates about nonparental care. Most kindergarten programs are only half-day and thus provide only limited child care and preparation for first grade. In Western Europe maternity and parental leave policies address infants' needs in the first year; custodial care programs are available for toddlers between the ages of one to three; and early education programs are normally provided for *nearly all* three- to six-year-olds. The cost and availability of programs for toddlers are similar to what we find in the United States. But even here, most programs are government subsidized to reduce costs for parents, and many have evolved from being a mainly custodial to being more educational in approach (see Corsaro & Emiliani, 1992).

The biggest difference between the United States and Western Europe is the extensiveness and overall quality of early education programs for three-to-six-year-olds. Almost all European countries offer quality programs at a low cost. Although early education teachers have generally less training and are normally paid somewhat less than elementary and secondary teachers, their incomes are much higher on average than early education teachers in the United States. There are also much lower rates of teacher turnover in West European preschool programs, compared to those in the United States (see Lamb, Sternberg, Hwang, & Broberg, 1992). In countries like France and Italy, more than 90% of all three- to six-year-olds attend government-supported programs, and parents pay very low fees—primarily to cover the costs of meals (see Corsaro & Emiliani, 1992; Greenhouse, 1993). Programs in these two countries are seen as exemplars of the best early education in the world (Bohlen, 1995; Edwards, Gandini, & Forman, 1993). They are based on carefully developed early childhood curricula that stress social and language skills and bridge the child's transition from the family to the community and formal schooling (Corsaro, 1996). (In earlier chapters we saw how such programs in Italian preschools promote children's construction of peer cultures, which both enrich their childhoods and contribute to their development of social, language, and cognitive skills.)

In the United States day care and early education policies have several general features: "parent responsibility for selecting and paying for care, local government and market forces for regulation, limited government financing, and market forces to regulate supply" (Haskins, 1992, p. 279). This does not mean that the United States government does not support child care and early education. Haskins believes the government does a lot by providing early education for poor children through Head Start programs, tax credits to help offset child care costs (including the Earned Income Tax Credit for low-income families), and various block grants to states, which can be used to support day care and before- and after-school programs. It should be pointed out, however, that many of these programs are now under serious threat of cutbacks intended to balance the budget, and most are highly limited in meeting the needs of low-income and poor families. Head Start, for example, serves only about 35 percent of the very poor children who qualify for its program. Furthermore, Head Start is a highly limited program; in most instances, children attend for only three to four hours per day, four days a week, for eight months a year. Clearly, Head Start can not be seen as providing consistent child care for working mothers with low incomes, and, like many care and early education programs in the United States, it suffers from incoherent educational goals and high levels of teacher turnover.

The biggest problem with Head Start and most other moderately priced private day care and early education programs is the quality of such programs. As we noted above, such programs in the United States are primarily market driven. Therefore, a case could be made that the overall supply of day care in the United States is sufficient; however, the contention that the quality of affordable day care is adequate is extremely hard to defend (cf., Haskins, 1992). Numerous studies have pointed to problems with minimal safety standards, limited educational curricula, low staff pay, and high staff turnover in both family day care in private homes and larger day care centers (see *Bloomington Herald-Times*, 1994; Lamb, Sternberg, & Kettelinus, 1992; Lewin, 1990; Pear, 1994). Moreover, the cost of enrolling children in even moderately priced programs is difficult for working-class and low-income families to meet. Perhaps the biggest problem is low staff pay, especially in for-profit private centers where there are strong pressures to keep costs down. Several studies cited average early education teacher salaries in the range of $10,000 to $16,000 a year for 1990, barely above the poverty level. In fact, many early childhood teachers cannot afford to enroll their children in the programs in which they work! Not surprisingly, these low salaries are directly related to high teacher turnover, which is about 40 percent per year.

Overall, we see that the real issue is not so much how working parents and day care may be negatively affecting young children's lives, but rather how creative and committed community and government programs can help families adapt to and minimize the negative effects of these changes. Again we see a pattern wherein the United States has developed some policies and programs to aid middle- and upper-class families in dealing with these problems. Such families are given a period of unpaid family leave and moderate support (mostly through tax credits)—enough to buy adequate- to high-quality child care and early education. Working-class and low-income families, on the other hand, face much more difficult challenges (National Research Council, 1995). Mothers must quickly return to work after childbirth, and those child care and early education programs that are affordable are often of low quality.

Divorce and Its Effects on Children

In discussing divorce and its effects on children, we will look first at patterns in the overall increase in divorce in industrialized societies. We then will consider how laws regulating divorce and child support affect the economic security of women and children. Finally, we will review research on the social and psychological consequences of divorce for children and youth.

Patterns in divorce and economic consequences for women and children. A major change in family structure in the industrialized world has resulted from the dramatic increase in the number of divorces. Nowhere has this increase been more apparent than in the United States, where the number of children directly experiencing divorce rose from 463,000 in 1960 to 1,174,000 in 1980 (U. S. Bureau of the Census, 1992). The divorce rate peaked in the early 1980s and dipped slightly in the early 1990s, with the number of children experiencing divorce dropping to 985,000. Several factors have been attributed to the increase in the divorce rate, including the entrance of women into the work force, changing values and increasing individualism, liberalization of attitudes and laws regarding divorce, and economic pressures and family stress (see Furstenberg & Cherlin, 1991). Because all of these factors are interrelated, it is doubtful that any one cause can be singled out as more important than another. Comparative data from other industrialized countries, however, suggest that highly individualistic value systems and liberalization of divorce laws both seem to affect the divorce rate. Exhibit 10.2 presents divorce rates in selected industrialized countries for three time periods (1960, 1980, and 1986 to 1988). We can see a number of patterns. First, all of the countries experienced increasing divorce rates, with some leveling off (and in a slight drop in the United States) between 1980 and 1988. In Italy divorce was not legalized until 1973. The divorce rate rose to a high of 1.3 per 1,000 married women shortly after legalization (not shown in Exhibit 10.2) and then, as we can see, there was a drop to 0.8 in 1980 and a rise to 2.1 by 1988. This is similar to the large increases in the rate of divorce that occurred in other countries from 1960 to 1980. Second, we see major variations in the overall rate of divorce. The United States had the highest rate overall in 1988 at 20.7 per 1,000 married women. Four other countries (Canada, Denmark, Sweden, and Britain) had rates between 10 and 15. France and West Germany had rates between 5 to 10, while Japan and Italy had the lowest rates, at around 5 or less. Although it is difficult to explain these differences, several of the countries with the lowest rates (France, Italy, and Japan) have religious or collectivist values that are not favorable to divorce. Furthermore, France and Italy have required waiting periods of five to six years to complete dissolution.

Many commentators who see divorce as having strong negative effects on children point out the need to reconsider the liberalization of values and laws regarding divorce in the United States (Poponoe, 1992). We will return to this issue in Chapter 11. First, however, let's consider what we currently know about the economic effects of divorce on women and children. As we discussed in Chapter 4 and earlier in this chapter, separation and divorce often have severe negative economic consequences for women and children.

EXHIBIT 10.2

Divorce Rates for Selected Countries (1960–1988)

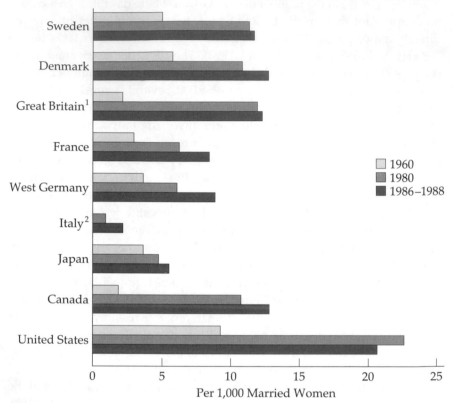

[1]Data prior to 1988 for England and Wales only.
[2]Divorce was not legal in Italy in 1960.

Source: Youth Indicators, Statistical Office of the European Communities, Demographic Statistics, 1988 and 1990; *U.S. Department of Health and Human Services, Nation Center for Statistics,* Monthly Vital Statistics Report, 1990.

The present system of child support in the United States often puts an enormous economic burden on women in the periods of separation and following divorce. Women who were unemployed before a divorce often find they must enter a job market for which they have limited skills or training. Most who are employed find that their meager incomes are not enough to maintain their and their children's former economic well-being. Many women and their children must live near or below the poverty line following divorce, as mothers work longer hours or combine work and further education and job training. Many women chose to remarry soon after divorce in an attempt to regain economic security (Sidel, 1992; Furstenberg & Cherlin, 1991). Children, of course, must share in and adapt to these economic difficulties. Children often have to relocate to smaller homes or rented apartments, have less money for their basic and leisure needs, and spend less time with both their fathers and mothers.

Many men in the United States pay little or no child support because they can get away with it. Lax enforcement of child support laws has been linked to traditional gender role ideology in the United States and to an overall reluctance in our society to face up to the consequences of divorce. Men, whether they pay support or not, often make out much better financially than their children and ex-wives following divorce. However, many men underestimate and rationalize such inequities, because they usually have less interaction with their children and frequently enter into new relationships or marriages in which they have new children to help support. In this way, many American men exchange old obligations for new ones; from their point of view they are not disregarding their family responsibilities but rather redefining them as they move from one marriage to the next (Furstenberg & Cherlin, 1991).

Things are quite different in Western European countries, where child support laws are more strictly enforced and where government takes up the slack for those who do not pay. Some changes are beginning to appear in the United States; as we will discuss in Chapter 11, these changes, which involve new and stricter methods of enforcing child support, may have a real impact on the economic consequences of divorce for children.

Social and psychological effects of divorce on children. Social and psychological effects of divorce on children are much harder to measure, interpret, and understand than are the economic consequences. And, although there has been a good deal of research in this area, the results are inconclusive. There are several interrelated challenges in estimating the social and psychological effects of divorce on children. First, most studies measure effects at one point in time; however, divorce and its consequences are *processes* that unfold over a long period of time (Furstenberg & Cherlin, 1991). For example, many studies estimate the short- and long-term consequences of divorce by way of interviews or surveys that estimate psychological well-being or through the collection of behavioral measures (school grades, drug use, sexual activity, criminal behavior) during separation or after divorce. As a result it is hard to know if these outcome measures were affected by preexisting conditions, such as the level of conflict in the family before separation and divorce, or certain individual characteristics of the children (Skolnick & Rosencrantz, 1994). A second problem is that some studies include matched groups of children who have not experienced divorce, but many do not. The issue here is that certain psychological and behavioral problems of the children may themselves have contributed to family instability, conflict, and eventual dissolution of the marriage. Without matched samples there is no way to sort out such effects.

With these cautions in mind we can turn to a summary of findings on the consequences of divorce for children. These were presented in a recent book by Furstenberg and Cherlin (1991). In terms of short-term psychological effects, Furstenberg and Cherlin point to two types of disorders that may result from divorce: **externalizing disorders** ("acting out" behaviors such as aggression, disobedience, lying, and so on) and **internalizing disorders** (depression, anxiety, or withdrawal). Boys in high-conflict families (whether these conflicts lead to divorce or not) tend to show more aggressive and antisocial behavior. Aggressive behavior among boys during separation or after divorce is seen as possibly related to the fact that the boys most often live with the opposite-sex parent. Sometimes a pattern occurs in which acting out by boys is followed by overly harsh discipline or indulgence from mothers, which then leads to more acting out. For girls the findings are less consistent. In studies of divorced families, girls seem to do better after marital disruption; however, they may develop internalizing disorders that become apparent several years later.

Furstenberg and Cherlin stress the importance of matched samples of children from intact families in drawing conclusions about long term effects. They refer to one such study, which found that 34 percent of children from disrupted families had problems in school some eight years after the divorce, compared with 20 percent of children from intact families. Is this a significant finding? Yes and no, say Furstenberg and Cherlin. First, children from disrupted families clearly have more problems, but we do not know if (and certainly not how or why) these problems may be related to family experiences. Second, the *majority* of children from disrupted families (66 percent) in the study did not have problems in school. Other research, which looked at high school graduation rates, reported similar findings. In a final study discussed by Furstenberg and Cherlin, children from intact families in which there was a great deal of conflict between parents were doing no better, and were often doing worse, than the children of divorce.

Overall, we see that there are many methodological challenges to studying the effects of divorce on children, and the research is not conclusive (Skolnick & Rosencrantz, 1994). The research indicates that there is no definite path down which children of divorce progress. Still, the research does suggest some important strategies in reducing the negative effects of divorce on children. First, how the custodial parent (usually the mother) functions as a parent in the first months after a separation is of crucial importance. This is a critical time for children, who are trying to come to terms with the fact that their lives are changing in highly troubling and confusing ways. Further, some children tend to blame themselves for their parents' problems during this period. If the custodial parent can keep the family functioning in line with established and predictable routines, the children generally will do well.

Here again we see, as we have throughout this book, the importance of familiar, everyday routines for security in children's lives. Of course, maintaining such routines is no small task for a custodial parent whose life may seem to be crumbling all around her. This is a time when both parents need to cooperate for the sake of the children—even though their partnership is coming apart. Such cooperation is an overwhelming challenge, and it is at this point in the divorce process that outside support from relatives, community organizations, and government agencies is most crucial.

A second key factor in minimizing the negative effects of separation and divorce on children is maintaining a low level of conflict between parents. Persistent, intense, and highly visible conflict during the separation and after divorce magnifies the negative impact of the disruption. Again, minimizing conflict while terminating a marriage is a tall order. Rather than lessening conflict, some divorcing couples become so caught up in anger and bitterness toward one another that they bring children into their disputes, at times even forcing them to take sides in bitter custody battles.

In a course I teach regularly on childhood and contemporary society, I ask my students to write a paper in which they reflect on problems in their own childhoods. Many students write about experiencing divorce. Time and time again they refer to the level of conflict between parents throughout the divorce process. Unfortunately, many students whose parents could not escape cycles of hostility and resentment still display anxiety and distress in their accounts, even if the divorce occurred many years in the past. Students' reports are much more positive and heartening in those cases where parents managed to put their bitterness aside and cooperate as best they could for their children. Such students often note that the experience was still stressful, but manageable. Furthermore, they felt that over time they developed a deeper respect and understanding of their parents' commitment to them.

Teen Pregnancy and Nonmarital Births

Perhaps no other change in family structure has been more controversial than the rising number of nonmarital births in Western industrialized societies. This issue seemed to reach its peak in the United States when a fictionalized television character, "Murphy Brown," was criticized by then vice president Quayle for deciding to have a child out of wedlock. Nonmarital births seem most disturbing to those who hold traditional values regarding family structure, because they are seen as a rejection of the two-parent family. However, the issue is intensified by the growing number of nonmarital births of adolescent girls, most especially poor minority youth. In this case, as we saw in Chapter 9, all the negative aspects of blaming the victim come to the fore. Debates about nonmarital births and what is best for the children and the children having the children become tinged with racism and stereotypes of the poor.

Let me be clear from the start. Teenage pregnancy, nonmarital births on the part of young girls, and abortion among youth are best avoided at all costs. They clearly are destructive of childhoods. That said, understanding the extent of the problem, interpreting its effects on children and youth, and doing something about it are indeed highly challenging tasks.

The dramatic rise in teen nonmarital births. What is the extent of the problem and how has it grown? Teen sexuality and pregnancy is clearly a global problem, but here we will restrict our discussion to industrialized countries, primarily the United States. In the United States measures of teen pregnancy over time are very unreliable because of difficulties in obtaining data on abortion, most especially before its legalization in 1973. However, by looking at birth rates and available data on abortion after 1973, it does appear that pregnancy rates among teenagers have not increased dramatically since the 1950s. From the turn of the century until the end of World War II, teen birth rates were stable at about 60 births per 1,000 women. In this period, teen birthrates were part of an overall baby boom and they nearly doubled to a peak of about 97 births per 1,000 in 1957. Teen births then began to decline and by 1975 were back down to a level of between 50 to 60 per 1,000 women, where they have remained until the present (Luker, 1991).

To accurately estimate teen pregnancy over time, however, we need to look not only at birth rates but also at abortion rates. As Kristin Luker points out, the abortion rate among teens rose from 27 to 42.9 abortions per 1,000 women between 1974 and 1980, but then remained steady until 1988. This pattern, argues Luker, "means that pregnancy rates, which rose modestly in the 1970s, have in recent years leveled off" (1991, p. 73).

What has been increasing dramatically in the United States is the percentage of *out-of-wedlock teen births*. The same pattern exists for teens as it does for all women fifteen to forty-four years of age: a steady increase from about 13 births per 1,000 women in 1950 to around 43 births per 1,000 women in 1990. However, underlying these overall rates are important racial and ethnic differences. The rate of out-of-wedlock births has been high for nonwhite teens for many years, rising from around 69 births to 88 births per 1,000 women between 1950 and 1990. The rate of nonmarital births to white teens is much lower than for nonwhite teens, but the rate has increased *at a much more dramatic rate,* rising from 5.1 births per thousand women in 1950 to nearly 31 births per thousand women in 1990 (Luker, 1991).

Before considering the possible factors underlying these changes and the consequences of teen births for both the young parents and their children, it is useful to consider comparative data from other industrialized countries. Here only limited data are available, but they indicate several clear patterns. First, the percentage of live births to unmarried women has increased in nearly all industrialized countries, but the rate of increase and the overall percentage varies dramatically across countries. In 1992 about 30 percent of babies born in the United States were born to unmarried women. In Sweden, nearly half of all births were attributed to unmarried women, while the share was 46 percent in Denmark, 33 percent in France, and 31 percent in the United Kingdom. In all these countries there have been dramatic increases in nonmarital births since 1960, when nonmarital births made up only about 10 percent of total births. On the other hand, several other industrialized countries also have seen increases, but the percentage of births to unmarried women remains low—around 10 percent in West Germany and less than 6 percent in Greece, Italy, and Japan (Russell, 1995; U.S. Department of Health and Human Services, 1990; Statistical Office of the European Communities, 1990).

Second, the United States has higher teen pregnancy, abortion, and birth rates than almost all other developed nations of the world (Jones et al., 1985; Westoff, Calot, & Foster, 1983). Available data comparing the United States with several West European countries are somewhat out of date (they were collected in 1980); still, they are informative. Exhibit 10.3 shows that the pregnancy rate for fifteen-to-nineteen-year-old girls in the United States was more than double that of four of the other nations studied (Canada, England/Wales, France, and Sweden) and more than six times that of the Netherlands. It is important to point out that these differences cannot be explained simply in terms of racial differences in teen pregnancy in the United States. In 1980 the pregnancy rate for white teens was 83 per 1,000 women, still much higher than the rate in the other countries (Jones et al., 1985, p. 55). Still, race and ethnicity are important factors, especially with the increasing percentage of Hispanics in the teenage population in the United States in recent years. In fact, while the overall pregnancy and birthrates of Hispanics are lower than those of blacks in the United States, Hispanics accounted for 84 percent of the increase in teen births between 1987 and 1992 in the United States (Russell, 1995). This fact suggests that the differences between the United States and the other countries for 1980 comparisons may be increasing.

Particularly striking in Exhibit 10.3 is the fact that the abortion rate alone in the United States was "about as high as, or higher than, the overall teenage pregnancy rate in any of the other countries" (Jones et al., 1985, p. 56). It should be noted, however, that the overall proportion of abortions to live

EXHIBIT 10.3

Pregnancy, Abortion, and Birth Rates for Women Ages 15 to 19 in Selected Countries (1980)

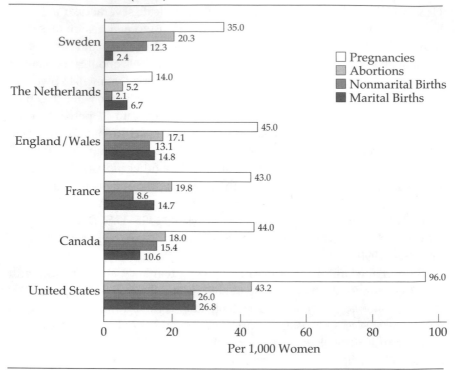

Source: Adapted from Jones et al., 1985.

births as an outcome of pregnancy does not vary a great deal across the five countries, with abortion being the most frequent outcome of pregnancy in every country except the Netherlands. We also know, as noted above, that the abortion rate has leveled off in the United States, but it is still much higher than in most other industrialized countries.

Finally, what is of most interest to us here is the rate of nonmarital births. We see that the pattern is similar to that for the overall pregnancy rate. The American rate of 26 nonmarital births per 1000 fifteen-to-nineteen-year-olds is about double the rate for Canada, England/Wales, and Sweden, triple the rate in France, and more than ten times the rate in the Netherlands! Another interesting factor to point out is that *although the percentage of nonmarital births is as high or higher for all women* in several of the countries compared to the United States, we see *big differences in the rate of nonmarital births for teens* between the United States and the other countries. This finding is in line with the fact that many unmarried mothers in Europe are older and are in stable, if not marital, relationships (Russell, 1995).

Possible cause of increases in teen nonmarital births. These comparative data put us in a better position for evaluating the many factors that most influence teen pregnancy, abortion, and nonmarital births in the United States. One of the reasons offered for increases in nonmarital birth rates among teens in all industrialized countries is that young women are delaying marriage but are becoming involved in sexual activity at younger ages than in the past. One important factor here is the declining age of puberty due to nutritional and other changes. At the turn of the century the average age at menarche for adolescent females was 14.8 years, while in 1988, the average age was 12.5 years. Some adolescents begin to menstruate as early as 10 years of age (Alan Guttmacher Institute, 1994).

The initiation of sexual activity among females is influenced by several factors. The onset of puberty strongly affects sexual initiation for males, but its effects are mediated by a host of factors for females. Puberty strongly influences whether black females will initiate sexual activity at an early age; however, for white females family structure and the sexual activity of their friends have more influence than the onset of puberty (Alan Guttmacher Institute, 1994; Udry & Billy, 1987). Despite these variations, it is still true that contemporary youth in industrialized society will live on average nearly a decade of their lives as sexually mature and single (Luker, 1991). Therefore, given that teens were more sexually active (with more sexual partners) in the 1980s than they were twenty years earlier, it is not surprising that we have seen some increase in nonmarital births. It is doubtful, however, that this increase in sexual activity over a longer period of time can in and of itself explain the dramatic rise in nonmarital births in the United States. Nor can it explain the differences we see in the nonmarital birth rate of the United States as compared to most West European countries, where teens also face a long period of sexual maturity prior to marriage and where they report similar levels of sexual activity (Jones et al., 1985).

A second factor to consider is teens' knowledge about reproductive processes and contraception, as well as their access to contraception and abortion services. Here, the United States seems far behind most West European countries, where extensive sex education programs in schools begin in the early grades and contraceptive devices and services are widely available in clinics and pharmacies. In general, there is more openness and tolerance of teenage sexual activity in the European countries than there is in most of the United States and in parts of Canada.

One reason for the more successful experience of the European countries may be that public attention is generally less focused on the *morality* of early sexual activity and more focused on the search for *ways to prevent* increased teenage pregnancy, abortions, and childbearing. In the United States contentious debates arise about whether sex education and the availability of contraceptives will increase sexual activity among teens and result in even higher rates of teen pregnancy and births. But surely the dramatic differences we see in pregnancy, abortion, and birthrates when we compare the United States to West European countries does not support such beliefs. Furthermore, American teenagers seem to have inherited the worst of all possible worlds regarding their exposure to messages about sex. Movies, music, radio, and TV tell them that sex is romantic, exciting, titillating; premarital sex and cohabitation are familiar ways of life among the adults around them; and their own parents or their parents' friends are often divorced or separated but involved in sexual relationships. In spite of this, adults continually send teens the message "Good girls should just say no" to the expected sexual advances of boys and young adult males. Almost nothing that they see or hear about sex informs them about contraception, the importance of avoiding pregnancy, and the responsibility of both females and males in sexual activity (Jones et al., 1985; Kisker, 1985).

Large numbers of American youth do manage to navigate successfully through what Luker refers to "as the reproductive minefield of extended adolescence" without experiencing (or causing) pregnancy, making decisions about abortion, or bearing children in or out of wedlock (1991, p. 79). How do these teens differ from those who are not successful? Although many who move through the period unscathed are less sexually active and in some cases even abstinent, many others are sexually active but take care to avoid pregnancy or, if they become pregnant, rely on abortion.

Let's return now to the issue of poverty, which is so often the central factor for the social problems of children. In the United States teen birthrates are highest for those who have the greatest economic disadvantage. Interestingly, in the current debate about teenage pregnancy this general finding is often interpreted to mean that teenage childbearing *causes* poverty, rather than the other way around. As we saw in the last chapter, the next step in this way of thinking is that many welfare programs that provide assistance for unmarried mothers create a financial incentive for young poor women to bear children outside of marriage. Thus, welfare policies themselves cause poverty (Murray, 1984).

Let's begin with the second part of the argument—that welfare policies contribute to high rates of teen pregnancy and births. First, such an argument clearly is not supported by the comparative data we discussed above. Let's return to Exhibit 10.3. All of the other countries provide more extensive benefits to poor mothers (including child care, medical care, food supplements, housing and family allowances) than those provided in the United States

(Jones et al., 1985). Yet these countries all have substantially lower teen pregnancy, abortion, and marital and nonmarital birth rates.

Many conservatives eschew such comparative data, arguing that what might work in the more collectivist welfare states of Western Europe will not work in the United States. On the surface, such an argument may seem to have merit. For example, from 1976 to 1992, about 42 percent of all single women receiving Aid for Families with Dependent Children (AFDC) in the United States were, or had been, teenage mothers (American Psychological Association, 1995; GAO Report, 1994, p. 8). But is there evidence that specific United States welfare policies play a significant role in adolescents' fertility-related behavior? While researchers on this question are not in complete agreement, recent reviews of the welfare incentive literature concluded that welfare benefits do not serve as a reasonable explanation for variations in pregnancy and childbearing rates among unmarried adolescents (American Psychological Association, 1995). What the research did find is that poverty, race and ethnicity, and education—not specific welfare policies—have the most significant effects on teenage childbearing. Luker nicely summarizes the general findings of this research.

> First, since poor and minority youth tend to become sexually active at an earlier age than more advantaged youngsters, they are 'at risk' for a longer period of time, including years when they are less cognitively mature. Young teens are also less likely to use contraceptives than older teenagers. Second, the use of contraception is more common among teens who are white, come from more affluent homes, have higher educational aspirations, and who are doing well in school. And, finally, among youngsters who become pregnant, abortions are more common if they are affluent, white, urban, of higher socio-economic status, get good grades, come from two-parent families, and aspire to higher education. Thus more advantaged youth get filtered out of the pool of young women at risk of teen parenthood. (1991, p. 76)

"But wait a minute!" say conservatives and also many Americans who view problems like teenage pregnancy individualistically rather than structurally. Why can't these disadvantaged teens act more responsibly and sensibly, more like their advantaged counterparts? In this view, notes Luker, the teenage pregnancy problem is cast as a universal: Everyone is a teenager once and teenagers must control their impulses and be responsible about their futures (Luker, 1991, p. 81). But here's the rub. Teenagers are not all the same. Many are not well prepared for the challenges of puberty, do not have support from caring adults when they make difficult decisions, and do not have parents who can or will bail them out when they make mistakes. In fact, as we discussed in Chapter 9, many economically disadvantaged girls not only lack supportive caring adults in their lives, *they also must often fight off adult sexual abuse and coercion.* Finally, and perhaps most important, many poor youth are different from middle-class and wealthy teens in that they see little hope that their lives will improve—there are no bright horizons in their futures. As a result, they often drift into pregnancy and then into parenthood (Furstenberg, Brooks-Gunn, & Lansdale, 1989).

Consequences for teen parents and their children. Given the relationship between poverty and teen pregnancy, it should not be surprising that many researchers have found it difficult to "sort out the effects of early childbearing from the selective factors that lead some youth to become teen parents" (Furstenberg, Brooks-Gunn, & Chase-Lansdale, 1989, p. 315). For most teen mothers early childbearing immediately worsens their quality of life and often leads to a number of negative consequences as far as their educational, economic and marital futures are concerned. Short-term studies have found that teen mothers are more likely to drop out of school, fail to find stable and remunerative employment, and enter into stable marriages than are women who begin childbearing in later life (Furstenberg, Brooks-Gunn, & Chase-Lansdale, 1989; Hofferth & Hayes, 1987). In a rare long-term study, however, Furstenberg and his colleagues found that although teen mothers did not do as well as later childbearers, most teen mothers managed to stage a recovery in later life (Furstenberg, Brooks-Gunn, & Chase-Lansdale, 1989). The key to such recoveries was the women's successes in educational achievement, fertility control, and stable marriages.

What do we know about the lives of children of teen mothers? We have frequently discovered in our exploration of childhood in this book that many things are assumed about children's lives even though the detailed study and research required to really understand them or to do something about them is lacking. We see this pattern again when it comes to teenage pregnancy. As Furstenberg, Brooks-Gunn, and Chase-Lansdale note, "it is commonly presumed that early childbearing adversely affects children, although only a limited amount of evidence has been marshaled to demonstrate this seemingly obvious proposition" (1989, p. 316). One wonders how much more we might know about the everyday lives of teen mothers and their offspring if we had invested as much research funding and time in direct studies of them as we have in trying to find a relationship between welfare spending and teenage pregnancy.

In any case, we do know some things. Generally, children born to teenage mothers are at a developmental disadvantage compared with children born to older mothers. For younger children, these differences are much more likely to be observed in sons than in daughters, with sons of teenage mothers being more aggressive and lacking self-control compared to sons of older mothers. In adolescence, school achievement is markedly lower among offspring of teenage mothers, and these youth display behavioral problems and a lack of interest in learning compared to that displayed by children of older mothers (Furstenberg, Brooks-Gunn, & Chase-Lansdale, 1989). However, a wide range of factors are associated with having a teenage mother (for example, disadvantaged neighborhoods, low-quality schools, lower education of mother, emotional problems of the mother, and so on), and it is not clear which of these factors may account for these differences.

Overall, the findings suggest that a number of preventive programs, including those that provide sex education, promote abstinence or the delay of sexual activity, and provide contraceptive and family planning services are needed to combat teen pregnancy and offset its consequences. These programs should be aimed at various age groups and should provide supportive or ameliorative services as well (prenatal care, parenting classes and child care). As we will discuss in Chapter 11, such programs hold much more hope for success than do recent welfare reform proposals, which seem to be aimed at shaming and punishing teenage girls.

Violence, Victimization, and the Loss of Childhood

In Chapter 9 we discussed the bogeyman syndrome or the general fear of the victimization of children in contemporary industrialized societies. These heightened fears about children's safety are, to a large degree, a reflection of our own adult anxieties about our lack of control in a rapidly changing world. Yet even if the world is a place no more dangerous (and perhaps even less dangerous) than it was in the past, violence and inhumanity do exist. Children, more than any other group, are the main victims of such evils—victims of anger, violence, and neglect in their societies, communities, and families. Children are at a high risk of victimization for several reasons, including (1) their dependency on adults, (2) their relatively small physical stature, and (3) the legal toleration of victimization (Finkelhor & Dziuba-Leatherman, 1994). Further, given their dependency on adults, children often have little choice regarding whom they associate with and where they live. These limited options are especially unfortunate for economically disadvantaged children who live in dangerous neighborhoods, because they increase their "vulnerability to both intimate victimization and street crime" (Finkelhor & Dziuba-Leatherman, 1994, p. 177). In our review we will concentrate primarily on child victimization in and outside the family in American society, with some comparison to other industrialized societies. We will not be able to address important recent work on children victimized by war and political violence (but see Dodge & Raundalen, 1991; Garbarino, Kostelny, & Dubrow, 1991 for recent discussions of this issue).

Child Abuse in the Family

There is only one thing worse than losing a child to tragic and unforeseen circumstances such as war, disease, or disaster. That is to lose a child through willful, intentional, and preventable acts of abuse. All too often, such acts occur right in the sanctity of the child's home—the place where he or she ought to feel safe and protected from harm.

When children are abused by caretakers, they are not only physically and emotionally harmed, they often blame themselves for the failings of those they trust and love. The consequences of abuse are thus doubly tragic and often long lasting. In some cases they even perpetuate more abuse; the abused child herself also becomes a child abuser.

Of course, no family is perfect. All families have their ups and downs. Most parents, excluding perhaps TV parents like Ward and June Cleaver, lose patience with their children and yell at them now and then. At times, regrettably, most parents give their preschooler, preadolescent, or adolescent a shake or slap on the bottom or face. Does this constitute child abuse? I do not think parents losing their patience once in a while is the same as child abuse, but I do think persistent striking, yelling, or belittling children is. Some parents may not think so. In fact, some may think any form of physical punishment is permissible if it is administered by a parent. I can understand this view of discipline since I got a few spankings in my time and probably deserved them. Yet to me it is a form of abuse. In our society we do not allow corporal punishment of adults; why should we allow it of children? A number of Scandinavian countries have passed laws against physical punishment in the home, and most countries in the industrialized world (except for Australia, Canada, and the United States) now forbid it in schools. To me, this is a step in the right direction.

It is clear that child abuse is not easily defined, nor is its prevalence easily estimated. This fact is due to the generally held value in most societies that children belong to their parents. As a result, any society's attempt to define and control child abuse immediately runs up against issues of family privacy, and the belief that people have the right to bring up their own children without government interference or regulation. Most agree, however, that there are limits to parental authority, and most **child abuse laws** and regulations revolve around the determination of *misuse of parental authority*. Most laws are generally in line with a definition offered by Landau: "Parental authority and power are misused when they are employed to damage the child either physically or emotionally or administered in any manner that reduces or limits the child's opportunity for normal growth and development" (1994, p. 116). However, a big problem in dealing with child abuse is in determining such misuses of power. **Child neglect**, the most common form of child abuse, is best defined as an omission or failure of parental responsibility to meet their children's needs in regard to health, development, and physical safety.

What is the extent of child abuse? Is it increasing? Does it vary across societies and across social classes and cultural groups within societies? Such questions cannot be readily addressed because of the difficulty in defining and measuring abuse. Also, until recently most countries did not even keep accurate records on child abuse. Things are changing mainly because of the work of child health advocacy groups. One of the few comparative studies of child abuse relied on a measure developed by the World Health Organization (WHO). This measure focused on child abuse that resulted in deaths in infancy. Clearly the measure underestimates abuse, but we can at least be somewhat confident of its accuracy since statistics on death are normally carefully collected and reported in industrialized countries. The WHO measure combined infant homicides with infant deaths from undetermined external causes. This measure was recently used to rank 23 countries in terms of the number of deaths per 100,000 live births between 1985 and 1990. Four countries (Denmark, the former Czechoslovakia, the United States, and the former Soviet Union) had rates between 8.1 and 10.1, with the United States rate estimated at 9.8 per 100,000 births. Nine other European countries, along with Australia, New Zealand, and Japan, had rates between 3.1 and 7.4, while seven countries (Canada, Poland, the Netherlands, Norway, Sweden, Italy, and Spain) had rates below 3.0 (Belsey, 1993).

In the United States there is a great deal of debate about the accuracy of reports of child abuse and whether or not the incidence of abuse is increasing. Most of the debate centers around statistics collected on child abuse since 1976. We can see in Exhibit 10.4 that there has been a dramatic increase in the number of reported cases of child abuse between the time that statistics were first kept in 1976, when 669,000 reports were made, up to 1995, when there were over 3 million reports. This rise does not mean, however, that there has been an increase in child abuse. There is no way of knowing the number of cases of abuse that occurred before 1976, and surely some of the increase in reports is due to greater public awareness of the problem. Furthermore, some have argued that many reports of abuse are "unfounded" and that exaggerated reports hamper child protective agencies and are an invasion of family privacy (Besharov, 1994; Family Research Council, 1994). Others have responded to these criticisms by characterizing them as attempts by conservatives to limit government intervention at all costs. These persons are adamant in their preference of family rights over children's rights (Finkelhor, 1994). In any case, such debates politicize the issue and in

EXHIBIT 10.4

Child Abuse and Neglect Reporting

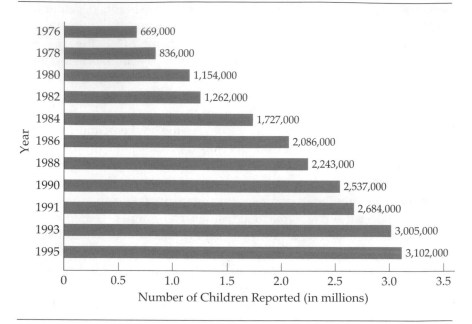

Source: American Humane Association; National Committee for the Prevention of Child Abuse.

many ways draw attention away from the serious efforts to do something about it.

Let's take the issue of what one side in the debate calls "unfounded" and the other "unsubstantiated" reports. These are reported cases of abuse that cannot be substantiated after investigation by child protective services. One side estimates that such cases make up as much as 65 percent of all reports, while the other side estimates that they make up about 47 percent. Let's take the conservative estimate and return to Exhibit 10.4. If we use this estimate of 65 percent of the cases being unsubstantiated, that still leaves *over a million cases of child abuse in 1995.* Now let's continue with this conservative approach and assume that *all* the cases in 1976 were substantiated (a very unlikely assumption). Using this very conservative method of estimation there is still a 62 percent increase in the number of cases of child abuse from 1976 (669,000) to 1995 (1,085,700). Surely, there is a major problem of child abuse in our country, and surely it has been increasing since the mid-1970s. In fact, a recent Gallup poll of American parents found that more than three million children are physically abused each year in the name of discipline (Lewin, 1995a).

As shocking as these statistics are, we still need to be careful about how we interpret the problem and decide on ways to prevent it. First, it is important to keep in mind that there are various types of child abuse. Of the substantiated cases of abuse in 1995, 54 percent were cases of child neglect; 25 percent physical abuse; 11 percent sexual abuse; 3 percent emotional abuse, and the remaining 6 percent "other" or "undefined." This distribution has remained fairly steady since 1976, with a slight recent drop in the number of cases of sexual abuse. The fact that the majority of cases are cases of neglect is somewhat heartening, because this problem is more easily attacked by preventive programs such as family education, child safety laws, and so on. Still the fact that child abuse continues to grow is a reflection of how deeply rooted it has become in our society.

Numerous and interrelated factors contribute to child abuse and neglect, including poverty, parental substance abuse, social isolation, and a lack of experience in caring for young children. Although abuse occurs in families from all social class groups, it occurs in a larger proportion of poor families where parents face a multitude of challenges and many have drug and other substance abuse problems. In February, 1994, Chicago police who were conducting a drug raid entered an apartment in the inner city only to find two toddlers sharing a bone with a dog. As police moved through the filthy, two-room apartment they found "buried beneath blankets and dirty clothes on the floor or crammed on top of two soiled mattresses" seventeen other children, ranging in age from one to fourteen (Terry, 1994, p. 1). The nineteen children were the offspring of at least four sisters, all in their twenties, who lived in the apartment with the children. Three of the mothers had been investigated in the past when one of the children had been born with drugs in his system. They also were investigated because of inadequate supervision of several of the children. On this day, as the children were being carried away through the cold toward a fleet of police cars, several asked for food, and one child pleaded with Officer Patricia Warner, "Would you be my mommy? Would you take me home" (Terry, 1994, p. 11).

City and state agencies that are supposed to care for and protect abused and neglected children are often overwhelmed by caseloads and lack of money. A recent survey of state welfare officials found that 70 percent of the respondents were seriously concerned about plans in Congress to provide states support for child welfare and related services through blockgrants that give the states near total responsibility for administration of the programs. These concerns were related not only to potential loss of funds, but also to what child welfare workers saw as a growing lack of federal leadership on this important issue (National Committee to Prevent Child Abuse, 1996).

Some of the effects of child abuse and child neglect are fatal, some leave physical injuries that may take years to recover from, and others leave permanent emotional scars that lead victims eventually to abuse their own children. Many such injuries may also have important developmental consequences that have not been investigated (Finkelhor & Dziuba-Leatherman, 1994). In 1995 an estimated 1,215 children died as a result of abuse or neglect. Eighty-five percent of the victims were younger than five years old; 45 percent were less than one year of age. About 46 percent of the perpetrators had current or prior contacts with local child protective services. The number of deaths in 1995 represents a slight drop from the year before. Even with increased attention to the problem of child abuse, however, the incidence of fatalities has changed little over the last ten years (National Committee to Prevent Child Abuse, 1996). The National Center on Child Abuse and Neglect estimated that nearly 318,000 children suffered serious or moderate physical injuries from child abuse and neglect in 1988.

There is some research on the short- and long-term effects of sexual abuse on children's mental health. It has been found that children who have been sexually victimized "appear to be at a nearly fourfold increased lifetime risk for any psychiatric disorder and at a threefold risk for substance abuse" (Finkelhor & Dziuba-Leatherman, 1994, p. 181). Finally, there is a great deal of evidence to support the contention that a history of victimization increases the chances that one will become a perpetrator of violence, abuse, or crime. As Finkelhor and Dziuba-Leatherman note, an important qualification in this regard "is that victims are not necessarily prone to repeat their own form of victimization" (1994, p. 181).

Education, prevention programs, and harsher penalties for repeated offenders are the best methods for dealing with this problem. A great deal of headway has been made in education with help from private child advocacy organizations and individual volunteers. Needed comprehensive prevention programs are being implemented slowly, however, because of their expense at a time when government budget constraints are severe. We will return in Chapter 11 to argue that a rethinking of priorities that balances short-term costs with long-term benefits is needed in dealing with this issue.

Child Victimization Outside the Family

As we saw in the preceding section the potential of victimization of young children is highest in the home and family. Yet, as children grow older and spend more time outside the home they encounter a whole new set of dangers. Loving and responsible parents often find they have less control over their children's security, while the dangers for children who grow up in unstable and threatening families increase dramatically. Children from all social class groups are bombarded with violent and sexual images from the media. Given advanced technology these images from television and movies reach children in all parts of the world. For middle-class parents in industrialized societies a new concern is computer technology and children's access to sexual images and even sexual predators over the Internet (*Newsweek*, 1995; *Time*, 1995). Such concerns are heightened because in many middle-class families children are more computer literate than their parents. Although there is much debate about the negative effects of the media on children versus the right of free speech, the media clearly has not developed its potential to support, challenge, and educate children and youth in positive ways. Does the media promote the violence and dangers of society, or merely reflect them? The answer is, probably both. We will return to discuss the role and potential of the media in children's lives in Chapter 11, but now let's turn to a consideration of the very real dangers children encounter in their everyday lives outside the family.

A much underestimated and understudied social problem for children is peer abuse. The topic of peer abuse usually calls to mind bullying and the general value in many societies that boys need to learn to stand up for themselves. One thinks of the memorable episode from the old *Andy Griffith Show*, in which Opie is tormented by a bully who keeps taking his lunch money. Barney wants to intervene, but Andy indirectly pushes his son to stand his ground by telling him a story of how a bully had once tried to steal his favorite fishing hole. In the end Opie takes on the bully and gets a black eye for his efforts. The bully, however, backs off and Opie keeps his lunch money.

The elements and message of this story are generally in line with what we know about the interpersonal nature of bullying and the individual characteristics of bullies and their victims from research done by clinical psychologists. (We considered this and other research on peer rejection earlier in the chapters on peer culture.) Surely, such individual-level research is useful, but it tells us very little about the sociocultural dimensions of peer abuse. Peer abuse, like peer interaction more generally, is socioculturally situated in children's lives. Peer abuse varies over time and place and is produced and resisted in various ways across cultural, social class, age, gender, racial, and ethnic groups (Ambert, 1995).

Let's consider three ways that a sociocultural approach captures the complexity of peer abuse in children's lives. First, recent research reveals that girls are the victims of peer abuse as frequently (or perhaps even more frequently) than boys. The most frequent type of peer abuse is verbal harassment, but girls are often victims of physical and sexual assault by peers. Their tormentors are often boys. Some are classmates they do not even like and try to avoid, while others are their boyfriends with whom they are intimately involved (Ambert, 1995; Eder, 1995; Stein, 1993). A recent telephone interview study of eleven-to-seventeen-year-old children by the child advocacy group *Children Now* found that 40 percent of girls ages fourteen to seventeen said they had a friend in their age group who had been hit or beaten by a boyfriend (Lewin, 1995a). These findings are generally in line with earlier research on the issue and demonstrate its seriousness (Ambert, 1995; Henton & Cate, 1983).

Second, a sociocultural approach to peer abuse would take sexual orientation into account. Thorne points out that lesbian and gay adolescents, unlike heterosexual youth, have no public rituals to validate their desires: "There are no affirming markers about what they are feeling and thinking" (Gagon, 1972, p. 238 as quoted in Thorne, 1993, p. 154). In fact, lesbian and gay youth witness markers to sexual orientation used in highly negative ways; terms like *fag* and *queer* are highly insulting in the peer cultures of preadolescents and adolescents. Further, in her study of peer interaction in middle schools, Eder found that social isolates were often labeled as "queer" and "fag" because "they were perceived to lack the very social characteristics that represented the rigid gender and sexual roles" in the peer culture (1995, p. 155). These findings capture the challenging circumstances lesbian and gay youth face in adolescent peer cultures. Such features of adolescent culture contribute to problems of low self-esteem among lesbian and gay youth, which in turn may be related to high rates of suicide among these youth. Much more research is needed in this area. However, there is more public recognition of the problem as evidenced in Massachusetts, for example, where Governor Weld has formed the Commission of Gay and Lesbian Youth to develop strategies to combat gay teen suicide.

Finally, a sociocultural approach to peer abuse also draws our attention to the importance of social class and minority status. The *Children Now* study found that "minority children face a rougher world than white children do, reporting greater exposure to gangs and drugs and more fear of violence and crime" (Lewin, 1995a, p. 17). Other research and recent statistics on the tremendous rise of violent crime in poor neighborhoods and schools in the inner city and even small towns are in line with this finding (Garofalo, Siegal, & Laub, 1987; Hagan, 1994; Morgan & Zedner, 1992). Much of this violence is related to crime and gang activity. The majority of children who live in impoverished environments do not engage in illegal activities. They do, however, despite their own best efforts and those of their parents, often find themselves caught up in violence perpetrated by other children.

Another recent story from Chicago captures the tragic nature of violence and poverty for children. On a night in late August 1994, a member of a street gang stepped out of the shadows between two storefront churches on Chicago's far south side and started shooting wildly at a group of teenagers playing football. When the gunfire stopped, a fourteen-year-old girl lay dead, killed by a bullet apparently meant for someone else. At first, the shooting appeared to be another senseless, though increasingly common, story of innocents slaughtered in the streets (*New York Times*, 1994, p. 1). What sets this incident apart from other such shootings, though, is the neighborhood in which the shooting occurred and the age of the suspected assailant.

The neighborhood in which the shooting occurred is in a working-class area of single-story homes with well-kept yards. There had been so much gang trouble in the neighborhood before the shooting that parents kept their children near their homes. A makeshift basketball backboard and hoop was erected on a curbside by parents to dissuade their children from playing at the local school, which they felt was too dangerous. In spite of these precautions, Shavon Dean was shot and killed and another boy was seriously wounded. The police's prime suspect was an eleven-year-old boy. The boy had many prior serious scrapes with the law (including arson, auto theft, and armed robbery), and police suspected he had been recruited by older gang members to carry out the shooting. He was living with his grandmother after having been taken away from his mother at age three, when social workers discovered cigarette burns on his body and other signs of physical abuse. The Chicago Police Superintendent described the boy as dangerous but "still an eleven-year-old" who fell through the cracks of the city's social services.

How did this tragic story end? The eleven-year-old boy was never apprehended by police. He never had his day in juvenile court. He did not end up in prison. Five days after the shooting, on Friday, September 2, 1994, the headline in the *Chicago Tribune* read: ROBERT: EXECUTED AT 11. Although Robert's last name and that of his mother and grandmother made all the national papers and television news programs on that day, we'll use only his first name. Robert was found dead in a tunnel under the tracks of the South Shore Railroad with two bullets in the back of his head. He had been killed execution style. Two other gang members, a fourteen-year-old and a sixteen-year-old, were arrested for Robert's murder. Police believe their motive was to keep Robert from talking. At the news of her grandson's death, Robert's grandmother sobbed, "He's a baby. He's just a baby." Exactly the same words were uttered by the grief-stricken aunt of Shavon Dean upon hearing the news about Robert. When Robert was found dead, he was wearing a T-shirt with the image of a cartoon character, the Tasmanian Devil, printed on it.

As sad as this story is, it is even more tragic when one realizes that more and more children are, like Shavon Dean, being caught up in the crossfire of violence in the United States. Some but certainly not all of this violence and crime is gang-related; much of it is perpetrated on children by adults. Earlier we noted the high homicide rates in the United States for black preadolescents and adolescents. While poor and minority youth are much more likely to experience violence in their lives than white, middle- and upper-class children, the overall homicide rates for children are much higher than any industrialized country. In 1990 more than 3,000 fifteen-to-nineteen-year-olds were murdered in the United States, a rate of nearly 17 per 100,000 children. This rate is much higher than that for our nearest competitor among industrialized nations, Canada, where the rate was 2.3 per 100,000. In Italy, the land of the Mafia, 109 teenagers were murdered in 1990, a rate of 2.1 per 100,000. Japan and Norway had the lowest rates in the industrial world— 0.3 per 100,000. In Norway only one fifteen-to-nineteen-year-old was murdered in 1990 (UNICEF, 1995a).

These differences are, of course, at least somewhat due to the wide availability of guns in the United States as compared to other countries. Yet the differences go well beyond differences in gun laws. The United States is a highly violent society. This violence touches twelve- to nineteen-year-old children as much or more than any other age group. The data in Exhibit 10.5 are perhaps the most striking of any I have presented in this chapter. They show the number of victims of violent crimes other than murder by age group in the United States in 1992. It is immediately clear that the odds of victimization are much higher in the lower age groups. Although the rates in the youngest of the three age groups do not vary substantially, it is amazing that the rates for twelve-to-fifteen-year-olds and sixteen-to-nineteen-year-olds are actually higher than the rate for twenty-to-twenty-four-year-olds, who are normally thought of as most vulnerable to violence because of their high activity levels and risk-taking. Finally, it is surprising how much higher the rates are for the youngest age group of twelve-to-fifteen-year-olds, compared to young and middle-aged adults. The rate for twelve-to-fifteen-year-olds is double that for twenty-five-to-thirty-four-year-olds, more than

EXHIBIT 10.5

Victims of Violent Crime Other than Murder in 1992 (by Age Group)

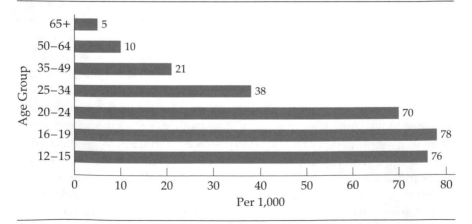

Source: Federal Bureau of Investigation; American Bar Association.

three times that of thirty-five-to-forty-nine-year-olds, and more than seven times that of fifty-to-sixty-four-year-olds.

These statistics again reinforce the extreme vulnerability and mistreatment of a significant proportion of children in our society. We can begin to understand why Nicholas's mother Angela sprays her children each morning with a religious oil and why Nicholas's younger brother, Willie, prefers the playground at McDonald's. "'There's a giant hamburger and you can go inside of it,' Willie said. 'And it's made out of steel, so no bullets can get through.'" (Wilkerson, 1993, p. 16).

Summary

In this chapter we reviewed a wide range of social problems that affect children's lives. We examined trends in child poverty and looked at its effects from a global perspective. Although there has been some progress in reducing malnutrition, improving health care, and expanding educational opportunities of children in many countries in the developing world, there have also been setbacks due to uneven economic development and the resulting austerity programs, which were instituted to address the debt crisis. We looked at how these economic trends have resulted in violence against street children in Brazil, the exploitation of urban child workers in Kenya, and the kidnapping or sale of children to work on farms and in sweatshops in India and Pakistan. One encouraging factor we saw in all these case studies was the emergence of nongovernmental organizations. These organizations, which are directed by caring adults and children with no government affiliation, promote change and address problems of child poverty and exploitation at the grass-roots level.

Although the majority of children in the Western industrialized countries live in secure economic circumstances and have bright futures, there has been a clear increase in the proportion of children living in poverty in the United States and several other industrialized countries. In contrast, most of the other countries in the industrialized world have much lower rates of child poverty and have had reductions or very modest increases in child poverty in recent years. Of central importance to this increase in child poverty in the United States are the dramatic structural changes in families since the 1950s. A major increase in the divorce rate and in the number of nonmarital births (especially to poor teenage girls and young women) has moved many women and children into poverty. The problem is worsened by the fact that the fathers of many of these children do not provide support to their offspring, nor have state or federal governments, until recently, passed stringent child support laws. Many other industrialized countries have not experienced family instability to the same degree as the United States. Additionally, most of these countries provide services for families including subsidized medical care, family leave, child care and early education that are vital to poor and working class families. As we saw in our review, the United States provides more extensive social welfare programs of this type for the elderly than for children. The end result has been a general trend in which the quality of lives of the elderly and children have moved in different directions—up for the elderly and down for children.

We also considered how changes in family structures affected children's lives in Western societies. In this review we focused on three important changes: the dramatic increase in the number of mothers of young children entering the work force, the major rise in the divorce rate, and the increasing number of nonmarital births among teenage girls. As an increasing number of mothers with young children entered the work force in the United States, some researchers questioned how the increasing need for child care affected the security of children's attachment to their mothers. One positive result of the debate over attachment has been an evaluation of the quality of affordable daycare and an examination of governmental policy regarding maternity and family leave, day care, and early education in the United States. The United States lags far behind almost all other industrialized countries regarding these issues. Many other countries have extensive programs of maternity and family leave as well as subsidized high quality early education programs.

The divorce rate has increased in all industrialized countries over the last thirty years, but the divorce rate and the number of children affected by divorce is much higher in some countries than in others, with the United States having the highest rates. Most of the best research on the effects of divorce on children has documented the negative economic consequences of divorce for women and children. Here again the United States does poorly when compared to other industrialized countries, primarily because the present system of child support in the United States puts an enormous economic burden on women in the periods of separation and following divorce. Social and psychological effects of divorce on children are much harder to measure, interpret, and understand than economic consequences, but there are important patterns in findings from the recent research. First, the studies show that in divorced families where there has been a great deal of conflict boys are more likely to display externalizing disorders (acting out behaviors like aggression, disobedience, and lying), while girls are more apt to display internalizing disorders (depression, anxiety, or withdrawal). Second, studies using matched samples of children from intact families have found that while children from disrupted families were more likely to show long-term effects (like problems in school), the majority of children from divorced families did not have such problems. Other studies have identified two key ways of minimizing the negative effects of divorce: (1) the custodial parent should keep the family functioning in line with established and predictable routines as much as possible; and (2) parents should maintain low levels of conflict in their dealings with each other in the presence of their children.

There has been a dramatic increase in teenage nonmarital births in the United States. For most teen mothers, childbearing, most especially in the early teen years and among girls from economically disadvantaged families, almost always worsens their quality of life and limits their futures and those of their children. More research is needed on the effects of teenage childbearing on teen mothers and their children. We do know, however, that many teen mothers and their children who are adversely affected by the early childbearing, overcome their problems later in life. Overall, these findings suggest a number of programs for combating the problem that are best aimed at specific age groups. The programs should be both preventive (providing sex education, promoting abstinence, making youth aware of family planning services) and, in cases where childbearing has occurred, supportive or ameliorative (providing prenatal care, parenting classes, and child care).

In the final section of this chapter we looked at violence and the victimization of children both in and outside the family. We considered what constitutes child abuse, the various types of child abuse, and trends in the incidence of abuse. Many abuse cases involve neglect, a problem that is more easily attacked through preventive programs like family education and child safety laws than are other types of abuse. However, there is a great need for more extensive programs and a greater awareness of the extent of the problem. The growing body of evidence indicates that a history of abuse increases the chances that a child will become a perpetrator of violence, abuse, or crime.

The extent of violence against children outside the family in the United States is a national tragedy. Children are often caught up in violence in their schools, neighborhoods, and wider communities. Much of this violence is at the hands of other children, and in recent years it has become much more lethal given the wide availability of handguns. While poor and minority children and youth are much more likely to experience violence in their lives than are white, middle- and upper-class children, the overall child homicide and violent crime rates are much higher in the United States than any other industrialized country.

The range and severity of problems young children face are very depressing. Yet, in this chapter we covered only some of the more serious challenges children face and we restricted our discussion primarily to the United States. There are times when those of us who study, work with, or act as advocates for children feel overwhelmed and pessimistic about the future of children and childhood. Problems related to child care and early education, teen pregnancy, child abuse, and violence in children's lives seem to grow as political rhetoric in support of "our children" seems to dwarf any real political action. Yet, there are reasons to be optimistic about childhood and its future. Change may be slow, but more individuals and groups are joining the debate, making financial contributions, and volunteering their time and energy to causes that help children. In the last chapter we will consider the future of childhood and discuss some major and many more modest proposals to improve children's lives.

11

The Future of Childhood

I began this book by recounting an everyday event in the life of some Italian preschool children involving their wonderful creation of a traveling bank. My point was to highlight the active participation of children in society and their creation of their own unique peer cultures. I followed this depiction with a brief summary of the bombing of the Alfred P. Murrah Federal Building in Oklahoma City, which killed 168 persons, 19 of them children who were attending a preschool in the building. The Oklahoma City bombing was a grim reminder that children are very much part of and affected by the adult world.

As I write the conclusion to this book it has been more than a year since the bombing in Oklahoma City. After several years away from the field, I am back again with children in an Italian preschool. This time I am in the city of Modena in the province of Emilia-Romagna—arguably the best place in all the world to be a preschool child. I am working in a *scuola materna* with a group of five-to-six-year-olds and their teachers, who have been together for three years. The children and teachers are all so comfortable with each other, so confident of their place in the interrelated peer and school local cultures.

Over the last five months the children have drawn me into the wonderful security of their world. Now it's mid-June and their time together is coming to an end in about a week. It's a time of anticipation. We have made two visits to the elementary school that most of the children will attend in the fall. I will be starting first grade with these kids, as I am studying this transition process. We met our prospective new teachers and their students. The teachers are now teaching fifth grade, but will move back to first grade in the fall. The big fifth graders took us under their wings, gave us a glimpse of their everyday lives in the school, served us a great snack, and sang songs with us. It's all very exciting!

It is also a time for reflection. The children will be leaving their preschool teachers and some of their classmates. This realization is coming gradually to the children, because for six-year-olds, the present—the here and now—seizes most of their attention. Just last week there was a *"festa di nonni"* ("party for grandparents") at the preschool. Many grandparents who live in the city attended. Some grandmothers worked with the boys and girls, making clothes for Barbie and other dolls, while other of the *nonne* went up to the kitchen with a group of kids to make dessert. Some grandfathers worked outside in the garden with one group, and one grandfather made kites. We later took these kites out into the yard, and the kids took turns flying them around. My job was fetching the wayward kites out of the trees without damaging them.

What I remember most, however, happened right before lunch. The kids sang several songs for their grandparents. They had been practicing and singing these songs all year; in fact, the previous month they had sung them at a festival in the center of the city, with other children from preschools all across town. I have heard these songs again and again. I know them by heart. As the children sang the first two songs, I sang along with them, softly mouthing the words. In the middle of the third song, the children, who were sitting in small chairs, lay their arms over each others' shoulders and began to sway with the music. Their faces were beaming. I looked at the grandparents. They were misty-eyed. So was I.

This story illustrates how the interweaving of the local cultures of the children's and adults' world clearly enriches the children's lives as well as the lives of the adults. I remember other events from children's lives that I have been fortunate enough to share over the last twenty years. I think about some upper-middle-class American kids who created a play scenario around a sandbox. In it they were the owners of an ice cream store, and they decided to donate some of their profits to "sick kids" in the hospital. I remember some Head Start boys who transformed the family play area into a barber shop, pretended to trim my hair and beard, held up two mirrors so I could inspect my haircut, front and back, and then carefully brushed me off with a whisk broom. I also recall a pretend phone conversation between two Head Start girls. The girls were pretending to be their mothers and were having a conversation about the demands of parenting in poverty. They talked about the difficulties of shopping and responding to their children's demands to be taken to the park when they did not have a car and the public transportation system was expensive and inadequate. They also talked sadly of their domestic lives, with one pretend mother saying, "My man's been hitting on me!" The other little girl's response broke my heart. "You got one and I don't have one," she said. "My kids been askin' for 'my Daddy.' They say, 'I want my Daddy, I want my Daddy,' all day." (See Corsaro, 1993; Rosier & Corsaro, 1993; Rosier, 1996).

Finally, I think of the children of Oklahoma City again and the kindergartners of Dunblane, Scotland. I am sad, but also surprisingly buoyed by this jumble of thoughts and emotions. The actions of confused, misguided, and cowardly adults took away the lives of those young children. However, although those children are no longer with us, the spirit of their lives in their families, their schools, and their communities is not diminished.

Shortly after the Oklahoma City tragedy, columnist Bob Herbert recounted a television interview of a firefighter and police office who tried to rescue one-year-old Baylee Almon. Baylee died, but, as Herbert notes, the effort to save her was typical of the response to the tragedy. In a television interview, the police officer who found her, Sergeant John Avera, said, "'I heard a baby crying and we started moving bricks and rocks . . . and we found two babies. The officer I was with took one down one hallway and I took my baby out the other way.'" *My baby*, stresses Herbert. The thought leads him to quote Plutarch: "Good fortunes will elevate even petty minds, and give them the appearance of a certain greatness and stateliness, as from their high place they look down upon the world; but the truly noble and resolved spirit raises itself; and becomes more conspicuous in times of disaster and ill fortune" (Herbert, 1995b).

The nature of the adult world has profound effects on childhood. Even in the most impoverished and threatening environments, however, children will appropriate and construct their own worlds. Children's actions in their peer cultures, families, schools, and other social institutions contribute much to the adult world. How can we enrich children's appropriations, constructions, and contributions? How can we make investments in children and their childhoods? How can we create a spirit of doing our best for our children, for their lives today as well as for their futures as adults? How can we sustain the noble and resolved spirit that was so evident in the aftermath of Oklahoma City, and channel it to address their needs every day of the year?

The Major Challenges

The major challenges to enriching the quality of children's lives are primarily economic. As we saw time and time again in Chapter 10, many of the social problems of children are linked to poverty. What types of government policies and actions are needed in confronting child poverty? In addressing this question we will focus primarily on American children, but we also will explore the responsibility of the United States and other industrialized countries for combating child poverty in the developing world.

Confronting Child Poverty in the United States
As we saw in Chapter 10, American middle- and high-income children are better off than their counterparts in other industrialized countries. In contrast, working-class and poor children in other Western nations enjoy living

standards that are significantly above those of similar children in the United States. How can we do better for our working-class and poor children while maintaining the economic security of children from more wealthy families? Here we can learn from other countries and also build on and expand successful American economic initiatives.

Economic investment in families and children. The United States is the most economically stratified country in the industrialized world, and the gap between rich and poor has been growing dramatically. Between 1983 and 1989 more than 60 percent of the wealth created went to the top 1 percent of the population, and 99 percent went to the top 20 percent (Carville, 1996, p. 78; also see Smeeding & Gottschalk, 1995). This trend not only contributes to the growing rate of child poverty, it also can have dire consequences for our society both economically and socially.

What can be done? Other countries have less disparity in income distribution than the United States because their citizens, especially the wealthy, pay more in taxes. Tax increases are not popular in the United States and are unlikely to be accepted. However, we already have some programs in place that could be expanded without big tax hikes. We also can make investments in human capital. What poor children need most are parents who have jobs that earn enough to keep their families out of poverty (Bianchi, 1993). We can train and educate people to be productive workers. This process also will generate new tax revenue and reduce welfare costs.

Consider, for example, the **Earned Income Tax Credit** (EITC). The EITC is a refundable tax credit for low-income families with children. It is an earned income support program that encourages work and self-sufficiency. Best of all, the EITC has been effective in alleviating poverty, and its expansion would do much to help reduce child poverty. Another way to help poor children is to enforce child support laws that require the absent parent (almost always fathers) to contribute to the economic security of their children. The Family Support Act of 1988 was a step in the right direction, and recent initiatives at the federal and state levels crack down even harder on deadbeat dads. Even with these efforts there still will be cases where the absent parent cannot or will not pay support. To address that fact the United States must, as many European countries have, act to institute a minimum guaranteed level of child support to single mothers (and fathers). One state, Wisconsin, has acted in this regard. Wisconsin included a "socially assured minimum benefit" as part of its general revision of the child support policy; the revision also included withholding child support from the salaries of noncustodial parents. The net result of these policy changes in Wisconsin: larger awards for custodial parents, and the awards are much more likely to be paid (Hewlett, 1993, p. 46).

Probably the most difficult problem for working poor families and their children in the United States is the lack of affordable health care. The United States subsidizes the cost of health care for only certain segments of the population (the disabled, the very poor, and the aged) through programs like Medicaid and Medicare. Other citizens have medical insurance as part of employment benefits, and a sizeable group, whose employers do not provide this benefit, must buy insurance on the open market. Many in this last group are working poor who cannot afford medical insurance and try to get by without it. The children in these families often see a doctor only when it is absolutely necessary. If a child becomes seriously ill, the parents can be thrown into serious debt and even bankruptcy. For the poor children of single parents, a child's illness may often mean leaving a job and turning to welfare to collect Medicaid (Rosier, 1996; Dugger, 1992).

Recent attempts in the United States to adopt a policy of universal health care resulted in dismal failure. The Clinton health plan was confusing to many Americans, who were bewildered by terms like *managed competition, employed mandates,* and *health alliances.* Also, the Clinton administration never really owned up to the fact the government would have to play a major role in universal health care. Republicans and health care lobbyists spent loads of money attacking and distorting the plan. The end result was that a lot of people, including many children in the United States, do not have access to basic health care. We can and must do better for our children. If we can provide subsidized health care for our aged, we can most certainly provide it for our young. Children's health and well-being "is as much a 'national investment' as are bridges, roads and environmental protection" (Danziger, Smeeding, & Rainwater, 1995, p. 27).

Family leave, child care, and early education. Although contributions to children's physical health and economic well-being can be seen as national investments in any society's future, a major theme of this book is that children's lives in the "here and now" are also worthy of appreciation, support, and enrichment. This fact holds true especially during children's first six years of life. As we have seen in previous chapters, the preschool years are a time of exploration and spontaneity. They are also a time of negotiation, accommodation, and communal sharing. Most of us have only vague memories of our experiences when we were young children. But positive experiences in these earlier years instill in us a spirit and a sense of security and confidence that we carry with us throughout our lives. Yet, the United States does less than most every other country in the industrialized world to support families with preschool children.

What can be done? As was the case with children's economic well-being, the United States has active programs to build on and several good models from Western Europe to emulate. What is most needed in the United States is an integrated and comprehensive policy that addresses maternity and family leave, child care, and early education. The Family and Medical Leave Act of 1993, which ensures job security for up to twelve weeks of unpaid leave, was a step in the right direction. However, the fact that the leave is unpaid discriminates against poor and working class families and children. The United States needs to go beyond limited employer-mandated programs and devise a policy that offers a substantial period of paid leave with opportunities for additional unpaid leave during the child's first year.

Most European countries have extensive family leave programs that are financed with contributions from employers, workers, and the government. Extended parental leave guarantees that a newborn infant can remain with her mother (or father) during most if not all of her first year of life. Not only is the period important for the infant's development, it also is the most demanding period for her parents and siblings. Thus, parental leave reduces stress and provides all family members with more time to accommodate to and to savor this important change in their lives.

What can be done to better address the child care and early education needs of one-to-six-year old children in the United States? The United States currently offers tax credits that primarily benefit middle-income families, and limited child care programs at the state level for poor families. It also has a compensatory education program, Head Start, for poor children, and all children can attend at least half-day kindergarten programs in their sixth year. As we saw in the last chapter, however, a major problem in the United States is the poor quality of the affordable private child care and early education services that are available. The situation is quite different in Europe, where child care and early education programs are often directly subsidized by national or local governments. Although child care for one-to-three-year olds is normally available only to working mothers, there has been a general expansion in the availability and quality of such care throughout Western Europe. High-quality early education programs for three-to-six-year-old children are widely available at low cost in Europe. France and Italy, for example, have developed excellent early childhood education programs for three-to-six-year-olds with near universal attendance (Corsaro & Emiliani, 1992; Hewlitt, 1993; Edwards, Gandini & Forman, 1993). Presently in Italy there is a movement away from a custodial to a more educational approach in its *asilo nido* programs for one-to-three-year-olds as well. This model refines educational ideas and philosophies first developed for the *scuola materna* for the needs of younger children.

The Italian preschool system did not spring up overnight. It was instituted in the late 1960s and has been expanded and improved over a thirty-year period. Any change in the United States would also be gradual and would build on the present system. A first step for the United States should be the identification of high-quality not-for-profit child care and early education programs. Not-for-profit programs are generally higher quality, and they are better able to train, compensate, and retain teachers and staff, compared to for-profit centers, where the curriculum and staff salaries are primarily based on profit margin. High-quality not-for-profit programs could be targeted for government subsidies to support curriculum expansion, lower fees, and scholarships for economically disadvantaged children. Head Start, which now serves only about 30 percent of all eligible children, should be expanded to cover all eligible children. It should also be expanded from half- to full-day programs and made available year-round to help working parents (Bianchi, 1993; Danziger & Stern, 1990). Some not-for-profit early education programs also could serve as models for an expanded Head Start that still would focus on children from poor families, but would move away from some of the negative aspects of its compensatory curriculum (Corsaro, 1996; Corsaro & Rosier, 1992). Finally, subsidized early education programs could be coordinated with kindergartens to smooth children's transition into elementary school. Many kindergarten programs that are now offered for only half-days need to be expanded to full-day to better meet the needs of families and children.

Although such programs would be costly, European examples have demonstrated creative ways of sharing such costs among employers, parents, and the average taxpayer. The European programs not only support families and enrich children's lives, they also free more parents to work and create satisfying and well-paying full- and part-time jobs in the area of child care and early education (Corsaro & Emiliani, 1992; Hewlitt, 1993).

Combating Child Poverty in Developing Countries

As we saw in the last chapter, child poverty in developing nations can be linked to a number of factors, including rapid urbanization, the global debt crisis, government corruption, ethnic violence, and the spread of infectious diseases such as AIDS. The best way to combat these problems and the resulting poverty is with increased aid from wealthy nations. Such aid is often referred to as official development assistance (ODA). ODA refers to aid from governments for humanitarian and development purposes. Military aid is specifically excluded. About two-thirds of ODA is given directly from one government to another; the remainder is channeled to various countries via international organizations and United Nations agencies. In addition, some aid is provided by voluntary organizations in the wealthy nations (UNICEF, 1995b).

Although the United States gave more total aid ($9.7 billion) than any other country except for Japan ($11.3 billion) in 1993, the United States ranks very low in terms of aid as percent of gross national product and aid per person when compared to other industrialized countries. The Scandinavian countries stand out, with Denmark contributing aid in the amount of nearly 1 percent of its gross national product. The amount of aid given per person is perhaps the most easily understandable statistic. Here the United States again ranks low. For example, the United States gave $38 per person, Canada gave $82 per person (near the average amount), and Denmark contributed the highest at $259 per person (UNICEF, 1995b).

The amount of foreign aid is far from the only issue to consider when talking about child poverty in developing countries. Just as important is how aid is distributed. A major problem in many countries in the developing world is that the aid is not used for programs that assist children, such as health and education programs. Even worse, substantial funds often are siphoned off by corrupt government officials. Recently, at the World Summit for Social Development, Norway introduced a 20/20 formula in which an allocation of an average of 20 percent of the recipient governments' national budgets and 20 percent of the donor countries' aid budgets, would go to basic social services. Norway's argument was that an increased allocation to basic social programs would substantially contribute to the objective of reaching the poorest people (UNICEF, 1995b). Others have argued that foreign donors and the international financial community should *not* give funds directly to national governments. Instead, donors should distribute the money themselves or give it to trusted nongovernmental organizations (NGOs) (Bradshaw, Buchman & Mbatia, 1994). As we saw in the last chapter, NGOs are coming to play a central role as advocates for children and youth in many developing countries.

Some More Modest Proposals to Enrich Children's Lives

We have discussed the need for major investments in children's economic, physical, and social well-being. It is clear that short-term investments, though costly, will more than pay off in the long run, because they greatly increase the likelihood that children will become productive members of their societies. However, years of neglecting a significant proportion of our children means we cannot expect immediate results. It will take great resolve, hard work, and patience. We need to get started.

There is a wide range of things nations, communities, and individuals are already doing to enrich the lives of children. There are also some new ideas that have yet to be tested. Many of these demand some degree of investment of time and energy, but have only modest economic costs. Let's discuss these proposals under the general categories of (1) enhancing the lives of families and children and (2) supporting families and children at risk.

Enhancing the Lives of Families and Children

One of the most important things that adults can do to enrich children's lives is to give them more of our time. What is needed most is everyday time for routine activities, talk, and play. Parents also need more time to participate in their children's lives outside the family, most especially in schools and community organizations. What children want and need is to engage in a little conversation at dinner, to play a game of catch or cards, to watch a TV show or video together, to take a walk in the park or to get an ice cream, to be tickled or tossed about before a bath, or to read a story before bed. Children want attention. They want adults to even act silly and laugh with them now and then, to show they care. What children get, though, time and time again, are promises: "I'll buy you that new toy tomorrow," "We'll go to a museum on Saturday," "We'll see that movie next Sunday, I promise." Sometimes parents deliver on these special promises and sometimes not; however, what children need is routine, relentless reminders, that they are important and that they are loved. Demanding work schedules and the hectic pace of everyday life in modern societies work against the natural expression of how much almost all parents really do love their children.

Another problem is family isolation. Families are smaller, grandparents and relatives often do not live nearby, and neighborhoods are less cohesive and communal than in the past. Children need more opportunities and space to collectively "weave their webs" with others. They need more diverse and supportive social fields and locales that can support their intricate weavings, and that can allow them to establish secure places in their local family, peer, school, and neighborhood cultures. Family isolation is intensified by the class, gender, and age segregation that exists in most modern societies. Let's look at these problems—lack of family time and family isolation—and discuss some proposals to lessen their negative effects on children's lives.

Work time, family time. Recently child advocates have called for "family-friendly" workplaces that better integrate parenting and paid work in modern societies (Hewlett, 1992, 1993; Leach, 1994; Louv, 1990). A key to their arguments is the general acceptance of the fact that modern post-industrial societies need not require or ensure consistent full-time employment for every adult. Such acceptance would allow for more part-time work, periods of unpaid work leaves, and more diversity in types of employment (Leach, 1994). Many of these advocates point to family leave policies in Sweden and other countries, which we discussed earlier. Employers in these countries have found that accommodation to such policies improves worker morale and productivity. The result is sustained economic growth despite what most American employers would see as excessive government regulation. In Sweden, for example, gross national product per capita has remained one of the highest in the world and is clearly competitive with that of the United States (Hewlett, 1993).

Sweden, of course, is not the United States. American business leaders resent what they see as government mandates and intrusion; unions worry about layoffs or benefit reductions for full-time workers. Many are concerned that women who opt for part-time work or unpaid leaves will suffer losses of seniority and promotions. The United States need not enact the full-scale social welfare programs of countries such as Sweden to make the workplace more family friendly. However, at least two of the three major challenges we noted above (paid family leave, universal health care for children, and government subsidized child care and early education) need to be addressed. If they are, major headway can be made, and a whole range of additional modest proposals could result in more time for parents to be with and nurture their children.

Consider how the enactment of policies like paid family leave and universal health care (policies that have clear, immediate, positive effects on children's lives) could bring about ripple effects in the workplace that benefit families more generally. If the United States adopted family leave and universal health care programs whose costs were shared by employers, workers, and the government, many businesses could temporally replace fulltime employees who need to be with their infants, with part-time workers who are parents of preschool or elementary school children. These part-time employees could enter the work force with the assurance that their children's health care needs are covered. The parents would also gain valuable work experience.

Affordable government-subsidized child care and early education programs create a whole range of options for parents. They allow some to opt for full-time work, others part-time, and they allow others the opportunity to further their education and job skills. Also, as we noted earlier, government subsidy of not-for-profit child care and early education programs can result in the much needed professionalization of child care workers and early education teachers. With better training, pay, and promotion possibilities many talented and caring adults would have the opportunity to enter a profession they find rewarding and satisfying. In addition, a whole range of full- or part-time job opportunities for support staff could be created. This is a good example of how programs that help children and families can put people to work in a range of public and private sector jobs.

While the United States strives to meet these major challenges, a number of more modest experiments designed to make the workplace more family friendly are already being tried out here and in other countries. Most of these new ideas involve various types of flexible work schedules. For example, some companies in the United States and Europe offer flexible working hours, compressed work weeks, job-sharing, and at-home arrangements to give their employees more blocks of time to be with their children. In Europe, for example, some companies offer weekend work that pays the same for $2^1/_2$ ten-hour work days as it does for a full week. Companies can afford to do this because they reduce the number of hours of overtime pay. A number of recent studies have found that such programs and others that address family needs reduce job turnover and absenteeism, improve recruitment, increase worker morale and productivity, and enhance company image (Hewlett, 1993, p. 47; Leach, 1994, pp. 225-39).

Child advocate Penelope Leach notes that such programs move parents' working hours closer to her ideal goal: "No child under 3 has more than six hours a day of day care and no child under 8 comes home to an empty house, but has one parent there" (as quoted in Kinkead, 1994, p. 35). I would argue further that flexible work hours can give at least one parent the opportunity to routinely pick up their children from day care, early education, and elementary school programs with less haste and tension. Picking children up from day care and school is often a wearisome task for parents in a hurry. I am reminded of a story I once heard about a physician who rushed into a day care center, grabbed his child's coat and hat and called out to his five-year-old son, "Coat, hat, we're out of here!" The boy, happily constructing a lego house with two other children and a teacher, looked up and said, "I don't want to be a doctor when I grow up!" But with more flexible work hours and more time, this mundane and often tedious activity (from parents' perspective) can be transformed into a routine that is exciting for young children and relaxing and emotionally satisfying for parents. Instead of picking up children and rushing home to fix dinner, parents and kids can take a quick trip to the store to pick up some ice cream for after dinner, stop by a nearby park for play, swing by grandparents' or friends' homes for a short visit, or just drive or walk around the neighborhood.

Recently some headway has been made on this front with the consideration of legislation that would increase flexibility in working hours across the American work place. Both President Clinton and the Republican Congress have proposed legislation that would allow workers to take off up to two weeks a year in exchange for the overtime they work. Under Clinton's plan an employee could take $1^1/_2$ hours of compensatory flex time for each hour of overtime worked, with a limit of 80 hours annually. The plan also would enable workers to take up to 24 hours a year of unpaid time for family obligations—to attend parent-teacher conferences or to care for elderly parents. The American plans are a far cry from the more extensive and paid leave policies of Sweden and other European countries, and one worries about how they will apply to small businesses and firms that employ mainly less-skilled workers. But they are a step in the right direction. Also, if they work to improve worker morale and productivity, as other voluntary experiments of this type have, then they could lead to more extensive programs.

Breaking down the isolation of families with children. In most modern industrialized societies there is increased segregation of families with children from other members of society by class, race, ethnicity, gender, and age. Such segregation is especially difficult for poor families in the United States, who often live in neighborhoods where drug dealers and violent crime threaten the futures and the very lives of their children. Our earlier discussion of Nicholas and his family clearly depicted the minimal support available in many inner-city neighborhoods. Recent studies have found that the resiliency of the extended black family structure, and especially the supportive role of grandmothers, is being severely challenged by the extreme poverty and violence of many inner-city areas (Heath, 1989; Hill, 1990; Rosier, 1996; Stack, 1974). Single working mothers struggling to survive in such circumstances often "resent their status as invisible women, going unnoticed in neighborhoods most often portrayed as havens for crime, drugs, and welfare dependency, rarely for workaday striving" (Dugger, 1992). In her highly insightful ethnography of nine families living in poverty, Katherine Rosier found that single mothers often purposefully cut themselves and their children off from neighbors whom they saw as bad and threatening influences (Rosier, 1996). The mothers contrasted their own values of hard work and decency with what they saw as the irresponsibility of others, who had given in to drugs, crime, or welfare dependency (also see Anderson, 1994). However, this survival strategy further isolated these mothers, who felt they could not risk venturing into the community to seek out others like themselves.

In cases such as these, community organizations are needed to bring such families together for mutual support and to reach out to other families who have succumbed to the difficult challenges of poverty. As we saw with Nicholas's family, religious organizations offer spiritual and community support of this type. However, in many cases churches have abandoned inner-city areas and have moved to more stable working- and middle-class neighborhoods. Those that remain often offer basic religious services to congregations that live primarily outside the inner-city area, and community social services often are curtailed. A major reason, of course, is high rates of violent crime, a problem we take up in the next section.

A major contributor to family isolation among all social class groups in industrialized societies is age segregation. The fragmentation of institutions according to age and the high level of social mobility in modern societies "has meant that interaction of persons of different ages occurs less and less frequently and is of diminishing social significance" (Schildkrout, 1975, p. 111). Most societies will never again experience the close personal relations among generations (in terms of responsibilities and obligations) that prevailed in preindustrial societies. Some have argued that most people would not find a return to such close relations desirable (Qvortrup, 1994b). However, the degree of age segregation that exists in the United States is truly unfortunate, because the young and the elderly have so much to offer each other.

One thing that has continually struck me during my stays in Italy is the active involvement of older people in everyday life. In the cities in northern Italy where I have lived the elderly are everywhere: in parks, public squares, churches, and shops. It is not unusual to see sixty-, seventy-, and even eighty-year-old men and women navigating bicycles through heavy city traffic. When they are out and about, many of Italy's elderly are on their way to visit grandchildren or to pick them up from school. During my many hours of participant observation in Italian preschools I have found that the two most common phrases in the children's vocabularies are: "*mia nonna*" and "*mio nonno*" ("my grandma" and "my grandpa"). And grandparent involvement does not stop with preschool; at least 40 percent of the adults who take and pick up children from my daughter's elementary school in Modena, Italy, are grandparents. Grandparents caring for and spending time with their grandchildren are so much a part of everyday life in Italy that their activities are even depicted on street signs. As we see in Exhibit 11.1, signs that mark bike and walking paths in Modena clearly depict frequent users of these lanes: granddads and their granddaughters.

Even Italy, however, is experiencing more and more social mobility, so some grandparents live in towns and cities other than those in which their grandchildren live. But this change does not mean that activities cannot be devised to bring children and the elderly together, even if they are not all directly related. In the introduction to this chapter, I discussed my recollection of Grandparents Day at a *scuola materna* in Modena. As we can see from the pictures in Exhibits 11.2 and 11.3 of some of the activities that occurred that day, all of the children at Grandparents Day benefitted from interaction with the grandparents, even if their own grandparents could not attend. In Exhibit 11.2 a grandmother smiles proudly as her grandson whips up her traditional family dessert; another child looks on. In Exhibit 11.3 a young boy sits at a table where his grandfather has been making kites; several of his classmates pose for a picture with them.

EXHIBIT 11.1

Sign Marking Bicycle and Walking Paths in Modena, Italy

Undoubtedly there are Grandparent Days in schools in the United States. But these rare occasions need to be expanded to become every-year traditions in all schools. We also need to reach out to the elderly in our communities, many of whom are isolated, to serve as surrogate grandparents for neighborhood children whose own grandparents may live far away. Such programs could involve safe transportation for the elderly where public transit is limited and there are concerns about security. Why should we stop with

EXHIBIT 11.2

Grandmother and Grandson Prepare Dessert in
Scuola Materna in Modena, Italy

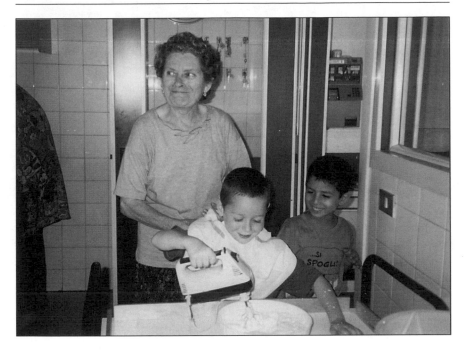

programs like "Meals on Wheels," when the elderly need *companionship* as much if not more than nutrition? We all need more opportunities to engage in routine collective activities with others.

We need not stop with programs for the very young and the elderly. It would be highly useful to bring the elderly together with preadolescents and adolescents, an age group many of the elderly have come to fear in the United States. Recently in Belleville, New Jersey, the local high school sponsored their second annual "senior prom" for all elderly members of this community of 34,000 near Newark. Teenage students were on hand to serve refreshments, chat, and dance with "the strangers of their grandparents' or, maybe, great grandparents' era" (Hanley, 1996). The elderly also have an open invitation to attend classes at the Belleville high school at no cost, and many have taken the high school up on its offer. Such programs turn strangers into friends and, as Belleville's school superintendent noted, the programs have done a lot to allay older citizens' concerns about education budgets.

EXHIBIT 11.3

Grandfather Makes a Kite for Children in a
Scuola Materna in Modena, Italy

Supporting Families and Children at Risk

Families and children need special help and support at times of major disruption and instability, which put families and children at physical, emotional, and social risk. Unemployment, family illness, family conflict, separation and divorce, and living in threatening and violent environments all take a toll on families and children. During these times parents and children need to help one another, and to do that, they also need support from outside the family. Communities, including voluntary and government organizations, need to play more of a role than they now do. What is needed, most especially in the United States, is a revigorization and celebration of **civic engagement**, people's connections with and participation in the life of their communities (Putnam, 1996).

As I argued earlier, although there has been a long debate about the breakdown of family values only recently have some begun to discuss our collective responsibility as citizens to act to help families and children in times of need. What often clouds fruitful debate about the need for civic participation, however, is an insistence that the traditional two-parent family is best. Many children in single-parent families are, for all sorts of reasons, better off than they would be if their parents had entered into loveless marriages or had continued in failed and unhappy ones. Further, families with caring adults are what is important for children. When there is more than one caring adult, all the better. In fact, as we saw in Chapter 4, children in many societies are cared for by a wide range of adult and peer caretakers. We can appreciate family diversity and still help children in need. Let's consider some of the major risks that families and children face and evaluate some proposals for how communities can help families at risk help themselves and their children.

Supporting families and children of divorce. The ease with which marriages can be dissolved and men can avoid supporting their families in the United States is shameful. There is much debate about returning to more restrictive divorce laws and especially to doing away with what is called "no fault" divorce. Under **no-fault divorce statutes,** a divorce is granted even if only one spouse wants it. I believe that doing away with no-fault laws is unwise, because the end result of such action may well be more expensive and acrimonious divorces.

Still, there is reason to question the quickness with which divorces are currently granted in the United States. Many European countries require a two- to six-year waiting period in granting divorces, while in the United States most states have done away with waiting periods of a year or more. Waiting periods require married couples to carefully evaluate their marital problems and to consider the effects of divorce on their children, and they prevent fathers and mothers from rushing quickly into new marriages. In many troubled marriages there can be compelling circumstances (such as intense conflict and spouse or child abuse) that require that legal separations be easily and swiftly obtained. However, even in these cases, quick divorce and remarriage usually is not in the best interest of children. In Italy and France longer waiting periods are closely tied to strict rules of child support. In France, for example, divorce requires a six-year waiting period, and the husband is bound to support his wife and children in their current lifestyle (Glendon, 1987; Hewlett, 1993).

In addition to benefitting from longer waiting periods, children of families undergoing divorce would also benefit from their parents' having to attend court-ordered classes or workshops in which they learn how to cope with their children's needs during the divorce process. Such required courses are becoming commonplace in the United States. There are now more than five hundred court-affiliated parent-education programs for divorcing parents in forty-one states. The courses are normally established under local court rules and are taught in family court or by local social service agencies. Two states, Connecticut and Utah, require classes statewide, and a number of other states are considering doing the same (Lewin, 1995b). The courses focus on getting parents to view their situation from their children's perspective. They often include parental viewing of videotaped skits of typical parental conflicts occurring in front of children, as well as interviews of real children who have experienced bitter divorces. They also stress the benefits of parents working together to raise their children, and the costs (financial and emotional) of court battles to work out custody agreements.

There is always, however, in programs of this type, a danger of espousing formulaic solutions and what some observers see as the "unpleasant tinge of the therapeutic state" (Lewin, 1995b). Also, some parents and their lawyers resent the classes and see them as intrusions in the legal process of divorce. Surveys of parents who have completed divorce education, however, show that they strongly approve of the courses. In Connecticut, for example, 90 percent of the parents surveyed after completing the classes approved of the requirement. As one father noted, "When they show you these heartbreaking interviews with real kids, you see how devastating it is for the kids, and you think a little less about your next move in court, and more about how it will be for your child" (Lewin, 1995b, p. A8).

Reducing the risk of child abuse. Every time I teach my course on childhood in contemporary society I ask my class (normally around ninety students) if they had a course on driver's education in high school. The hand of nearly every student immediately shoots up. Then I ask how many had a course on children, child development, or child care and child rearing. Now there are many fewer hands, usually about thirty-five or forty at most. And this is in classes that are normally about 75 to 80 percent female! It seems we feel it is more important to prepare our children to be drivers than parents.

One of the reasons many school districts shy away from teaching parenting is that it can be controversial. The same people who want religion and morality in the schools often balk at courses on parenting. A course on children and parenting? Why, that's an invasion of parents' rights. Child rearing is a private matter.

Surely, courses that prepare children and adolescents for parenthood can be developed and encouraged as important options, if they are not required classes. What should be the nature of the curriculum in such courses? We certainly need to get beyond courses that are often aimed at less-academic female students and that focus only on practical skills (Leach, 1994). We need courses that both inform students about children and also celebrate the wonder of children. Students need to do more than bathe a borrowed baby or make a one-time trip to a day care center.

What is needed is a series of projects that involve reading, discussing, doing, re-creating, and evaluating. Especially useful would be to require students to engage in a series of activities with young children and to reflect on and evaluate those experiences. Because of small families and the age segregation that exists in American society, such activities do not occur routinely in preadolescents' and adolescents' (especially males') everyday lives. But here again, a little ingenuity can go a long way. Boys can babysit as well as girls. And most adolescents have relatives, friends, or neighbors who have young children with whom they can spend time and get to know better. Think back to our earlier discussion of how nice it would be if parents could routinely pick up their young children from day care, preschool, or elementary school each day and then spend time with them in conversation and play. Why couldn't an adolescent relative or friend take the role of parent in this routine once or twice a week? This would be an excellent field project in a course on children and parenting. In such a project everyone benefits—young children, their older adolescent friend or relative, and the parents. It is also just one of many possible ways to prepare preadolescents and adolescents for parenting.

Classes on childhood, children, and parenting in middle school and high school can do much to prepare youth for their coming transition to parenthood. But how can we help today's parents deal with the major responsibilities and demands of caring for infants and young children? We know from our earlier discussion in Chapter 10 that the most common form of child abuse is neglect. A frequent factor in neglect is family isolation, stress, and substance abuse. How can we reach out to families in need of help because of one or several of these factors?

Great Britain reaches out to families with newborns through its program of national health visitors. Health visitors spend time talking with and advising all new parents (usually mothers) before and after the birth of a child. Again, there is some debate about costs of the program, the intrusion of the state into private family affairs, and the feminization and middle-class therapeutic aspect of these services (Mayall, 1996). Still, such services provide attention, care, and advice to many families, especially those living in poverty and isolation.

Although such universal child health programs do not exist in the United States, voluntary programs to help families at risk for child abuse and neglect are becoming more widespread. Such programs usually involve social workers who make house calls to troubled families, or family resource centers where parents can go to seek help. Many existing programs are modeled after one begun in Hawaii in the mid-1980s and after another project sponsored by the National Committee to Prevent Child Abuse in Chicago, which refined and expanded the Hawaii program. Such programs are controversial because of their expense, the fear of government intrusion, and difficulties in evaluating their effectiveness. Yet, there have been reductions in reports of child abuse in the communities served.

Programs to prevent child abuse may be the most important thing we can do to help America's children. As James Garbarino has most eloquently stated, "'If you take almost any major social problem in America and treat it like those nested Russian dolls, what you will get to is that child abuse would be the last doll—because it is such a profound wound in developing children" (as quoted in Lev & Brandon, 1994, p. D5).

Protecting children from abuse and violence outside the family. As we discussed in Chapter 10, a growing number of children's lives are disrupted, permanently scarred, or brought to an end by persistent abuse and violence in their schools, neighborhoods, and communities. Children are abused and harassed by peers and teachers in schools, exploited by employers in the workplace, assaulted and murdered by criminals, and maimed and killed by the bombs and bullets of wars. What can be done to reduce the shameful record of violence against children? A first step is speaking up and challenging world leaders and all citizens to become more aware of the extent of the problem. The next step is the enactment of a whole range of programs that little by little may help to turn the tide and make the world safer for children and youth.

Some gains have been made in the area of abuse and harassment in schools through growing recognition of the problem, research on its extensiveness and underlying causes, and programs to educate students about their rights and responsibilities (Besag, 1989; Ambert, 1995; Eder, 1995). These developments may lead to some of the same positive results that occurred after the long-neglected problem of sexual abuse in the workplace was finally addressed in a serious manner.

Although the exploitation of child workers can occur anywhere in the world, as we saw in Chapter 10, it is primarily concentrated in developing countries. Ultimately, the political leaders, parents, and children in these countries will have to lead the way in combating this evil. This has already occurred in countries like Pakistan and India. In these countries children have actively proclaimed their rights even when this has meant sacrificing their lives for the cause (as in the case of young Iqbal Masih). Nonetheless, we can all fight against this problem by pushing for legislation that would ban the sale of goods produced by child labor in our country, and by lobbying American companies to stop contracting work to countries where children are exploited.

How do we help children of war? The world seems never at peace and children are the chief victims of its conflicts. I have touched only indirectly on this issue in this book, yet there clearly are things to be done. We can support a ban on the production of land mines in the United States and throughout the world; we can support the United Nations Convention on the Rights of the Child, which specifically addresses children's rights in war time; and, we can inform ourselves and take responsibility for our own government's military actions and policies in regard to children.

Finally, there are the war zones of America. The number of children and youth who are victims of violent crimes in the United States is appalling, shameful, and devastatingly sad. The causes of this tragedy are many and they are intricately interrelated: poverty, abuse, drugs, guns, fear, and despair. We saw all these elements played out in the life of Robert, the eleven-year-old hitman who was himself executed. Stories like Robert's, although almost incomprehensible, are becoming more and more usual. Two Chicago boys, ages twelve and thirteen, dropped a five-year-old from a high-rise building because he wouldn't steal candy for them. In Richmond, California, a six-year-old boy and his twin eight-year-old brothers slipped into a neighbor's apartment to steal a tricycle. The six-year-old dumped the neighbor's newborn baby from his bassinet and beat the infant nearly to death. Increasingly in American war zones both the victims and perpetrators are children.

What's to be done? First and foremost we need to get beyond our own emotions and concentrate on the *children* who have to deal with such violence every day of their lives. As sad as it may be, we need to focus less on the actual victims and perpetrators of these crimes once they have occurred and more on the children who continue to deal with relentless violence in their neighborhoods long after our memory of the shocking events begins to fade. We need to use the sad victimization of our children to spur us to help those still at risk, rather than pointing fingers at our political enemies and shouting, "moral breakdown!"

How can we help these children? How do we keep them safe? How do we prevent them from being tomorrow's victims or tomorrow's executioners? What these children need in their communities are more police, fewer guns, more caring adults, and more secure places to play and to be children.

Residents of high crime areas have long lamented the lack of police attention and protection in their communities (Anderson, 1994). Recently there has been a call to hire more police and to increase their visibility in high crime areas. Many experts point to recent drops in violent crime in New York and other major cities as an indication that this policy is working. The police, however, must focus on helping and defending minority children and youth, not on intimidating them.

We also must address the easy availability of handguns and assault weapons. As gun violence and crime have increased among youth, so has the belief among youth who are not involved in crime that they need guns to protect themselves. Recent restrictions on gun sales, as well as legislation like the Brady Bill, which requires a waiting period and also a background check, have helped. But it is still much easier to sell, buy, and own handguns and assault weapons in the United States than it is to buy, sell, or own a car. In 1994 handgun legislation offered up in Congress by Senator Bill Bradley and Representative Charles Schumer would have mandated, essentially, many of the same restrictions for handgun sale and ownership that exist for selling and owning a car. Unfortunately, the legislative initiative never became law. I can think of no worse crime than selling a gun to a minor. Yet it happens all the time, often without real threat of criminal prosecution.

Throughout this book I have argued for the importance of appreciating children's active construction of their own peer worlds and cultures. We have seen how children's construction of and participation in their peer cultures also contributes to reproduction and change in adult society. Children who live in violent communities are restricted from creating and participating in such cultures. There are few safe places in their worlds for them to be children. A New York City grade school teacher, Sara Mosle (1994), writes that her third grade students lived under virtual house arrest. Their neighborhoods were filled with violence and crime, and they were afraid to spend much time outdoors. Thus, they lacked the everyday opportunities most of us had as children to play and to learn to get along with their peers. These children missed the rudiments of social interaction like "how not to hog the ball, how to stop teasing a friend before it became unpleasant, how to settle a disagreement without resorting to a fight" (Mosle, 1994, p. 19). As a result Mosle found that her students were continually upset about minor slights from their peers, and she spent a lot of time teaching "conflict resolution" in her class. Still, her students loved school. They begged her to let them stay after school so that they could "have a chance to talk to one another, to talk to me, to watch the fish in the aquarium, play (if Miss Mosle was in a good mood) for just a little" (Mosle, 1994, p. 19).

Many of the preadolescents and adolescents who have been placed in the Camden County Youth Center where Mary Taylor Previte is the administrator have a lot in common with Sara Mosle's third graders (Previte, 1994). They too need a safe place to learn, to play, to be children. However, compared to the third graders, these youth have seen more violence, have been more likely to experience death firsthand, and have been in trouble themselves. In the detention center they talk about the violent experiences in their lives, trying to rid themselves of memories of domestic abuse or drive-by shootings. In these painful reflections some children even contemplate their own funerals. However, they also make desperate attempts to catch up on lost childhood during leisure activities, and they make dramatic academic gains. Like the third graders who want to stay after school, these youth often prefer the lockup center to their homes and neighborhoods. Consider the response of one fourteen-year-old after two former residents of the center were gunned down on a Candem street corner: "'Good thing I be here. Mighta been me dead out there'" (Previte, 1994, p. 17).

The best candidates for providing havens from violence in the inner city are youth organizations. We know from the research of Heath and McLaughlin (1993) that youth organizations like Boys and Girls Clubs, Police Athletic League (PAL) clubs, and YMCAs have been very successful in serving inner-city youth. These organizations often tailor program content and institutional processes to the interests of the youth in the community, and they incorporate young people into participatory roles of all sorts. Activities in the organizations provide youth with *a sense of worth* from being a member of a group or team; *a sense of belonging* from being needed within the organization; *a sense of responsibility* from being held accountable for contributing to the group and for adhering to set rules and expectations. Such organizations are also often administered by excellent role models who are committed to giving something back to the communities in which they grew up.

A big problem for youth organizations in inner cities is uncertain budgets and lack of continuous support from local communities and from national chapters of various organizations. Such organizations are, of course, not a cure-all for the problems of violence and crime in inner-city areas. However, with strong financial support from federal, state, and local governments and from individuals, they may very well be the best hope for providing the security so many of our children desperately need.

Acting Right Now

In this section we have evaluated programs for supporting families and children. Many of these programs are already in place and are working well. Most are administered by private voluntary organizations or local governments, and the overwhelming majority do not carry heavy costs for taxpayers. These programs and future initiatives that promise to help families and children do, however, need the support of all of us.

Recently the debate about family values has expanded and blossomed into a public discourse with great potential. Conservatives, mostly Republicans, deserve credit for initiating the debate. However, their views about the limits of big government and the decline of personal responsibility captures only one side of the issue. Liberals, mostly Democrats, who at first were mainly on the defense, have now responded that the problems American families face are deeply rooted in the economic conditions of modern societies. Now the debate has become more constructive, and modest (but real) proposals like workplace flexibility and leave time for parents may become a reality (Dionne, 1996).

Another positive outcome of the new family values debate is that both sides have challenged the media, most especially the visual media of television and film, to be more responsible. Here both liberals and conservatives have assailed the media position that their products only *reflect* the violent and sexual themes of our society. In many ways the media *is* a mirror of society and culture, but that mirror needs to be wide enough to reflect the diversity of our culture. Furthermore, the media, because of its great power, has an obligation to go beyond entertainment; it is obligated to inform and to educate its audience. In short, the media needs to join the debate about families and children, rather than to reflect, sensationalize, and contribute to the problems families and children face.

As individual citizens we all must heed this same challenge. We need to increase our civic engagement by contributing our time and money to a wide range of community organizations that help families with children. Many political leaders are calling for such civic involvement, and there is some evidence that volunteerism may be increasing in the United States, especially among young people (see Yates, 1995; Youniss & Yates, in press). We need to celebrate this fact and join the process.

Conclusion

In this final chapter I have presented many ideas and proposals for how we can invest in children and their childhoods. In line with the belief that children are active participants in society, I have argued that we need to enrich children's appropriations from the adult world, to encourage their constructions of their own peer cultures, and to better appreciate the contributions children can and do make to our adult worlds. Many of the social problems of children can seem overwhelming. Yet, the truth is that the majority of the world's children are actively creating and enjoying their childhoods. We need to do our best to create a commitment of responsibility among adults so that we can provide *all* children these same opportunities and experiences.

Our children are our future. How often we hear this obvious but true proverb. Cultures that invest in their children, that shelter, nourish, and challenge their young, that hold high expectations for their future generations will survive and flourish. *All* children live their childhoods only once. We adults have had our childhoods; for some they were happy and enriching, for others, unfortunately, sad and oppressive. We cannot have them back to live another way, nor can we live the lives of our children.

All too often individuals and societies try to justify their actions in terms of their effects on children's futures as adults. This focus on the future, on what our children will become, can often blind us to how we treat and care for our children in the present. Enriching the lives of all our children will produce better adults and will enable our children to participate actively and fully in their own childhoods and to contribute to the quality of our adult lives.

Cultures that appreciate and celebrate their children for who they are as well as for who they will become are the cultures that will lead us most successfully into a new century. Yes, our children are our future. And if there is one point, moral, or insight that I would have you take from this book it is: *The future of childhood is the present.*

References

Abrahams, R. (1975). Negotiating respect: Patterns of presentation among black women. In C. Farrer (Ed.), *Women and folklore* (pp. 58–80). Austin, TX: University of Texas Press.

Adler, P. A., Kless, S., & Adler, P. (1992). Socialization to gender roles: Popularity among elementary school boys and girls. *Sociology of Education, 65,* 169–187.

Ainsworth, M., Blehar, M., Waters, E., & Wall, S. (1978). *Patterns of attachment: A psychological study of the strange situation.* Hillsdale, NJ: Lawrence Erlbaum Associates.

Alan Guttmacher Institute (1994). Sex and America's teenagers. New York: Alan Guttmacher Institute.

Alanen, L. (1990). Rethinking socialization, the family and childhood. In P. A. Adler, P. Adler, N. Mandell, & S. Cahill, *Sociological Studies of Child Development,* Vol. 3, (pp. 13–28). Greenwich, CT: JAI Press.

Alston, L. (1992). Children as chattel. In E. West & P. Petrick (Eds.), *Small worlds* (pp. 208–231). Lawrence, KS: University Press of Kansas.

Ambert, A. (1986). Sociology of sociology: The place of children in North American sociology. In P. Adler, & P. Adler (Ed.), *Sociological studies of child development* Vol. 1, (pp. 11–31). Greenwich, CT: JAI Press.

Ambert, A. (1995). Toward a theory of peer abuse. *Sociological Studies of Children, 7,* 177–205.

American Psychological Association (1995). Testimony submitted to the House of Representatives Ways and Means Subcommittee on Human Resources on the subject of Strategies for reducing nonmarital childbearing among adolescents: Effective policy responses. 3 February.

Anderson, E. (1994, May 5). The code of the streets. *Atlantic Monthly, 273,* pp. 81–94.

Ariès, P. (1962). *Centuries of childhood.* New York: Vintage.

Asher, S. & Coie, J. (Eds.) (1990). *Peer rejection in childhood.* New York: Cambridge University Press.

Barlow, K. (1985). Play and learning in a Sepik society. Paper presented at the annual meetings of the American Anthropological Association. Washington, DC.

Barnes, M. & Vangelisti, A. (1995). Speaking in a double-voice: Role-making as influence in preschoolers' fantasy play situations. *Research on Language and Social Interaction, 28,* 351–389.

Belsey, M. (1993). Child abuse measuring a global problem. *World Health Statistics Quarterly, 46.*

Belsky, J. (1988). The "effects" of infant daycare reconsidered. *Early Childhood Research Quarterly, 3,* 35–272.

Belsky, J. (1989). Infant-parent attachment and day care: In defense of the strange situation. In J. Lande, S. Scarr, & N. Gunzenhauser (Eds.), *Caring for children: Challenge to America* (pp. 3–48). Hillsdale, NJ: Lawrence Erlbaum Associates.

Belsky, J. & Rovine, M. (1988). Nonmaternal care in the first year of life and the security of infant-parent attachment. *Child Development, 59,* 1157–167.

Bell, E., Haas, L., & Sells, L. (1996). (Eds.). *From mouse to mermaid.* Bloomington, IN: Indiana University Press.

Benin, M. & Edwards, D. (1990). Adolescents' chores: The difference between dual- and single-earner families. *Journal of Marriage and the Family, 52:* 361–73.

Bereiter, C. & Engleman, S. (1966). *Teaching disadvantaged children in the preschool.* Englewood Cliffs, N J: Prentice-Hall.

Berentzen, S. (1984). Children constructing their social world. University of Bergen: Bergen Studies in Social Anthropology, No. 36.

Bernstein, B. (1981). Codes, modalities, and the process of cultural reproduction: A model. *Language in Society, 10,* 327–363.

Besag, V. (1989). Bullies and victims in schools: A guide to understanding and management. Philadelphia: Open University Press.

Besharov, D. (1994). The extent of child abuse is exaggerated. In K. de Koster (Ed.), *Child abuse: Opposing viewpoints,* (pp. 17–24). San Diego, CA: Greenhaven Press.

Best, J. (1990). *Threatened children: Rhetoric and concern about child-victims.* Chicago: University of Chicago Press.

Best, J. (1994). Troubling children: Children and social problems. In J. Best (Ed.), *Troubling children: Studies of children and social problems,* (pp. 3–19). New York: Aldine De Gruyter.

Best, R. (1983). *We've all got scars.* Bloomington, IN: Indiana University Press.

Bettelheim, B. (1976). *The uses of enchantment: The meaning and importance of fairy tales.* New York: Knopf.

Bianchi, S. (1993). Children of poverty: Why are they poor? In J. Chafel (Ed.), *Child poverty and public policy.* Washington, DC: The Urban Institute.

Blair, S. (1992). The sex-typing of children's household labor: Parental influence on daughters' and sons' housework. *Youth & Society, 24,* 178–203.

Bohlen, C. (1995, March 24). Tell these Italians communism doesn't work. *The New York Times,* p. A7.

Bourdieu, P. (1977). *Outline of a theory of practice.* New York: Cambridge University Press.

Bourdieu, P. (1991). *Language & symbolic power.* Cambridge, MA: Harvard University Press.

Bourdieu, P. (1993). Concluding remarks: For a sociogenetic understanding of intellectual works. In C. Calhoun, E. LiPuma, & M. Postone (Eds.), *Bourdieu: Critical perspectives,* (pp. 263–275). Chicago: University of Chicago Press.

Bourdieu, P., & Passeron, J. C. (1977). *Reproduction in education, society, and culture.* Beverly Hills, CA: Sage.

Bradshaw, Y. (1993). New directions in international developmental research: A focus on children. *Childhood, 1:* 134–142.

Bradshaw, Y. Buchmann, C., & Mbatia, P. (1994). A threatened generation: Impediments to children's quality of life in Kenya. In J. Best (Ed.), *Troubling children: Studies of children and social problems,* (pp. 23–45). New York: Aldine De Gruyter.

Bradshaw, Y., Noonan, R., Gash, L., & Sershen, C. B. (1993). Borrowing against the future: Children and third world indebtedness. *Social Forces, 71,* 629–656.

Bradshaw, Y. & Wallace, M. (1996). *Global inequalities.* Thousand Oaks, CA: Pine Forge Press.

Briggs, J. (1992). Mazes of meaning: How a child and culture create each other. In W. Corsaro & P. Miller (Eds.), *Interpretive approaches to children's socialization,* (pp. 25–50). San Francisco: Jossey-Bass.

Bruner, J. (1986). *Actual minds, possible worlds.* Cambridge, MA: Harvard University Press.

Bruner, J. & Sherwood, V. (1976). Peekaboo and the learning of rule structure. In J. Bruner, A. Jolly, & K. Sylva (Eds.), *Play: Its role in development and evolution* (pp. 277–285). New York: Basic Books.

Brunvand, J. (1981). *The vanishing hitchhiker.* New York: Norton.

Budwig, N. Strage, A., & Bamberg, M. (1986). The construction of joint activities with an age-mate: The transition from caregiver-child to peer play. In J. Cook-Gumperz, W. Corsaro, & J. Streeck (Eds.), *Children's worlds and children's language* (pp. 83–108). Berlin, Germany: Mouton.

Burtless, G. (1994). Public spending on the poor: Historical trends and economic limits. In S. Danziger, G. Sandefur, & D. Weinberg (Eds.), *Confronting poverty: Prescriptions for change.* New York: Russell Sage Foundation.

Cahill, S. (1986). Childhood socialization as a recruitment process: Some lessons from the study of gender development. *Sociological Studies of Child Development, 1,* 163–186.

Carlsson-Paige, N. & Levin, D. (1987). *The war play dilemma: Children's needs and society's future.* New York: Teachers College Press.

Carville, J. (1996). *We're right, they're wrong.* New York: Random House.

Cherlin, A. (Ed.) (1988). *The changing American family and public policy.* Washington, DC: Urban Institute Press.

Chira, S. (1996, April 21). Infant's trust found unhurt by child care. *The New York Times, Times Fax Internet Edition,* p. 1.

Clark, C. (1995). *Flights of fancy, leaps of faith.* Chicago: University of Chicago Press.

Clarke-Stewart, K. (1989). Infant day care: Maligned or malignant? *American Psychologist, 44,* 66–73.

Clerkx, L. & Van Ijzedoorn, M. (1992). Child care in a Dutch context: On the history, current status, and evaluation of nonmaternal child care in the Netherlands. In M. Lamb, K. Sternberg, C. Hwang, & A. Broberg (Eds.), *Child care in context: Cross-cultural perspectives,* (pp. 55–80). Hillsdale, NJ: Lawrence Erlbaum Associates.

Coie, J. & Dodge, K. (1988). Multiple sources of data on social behavior and social status in the school: A cross-age comparison. *Child Development, 54:* 1400–1416.

Connell, R. (1983). *Which way is up? Essays on class, sex, and culture.* Boston: Allen and Urwin.

Connell, R. (1987). *Gender and power: Society, the person and sexual politics.* Stanford, CA: Stanford University Press.

Connolly, K. & Smith, P. (1978). Experimental studies of the preschool environment. *International Journal of Early Childhood, 10,* 86–95.

Corsaro, W. (1979). "We're friends, right?": Children's use of access rituals in a nursery school. *Language in Society, 8,* 315–336.

Corsaro, W. (1985). *Friendship and peer culture in the early years.* Norwood, NJ: Ablex.

Corsaro, W. (1988). Routines in the peer culture of American and Italian nursery school children. *Sociology of Education, 61,* 1–14.

Corsaro, W. (1990). The underlife of the nursery school: Young children's social representations of adult rules. In B. Lloyd & G. Duveen (Eds.), *Social representations and the development of knowledge* (pp. 11–26). Cambridge, UK: Cambridge University Press.

Corsaro, W. (1992). Interpretive reproduction in children's peer cultures. *Social Psychology Quarterly, 55,* 160–177.

Corsaro, W. (1993). Interpretive reproduction in children's role play. *Childhood, 1,* 64–74.

Corsaro, W. (1994). Discussion, debate, and friendship: Peer discourse in nursery schools in the US and Italy. *Sociology of Education, 67,* 1–26.

Corsaro, W. (1996). Transitions in early childhood: The promise of comparative, longitudinal, ethnography. In R. Jessor, A. Colby, & R. Shweder (Eds.), *Ethnography and human development,* (pp. 419–457). Chicago: University of Chicago Press.

Corsaro, W. (1996). Early education, children's lives, and the transition from home to school in Italy and the United States. *International Journal of Comparative Sociology* xxxvii, 121–139.

Corsaro, W. & Eder, D. (1990). Chldren's peer cultures. *Annual Review of Sociology, 16,* 197–220.

Corsaro, W. & Eder, D. (1995). Development and socialization of children and adolescents. In K. Cook, G. Fine, & J. House (Eds.), *Sociological perspectives on social psychology* (pp. 421–451). New York: Allyn & Bacon.

Corsaro, W. & Emiliani, F. (1992). Child care, early education, and children's peer culture in Italy. In M. Lamb, K. Sternberg, C. Hwang, & A. Broberg (Eds.), *Child care in context: Cross-cultural perspectives* (pp. 81–115). Hillsdale, NJ: Lawrence Erlbaum.

Corsaro, W. & Heise, D. (1990). Event structure models from ethnographic data. *Sociological Methodology, 20,* 1–57.

Corsaro, W. & Maynard, D. (1996). Format tying in discussion and argumentation among Italian and American children. In D. Slobin, J. Gerhardt, A. Kyratzis, & J. Guo (Eds.), *Social interaction, social context and language: Essays in honor of Susan Ervin-Tripp* (pp. 157–174). Mahwah, NJ: Lawrence Erlbaum Associates.

Corsaro, W. & Molinari, L. (1990). From *seggiolini* to *discussione*: The generation and extension of peer culture among Italian preschool children. *International Journal of Qualitative Studies in Education, 3,* 213–230.

Corsaro, W. & Rizzo, T. (1988). *Discussione* and friendship: Socialization processes in the peer culture of Italian nursery school children. *American Sociological Review, 53,* 879–894.

Corsaro, W. & Rizzo, T. (1990). Disputes in the peer culture of American and Italian nursery school children. In A. Grimshaw (Ed.), *Conflict talk* (pp. 21–66). New York: Cambridge University Press.

Corsaro, W. & Rosier, K. (1992). Documenting productive-reproductive processes in children's lives: Transition narratives of a Black family living in poverty. In W. Corsaro &

P. Miller (Eds.), *Interpretive approaches to children's socialization*, (pp. 69–93). New Directions for Child Development, No. 58, San Francisco: Jossey-Bass.

Corsaro, W. & Rosier, K. (1994). Transition narratives and reproductive processes in the lives of black families living in poverty. Paper presented at the XIII World Congress of Sociology, Bielefeld, Germany.

Damon, W. (1977). *The social world of the child*. San Francisco: Jossey-Bass.

Danziger, S., Smeeding, T., & Rainwater, L. (1995). The western welfare state in the 1990s: Toward a new model of antipoverty policy for families with children. Luxembourg Income Study Working Paper Number 128. Walferdange, Luxembourg.

Danziger, S. & Stern, J. (1990). The causes and consequences of child poverty in the United States. *Innocenti Occasional Papers*, Number 10. Florence, Italy: UNICEF International Child Development Centre, November.

Davies, B. (1982). *Life in the classroom and playground: The accounts of primary school children*. Boston: Routledge and Kegan Paul.

Davies, B. (1989). *Frogs and snails and feminist tales*. Boston: Allen & Unwin.

deMause, L. (1974). The evolution of childhood. In L. deMause (Ed.), *The history of childhood* (pp. 1–74). New York: Harper & Row.

Denzin, N. (1977). *Childhood socialization*. San Francisco: Jossey-Bass.

Dionne, E., Jr. (1996, June 29–30). A healthy 'family values' debate. *The International Herald Tribune*, p. 6.

Dodge, C. & Raundalen, M. (1991). *Reaching children in war: Sudan, Uganda and Mozambique*. Uppsala, Sweden: Scandinavian Institute of African Studies.

Dugger, C. (1992, March 31). Tiny incomes, little help for single mothers. *The New York Times*. pp. A1, A16.

Dunn, J. (1988). *The beginnings of social understanding*. Cambridge, MA: Harvard University Press.

Dunn, J. & Kendrick, C. (1982). *Siblings: Love, envy and understanding*. Cambridge, MA: Harvard University Press.

Eder, D. (1988). Building cohesion through collaborative narration. *Social Psychology Quarterly*.

Eder, D. (1995). *School talk: Gender and adolescent culture*. New Brunswick, NJ: Rutgers University Press.

Eder, D. & Parker, S. (1987). The cultural production and reproduction of gender: The effects of extra-curricular activities on peer group culture. *Sociology of Education, 60*, 200–213.

Edwards, C., Gandini, L., & Forman, G. (Eds.) (1993). *The hundred languages of children*. Norwood, NJ: Ablex.

Ellis, S., Rogoff, B., & Cromer, C. (1981). Age segregation in children's social interaction. *Developmental Psychology, 17*, 399–407.

Evaldsson, A. (1993). *Play, disputes and social order: Everyday life in two Swedish after-school centers*. Linköping, Sweden: Linköping University.

Eyer, D. (1993). *Mother-infant bonding: A scientific fiction*. New Haven, CT: Yale University Press.

Family Research Council (1994). Government intervention can be harmful. In K. de Koster (Ed.), *Child abuse: Opposing viewpoints*, (pp. 41–47). San Diego, CA: Greenhaven Press.

Fein, G. (1981). Pretend play: An integrative review. *Child Development, 52*, 1095–1118.

Fernie, D., Davies, B., Kantor, R., & McMurray, P. (1993). Becoming a person in the preschool: Creating integrated gender, school culture, and peer culture positionings. *Qualitative Studies in Education, 6*, 95–110.

Fernie, D., Kantor, R., & Whaley, K. (1995). Learning from classroom ethnographies: Same places, different times. In A. Hatch (Ed.), *Qualitative research in early education settings* (pp. 155–172). Westport, CT: Greenwood.

Fine, G. A. (1987). *With the boys: Little league baseball and preadolescent culture*. Chicago: University of Chicago Press.

Finkelhor, D. (1994). The extent of child abuse is not exaggerated. In K. de Koster (Ed.), *Child abuse: Opposing viewpoints*, (pp. 25–33). San Diego, CA: Greenhaven Press.

Finkelhor, D. & Dziuba-Leatherman, J. (1994). Victimization of children. *American Psychologist, 49*, 173–183.

Fish, S. (1980). *Is there a text in this class? The authority of interpretive communities*. Cambridge, MA: Harvard University Press.

Formanek-Brunell, M. (1992). Sugar and spite: The politics of doll play in nineteenth-century America. In E. West & P. Petrik (Eds.), *Small worlds: Children and adolescents in America, 1850–1950* (pp. 107–124). Lawrence, KS: University Press of Kansas.

Frønes, I. (1995). *Among peers: On the meaning of peers in the process of socialization.* Oslo, Norway: Scandinavian University Press.

Furstenberg, F., Brooks-Gunn, J., & Chase-Landale, L. (1989). Teenaged pregnancy and childbearing. *American Psychologist, 44,* 313–320.

Furstenberg, F. & Cherlin, A. (1991). *Divided families: What happens to children when parents part.* Cambridge: Harvard University Press.

Gagon, J. (1972). The creation of the sexual in early adolescence. In J. Kagan & R. Coles (Eds.), *Twelve to sixteen* (pp. 231–257). New York: Norton.

GAO (May 1994). Families on welfare: Sharp rise in never-married women reflects societal trend. Report to the Chairman, Subcommittee on Human Resources, Committee on Ways and Means, House of Representatives.

Garbarino, J., Dubrow, N., Kostelny, K., & Pardo, C. (1992). *Children in danger: Coping with the consequences of community violence.* San Francisco: Jossey-Bass.

Garbarino, J., Kostelny, K., & Dubrow, N. (1991). *No place to be a child: Growing up in a war zone.* Lexington, MA: Lexington Books.

Garnsey, P. (1991). Child rearing in ancient Italy. In D. Kertzer & R. Saller (Eds.), *The family in Italy* (pp. 48–65). New Haven, CT: Yale University Press.

Garofalo, J., Siegel, L., & Laub, J. (1987). School-related victimizations among adolescents: An analysis of National Crime Survey narratives. *Journal of Quantitative Criminology, 3,* 321–338.

Garvey, C. (1984). *Children's talk.* Cambridge, MA: Harvard University Press.

Geertz, C. (1973). *The interpretation of cultures.* New York: Basic Books.

Genovese, E. (1974). *Roll, Jordan, roll: The world that slaves made.* New York: Pantheon Books.

Giddens, A. (1991). *Modernity and self identity.* Stanford, CA: Stanford University Press.

Gilligan, C. (1982). *In a different voice: Psychological theory and women's development.* Cambridge, MA: Harvard University Press.

Gillis, J. (1985). Review of *Forgotten Children* by Linda Pollock. *Journal of Interdisciplinary History, XVI,* 142–44.

Ginsburg, H. & Opper, S. (1988). *Piaget's theory of intellectual development.* (Third Edition). Englewood Cliffs, NJ: Prentice Hall.

Giroux, H. (1996). *Fugitive cultures: Race, violence, and youth.* New York: Routledge.

Glendon, M. (1987). *Abortion and divorce in western law: American failures, European challenges.* Cambridge, MA: Harvard University Press.

Goffman, E. (1961). *Asylums.* Garden City, NJ: Anchor.

Goffman, E. (1974). *Frame analysis.* New York: Harper & Row.

Goldstein, J. (1994). (Ed.), *Toys, play, and child development.* New York: Cambridge University Press.

Gomme, A. (1964). *The traditional games of England, Scotland, and Ireland.* Vol. 2. New York: Dover.

Göncü, A. (1993). Development of intersubjectivity in social pretend play. *Human Development, 36,* 185–198.

Goodman, E. (1995, February 21). Perhaps the word 'jailbait' should return to society's vocabulary. *Bloomington, Indiana, Herald Times,* p. A6.

Goodnow, J. (1988). Children's household work: Its nature and functions. *Psychological Bulletin, 103,* 5–26.

Goodwin, M. (1985). The serious side of jump rope: Conversational practices and social organization in the frame of play. *Folklore, 98,* 315–30.

Goodwin, M. (1990). *He-said-she-said: Talk as social organization among black children.* Bloomington: Indiana University Press.

Goodwin, M. (In press). Games of stance: Conflict and footing in hopscotch. In S. Hoyle & C. Adger (Eds.), *Language practices of older children.* New York: Oxford University Press.

Gottman, J. (1983). How children become friends. *Monographs of the Society for Research in Child Development, 48,* (3, Serial No. 201).

Gottman, J. (1986). The world of coordinated play: Same- and cross-sex friendships in young children. In J. Gottman & J. Parker (Eds.), *Conversations among friends: Speculations on affective development.* New York: Cambridge University Press.

Grant, L. (1984). Gender roles and statuses in school children's peer interactions. *Western Sociological Review, 14,* 58–76.

Greenberger, E. & Steinberg, J. (1986). *When teenagers work.* New York: Basic Books.

Greenhouse, S. (1993, November 14). If the French can do it, why can't we? *The New York Times Magazine,* pp. 59-61.

Griswold, W. (1994). *Cultures and societies in a changing world.* Thousand Oaks, CA: Pine Forge.

Gubrium, J. & Holstein, J. (1990). *What is family?* Mountain View, CA: Mayfield Publishing.

Hagan, J. (1994). *Crime and disrepute.* Thousand Oaks, CA: Pine Forge.

Haight, W. & Miller, P. (1993). *Pretending at home: Early development in sociocultural context.* Albany: State University of New York Press.

Hanawalt, B. (1986). *The ties that bind: Peasant families in medieval England.* New York: Oxford.

Hanawalt, B. (1993). *Growing up in medieval London.* New York: Oxford University Press.

Handel, G. & Whitchurch, G. (Eds.) (1994). *The psychosocial interior of the family.* New York: Aldine.

Hanley, R. (1996, May 10). With a prom and classes, schools court elderly for budget support. *The New York Times, Internet Fax Edition,* p. 6.

Hare-Mustin, R. & Maracek, J. (1988). The meaning of difference: Gender theory, post-modernism, and psychology. *American Psychologist, 43,* 455–464.

Harkness, S. & Super, C. (1992). Shared child care in east Africa: Sociocultural origins and developmental consequences. In M. Lamb, K. Sternberg, C. Hwang, & A. Broberg (Eds.), *Child care in context: Cross cultural perspectives* (pp. 441–459). Hillsdale, NJ: Lawrence Erlbaum.

Harrisson, J., Reubens, B., & Sparr, P. (1983). Trends in numbers employed, 1960–1980. In B. Reubens (Ed.), *Youth at work: An international survey.* Totowa, NJ: Rowman & Allanheld.

Haskins, R. (1992). Similar history, similar markets, similar policies yield similar results. In M. Lamb, K. Sternberg, C. Hwang, & A. Broberg (Eds.), *Child care in context: Cross-cultural perspectives,* (pp. 267-280). Hillsdale, NJ: Lawrence Erlbaum Associates.

Hatch, A. (1986). Affiliation in a kindergarten peer group. *Early Child Development and Care, 25,* 305–317.

Heath, S. (1983). *Ways with words: Language, life and work in communities and classrooms.* New York: Cambridge University Press.

Heath, S. (1989). Oral and literate traditions among black Americans living in poverty. *American Psychologist 44:* 367–373.

Heath, S. (1990). The children of Trackton's children: Spoken and written language in social change. In J. Stigler, R. Shweder, & G. Herdt (Eds.), *Cultural psychology: Essays on comparative human development* (pp. 496–519). New York: Cambridge University Press.

Heath, S. & McLaughlin, M. (Eds.). (1993). *Identity & inner-city youth: Beyond ethnicity and gender.* New York: Teacher's College Press.

Henton, J. & Cate, R. (1983). Romance and violence in dating relationships. *Journal of Family Issues 4,* 467–481.

Herbert, B. (1995, April 22). The terrorists failed. *The New York Times,* p. 15.

Hernandez, D. (1993a). *America's children: Resources from family, government, and the economy.* New York: Russell Sage Foundation.

Hernandez, D. (1993b). *We, the American children.* (U.S. Bureau of the Census, WE-10), Washington, DC: U.S. Government Printing Office.

Hernandez, D. (1994). Children's changing access to resources: A historical perspective. *Social Policy Report, Society for Research in Child Development VIII,* no. 1, 23 pages.

Hewlett, S. (1992). *When the bough breaks: The cost of neglecting our children.* New York: Harper Collins.

Hewlett, S. (1993). *Child neglect in rich nations.* New York: UNICEF.

Hill, R. (1990). Economic forces, structural discrimination and Black family instability. In H. Cheatham & J. Stewart (Eds), *Black families: Interdisciplinary perspectives,* (pp. 87–105). New Brunswick, NJ: Transaction Books.

Hilton, J. & Haldeman, V. (1991). Gender differences in the performance of household tasks by adults and children in single-parent and two-parent and two-parent, two-earner families. *Journal of Family Issues, 12:* 114–130.

Hochschild, A. (1989). *The Second Shift.* New York: Viking.

Hofferth, S., Brayfield, A., Deich, S., & Holcomb, P. (1991). *National Child Care Survey, 1990.* Washington, DC: The Urban Institute Press.

Hofferth, S. & Hayes, C. (Eds.). (1987). *Risking the future.* (Vol. 2). Washington, DC: National Academy Press.

Howard, A. (1974). *Ain't no big thing: Coping strategies in a Hawaiian-American community.* Honolulu: University of Hawaii Press.

Howes, C. (1988). Peer interaction of young children. *Monographs of the Society for Research in Child Development, 48* (1, Serial No. 217).

Huesmann, L. & Eron, L. (Ed.) (1986). *Television and the aggressive child: A cross-cultural perspective.* Hillsdale, NJ: Lawrence Erlbaum.

Hunt, D. (1970). *Parents and children in history.* New York: Basic Books.

Hunt, P. & Frankenberg, R. (1990). It's a small world: Disneyland, the family, and the multiple re-representations of American childhood. In A. James & A. Prout (Eds.), *Constructing and reconstructing childhood: Contemporary issues in the sociological study of childhood.* London: Falmer Press.

Inkeles, A. (1968). Society, social structure and child socialization. In J. A. Clausen (Ed.), *Socialization and society,* (pp. 73–129). Boston: Little, Brown and Company.

James, A. & Prout, A. (Eds.). (1990). *Constructing and reconstructing childhood: Contemporary issues in the sociological study of childhood.* New York: Falmer Press.

Jenkins, P. (1992). *Intimate enemies: Moral panics in contemporary Great Britain.* New York: Aldine De Gruyter.

Jenks, C. & Edin, K. (1995). Do poor women have a right to bear children? *The American Prospect 20,* Winter, 43–52.

Jones, E., Forrest, J., Goldman, N., Henshaw, S., Lincoln, R., Rosoff, J., Westoff, C., & Wulf, D. (1985). Teenage pregnancy in developed countries: Determinants and policy implications. *Family Planning Perspectives, 17,* 53–63.

Katriel, T. (1985). *Brogez:* ritual and strategy in Israeli children's conflicts. *Language in Society, 16,* 467–90.

Katriel, T. (1987). *"Bexibùdim!":* Ritualized sharing among Israeli children. *Language in Society 16:* 305–20.

Kinkead, G. (1994, April 10). Spock, Brazelton, and now . . . Penelope Leach. *The New York Times Magazine,* pp. 32-36.

Kisker, E. (1985). Teenagers talk about sex, pregnancy, and contraception. *Family Planning Perspectives, 17,* 83.

Klein, J. (1996, April 29). The predator problem. *Newsweek,* p. 39.

Kline, S. (1993). *Out of the garden: Toys, TV, and children's culture in the age of marketing.* New York: Verso.

Knapp, M. & Knapp, H. (1976). *One potato, two potato: The secret education of American children.* New York: Norton.

Kochman, T. (1981). *Black and white: Styles in conflict.* Chicago: University of Chicago Press.

Kramer, M. (1995, July 3). The myth about welfare moms. *Time,* p. 21.

Kristof, N. (1996, April 15). Asia's plantations of the 90's. *International Herald Tribune,* p. 2.

Labov, W. (1972). *Language in the inner city: Studies in Black English vernacular.* Philadelphia: Pennsylvania University Press.

Ladd, G. (1992). Themes and theories: Perspectives on processes in family-peer relationships. In R. Parke & D. Ladd (Eds.), Family-peer relationships: Modes of linkage (pp. 1–34). Hillsdale, NJ: Lawrence Erlbaum.

Ladd, G., Profilet, S., & Hart, C. (1992). Parent's management of children's peer relations: Facilitating and supervising children's activities in the peer culture. In R. Parke & D. Ladd (Eds.), *Family-peer relationships: Modes of linkage* (pp. 215-254). Hillsdale, NJ: Lawrence Erlbaum.

LaFrenier, P. & Charlesworth, W. (1983). Dominance, attention, and affiliation in a preschool group: A nine-month longitudinal study. *Ethology and Sociobiology, 4,* 55–67.

Lamb, M., Sternberg, K., Hwang, C., & Broberg A. (Eds.) (1992). *Child care in context: Cross-cultural perspectives.* Hillsdale, NJ: Lawrence Erlbaum Associates.

Lamb, M. Sternberg, K., & Ketterlinus, R. (1992). Child care in the United States: The modern era. In M. Lamb, K. Sternberg, C. Hwang, & A. Broberg (Eds.), *Child care in context: Cross-cultural perspectives,* (pp. 207–222). Hillsdale, NJ: Lawrence Erlbaum Associates.

Landau, E. (1994). Many factors contribute to child abuse. In K. de Koster (Ed.), *Child abuse: Opposing viewpoints,* (pp. 114–122). San Diego, CA: Greenhaven Press.

Landry, D., & Forrest, J. (1995). How old are U.S. fathers? *Family Planning Perspectives, 27,* 159.

Lave, J. & Wenger, E. (1991). *Situated learning: Legitimate peripheral participation.* New York: Cambridge University Press.

Leach, P. (1994). *Putting children first: What our society must do—and is not doing—for our children today.* New York: Alfred Knopf.

Lehman, J. & Danziger, S. (1995). *Ending welfare as we know it: Values, economics, and politics.* Cambridge, MA: The Electronic Policy Network.

Lev, M. & Brandon, K. (1994, September 18). Teaching parents not to abuse. *The Indianapolis Star*, pp. D1, D5.

Lever, J. (1978). Sex differences in the complexity of children's play and games. *American Sociological Review, 43*, 471–483.

Lewin, T. (1990, March 15). Panel asks $5 billion to improve child care. *The New York Times*, pp. B1,7.

Lewin, T. (1995a, December 7). Parents poll finds child abuse to be more common. *The New York Times*, p. A17.

Lewin, T. (1995b, April 24). Now divorcing parents must learn how to cope with children's needs. *The New York Times*, p. A8.

Lewin-Epstein, N. (1981). Youth employment during high school: An analysis of high school and beyond. *Report No. NCES-81-249. National Center for Educational Statistics.*

Lichter, D., & Eggebeen, D. (1992). Child poverty and the changing rural family. *Rural Sociology, 57*, 151–172.

Lockheed, M. (1985). Some determinants and consequences of sex segregation in the classroom. In L. Wilkinson & C. Marrett (Eds.), *Gender influences in classroom interaction* (pp. 167–184). New York: Academic Press.

Lollis, S., Ross, H., & Tate, E. (1992). Parents' regulation of children's peer interactions: Direct influences. In R. Parke & D. Ladd (Eds.), *Family-peer relationships: Modes of linkage* (pp. 255–281). Hillsdale, NJ: Lawrence Erlbaum.

Louv, R. (1990). *Childhood's Future.* New York: Anchor.

Luker, K. (1991). Dubious conceptions: The controversy over teen pregnancy. *The American Prospect, Spring*, 73–83.

Lurie, A. (1990). *Don't tell the grown-ups: Subversive children's literature.* Boston: Little, Brown & Company.

Males, M. (1994, July 29). Why blame young girls? *The New York Times*, p. 27.

Males, M. & Chew, K. (1996). The ages of fathers in California adolescent births, 1993. *The American Journal of Public Health, 86*, 565–567.

Maltz, D. & Borker, R. (1982). A cultural approach to male-female miscommuni-cation. In J. Gumperz (Ed.), *Communication, language, and social identity* (pp. 196–216). New York: Cambridge University Press.

Manning, W. (1990). Parenting employed teenagers. *Youth & Society, 22*: 184–200.

Marshall, L. (1976). *The !Kung of Nyae Nyae.* Cambridge: Harvard University Press.

Martini, M. (1994). Peer interactions in Polynesia: A view from the Marquesas. In J. Roopnarine, J. Johnson, & F. Hooper (Eds.), *Children's play in diverse cultures* (pp. 73–103). Albany: State University of New York Press.

Mason, K., & Kuhlthau, K. (1989). Determinants of child care ideals among mothers of preschool-aged children. *Journal of Marriage and the Family, 51*, 593–603.

Mayall, B. (1996). *Children, health, and the social order.* Philadelphia: Open University Press.

Maynard, D. (1985). On the functions of social conflict among children. *American Sociological Review, 50*, 207–223.

Maynard, D. (1986). Offering and soliciting collaboration in multi-party disputes among children (and other humans). *Human Studies, 9*, 261–85.

McDowell, J. (1979). *Children's riddling.* Bloomington, IN: Indiana University Press.

McLanahan, S. (1994). The consequences of single motherhood. *The American Prospect, 18*, 48–58.

Mergen, B. (1992). Made, bought, and stolen: Toys and the culture of childhood. In E. West & P. Petrick (Eds.), *Small worlds: Children & adolescents in America, 1850-1950* (pp. 86–106). Lawrence, KS: University Press of Kansas.

Miller, P. (1982). *Amy, Wendy, and Beth: Learning language in South Baltimore.* Austin: University of Texas Press.

Miller, P. (1986). Teasing as language socialization and verbal play in a white, working-class community. In B. Schieffelin & E. Ochs (Eds.), *Language socialization across cultures* (pp. 199–212). New York: Cambridge University Press.

Miller, P., & Moore, B. (1989). Narrative conjunctions of caregiver and child: A comparative perspective on socialization through stories. *Ethos, 17*: 428–449.

Miller, P., Potts, R., Fung, H., Hoogstra, L., & Mintz, J. (1990). Narrative practices and the social construction of self in childhood. *American Ethnologist, 17*, 292–311.

Miller, P. & Sperry, L. (1987). The socialization of anger and aggression. *Merrill-Palmer Quarterly, 33*: 1–33.

Mishler, E. (1979). "Won't you trade cookies with the popcorn?": The talk of trades among six year olds. In O. Garnica & M. King (Eds.), *Language, children, and society: The effects of social factors on children's learning to communicate* (pp. 21-36). Elmsford, NY: Pergamon.

Morgan, J.,& Zedner, L. (1992). *Child victims: Crime, impact, and criminal justice*. Oxford, England: Clarendon Press.

Mosle, S. (1994, June 4). Who's playing games? *The New York Times*, p. 19.

Mueller, E. (1972). The maintenance of verbal exchanges between young children. *Child Development, 43*, 930–938.

Murray, C. (1984). *Losing ground: American social policy, 1950-1980*. New York: Basic Books.

Mussati, T. & Panni, S. (1981). Social behavior and interaction among day care center toddlers. *Early Child Development and Care, 7*, 5–27.

Nasaw, D. (1985). *Children of the city*. New York: Anchor.

National Center for Health Statistics (1990). Monthly Vital Statistics Report, 38.

National Committee to Prevent Child Abuse (1996). Annual fifty-state survey of child welfare officials. Chicago: National Committee to Prevent Child Abuse. Chicago, Illinois.

National Research Council (1995). Report on workshop on child care for low-income families. Institute of Medicine, Board on Children and Families, 10 April, Washington, DC.

New, R. (1994). Child's play—*una cosa naturale*: An Italian perspective. In J. Roopnarine, J. Johnson, & F. Hooper (Eds.), *Children's play in diverse cultures* (pp. 123–47). Albany: State University of New York Press.

New York Times (1994). 1 September.

New Yorker (1995). Cover. 11 September.

Newsweek (1975). The goblins will getcha. . . . 5 December, 77.

Newsweek (1995). No place for kids? A parents' guide to sex on the net. 3 July, 47–50.

Newsweek (1996). Death in Dunblane. 25 March, 8–17.

Nieuwenhuys, O. (1993). To read and not to eat: South Indian children between secondary school and work. *Childhood, 1*: 100–109.

Nsamenang, B. (1992a). Early childhood care and education in Cameroon. In M. Lamb, K. Sternberg, C. Hwang, & A. Broberg (Eds.), *Child care in context: Cross cultural perspectives* (pp. 441–459). Hillsdale, NJ: Lawrence Erlbaum.

Nsamenang, A. B. (1992b). *Human development in cultural context: A third world perspective*. Newbury Park, CA: Sage.

Ochs, E. (1988). *Culture and language development: Language acquisition and language socialization in a Samoan village*. New York: Cambridge University Press.

Opie, I. & Opie, P. (1959). *The lore and language of schoolchildren*. New York: Oxford University Press.

Opie, I. & Opie, P. (1969). *Children's games in street and playground*. Oxford, England: Clarendon Press.

Oswald, H., Krappman, L., Chowdhuri, I., & von Salisch, M. (1987). Gaps and bridges: Interactions between girls and boys in elementary school. In P. A. Adler & P. Adler (Eds.), *Sociological Studies of Child Development*, vol. 2 (pp. 205–223). Greenwich, CT: JAI Press.

Pakistanis silence youthful voice against child labor. (1995, April 1). *Chicago Tribune*, p. 6.

Paley, V. (1984). *Boys and girls: Superheroes in the doll corner*. Chicago: University of Chicago Press.

Paley, V. (1992). *You can't say, you can't play*. Cambridge, MA: Harvard University Press.

Parke, R. & Ladd, G. (1992). (Eds.), *Family-peer relationships: Modes of linkage*. Hillsdale, NJ: Lawrence Erlbaum.

Parker, S. (1991). *Early adolescent male cultures: The importance of organized and informal sport*. Ph.D. Dissertation, Indiana University, Bloomington, IN.

Parker, J. & Gottman, J. (1989). Social and emotional development in a relational context: friendship interaction from early childhood. In T. Brendt & G. Ladd (Eds.), *Peer relationships in child development,* (pp. 95–112). New York: Wiley.

Parrott, S. (1979). Games children play: Ethnography of a second-grade recess. In J. Spradley & D. McCurdy (Eds.), *The cultural experience,* (pp. 206–19). Chicago: Science Research Associates.

Parsons, T. & Bales, R. F. (1955). *Family, socialization and interaction process.* New York: The Free Press.

Pear, R. (1994, February 2). Audit of day care centers finds widespread problems. *The New York Times,* p. 24.

Piaget, J. (1932). *The moral judgment of the child.* London: Routledge & Kegan.

Piaget, J. (1968). *Six psychological studies.* New York: Vintage.

Pollock, L. (1983). *Forgotten children.* New York: Cambridge University Press.

Popenoe, D. (1992, December 26). The controversial truth: Two-parent families are better. *The New York Times,* p. 13.

Preston, S. (1984). Children and the elderly in the U.S. *Scientific American, 251,* 44–49.

Previte, M. (1994, August 17). What will they say at my funeral? *The New York Times,* p. 17.

Putnam, R. (1996). The strange disappearance of civic America. *The American Prospect, 24,* 34–50.

Quindlen, A. (1994, August 4). The passion to keep them safe. *The New York Times,* p. 11.

Qvortrup J. (1991). Childhood as a social phenomenon-an introduction to a series of national reports. *Eurosocial Report No. 36.* Vienna, Austria: European Centre for Social Welfare Policy and Research.

Qvortrup, J. (1993a). Nine theses about "childhood as a social phenomenon." In J. Qvortrup (Ed.), *Childhood as a social phenomenon: Lessons from an international project. Eurosocial Report No. 47* (pp. 11–18). Vienna, Austria: European Centre for Social Welfare Policy and Research.

Qvortrup, J. (1993b). Societal position of childhood: The international project childhood as a social phenomenon. *Childhood, 1,* 119–124.

Qvortrup, J. (1994a). Childhood matters: An introduction. In J. Qvortrup, M. Bardy, G. Sgritta, & H. Wintersberger (Eds.), *Childhood matters: Social theory, practice, and politics,* (pp. 1–23). Brookfield, VT: Avebury.

Qvortrup, J. (1994b). A new solidarity contract?: The significance of a demographic balance for the welfare of both children and the elderly. In *Childhood matters: Social theory, practice, and politics,* (pp. 319–334). Brookfield, VT: Avebury.

Rainwater, L. & Smeeding, T. (1995). Doing poorly: The real income of American children in a comparative perspective. Luxembourg Income Study Working Paper Number 127. Walferdange, Luxembourg.

Ramsey, P. (1991). *Making friends in school: Promoting peer relationships in early childhood.* New York: Teachers College Press.

Ratcliff, D. (1994). *An elementary school hallway: Social formations and meanings outside the classroom.* Ph.D. Dissertation, University of Georgia, Athens, GA.

Ratner, N. & Bruner, J. (1977). Games, social exchanges and the acquisition of language. *Journal of Child Language, 5,* 391–401.

Richert, S. (1990). *Boys and girls apart: Children's play in Canada and Poland.* Ottowa, Canada: Carleton University Press.

Rizzini, I., Rizzini, I., Munoz-Vargas, M., & Galeano, L. (1994). Brazil: A new concept of childhood. In C. Blanc (Ed.), *Urban children in distress: Global predicaments and innovative strategies,* (pp. 55–100). Langhorne, PA: Gordon and Breach.

Rizzo, T. (1989). *Friendship development among children in school.* Norwood, NJ: Ablex.

Rogoff, B., Mosier, J., & Göncü, A. (1989). Toddlers' guided participation in cultural activity. *Cultural Dynamics, 2,* 209–237.

Rosier, K. (1996). *Competent parents, Complex lives: A longitudinal study of low-income Black mothers and their children's transition into schooling.* Unpublished Ph.D. Dissertation. Indiana University, Bloomington, IN.

Rosier, K. & Corsaro, W. (1993). Competent parents, complex lives: Managing parenthood in poverty. *Journal of Contemporary Ethnography, 22,* 171–204.

Russell, C. (1995). Why teen births boom. *American Demographics,* September, 1–2.

Samuelson, S. (1980). The cooties complex. *Western Folklore, 39,* 198–210.

Sawyer, C. K. (1995). A developmental model of heteroglossic improvisation in children's fantasy play. *Sociological Studies of Children, 7*, 127–153.

Sawyer, C. K. (1997). *Pretend play as improvisation: Conversation in the preschool classroom.* Mahwah, NJ: Lawrence Erlbaum Associates.

Schieffelin, B. (1990). *The give and take of everyday life: Language socialization of Kalui children.* New York: Cambridge University Press.

Schieffelin, B. & Ochs, E. (Eds.) (1986). *Language socialization across cultures.* New York: Cambridge University Press.

Schildkrout, E. (1975). Age and gender in Hausa society: Socio-economic roles of children in urban Kano. In J. LaFontaine (Ed.), *Sex and age as principles of social differentiation,* (pp. 108–137). New York: Academic Press.

Schofield, J. (1982). *Black and white in school.* New York: Praeger.

Schorr, L. (1988). *Within our reach: Breaking the cycle of disadvantage.* New York: Anchor.

Schwartzman, H. (1978). *Transformations: The anthropology of children's play.* New York: Plenum.

Seiter, E. (1993). *Sold separately: Parents & children in consumer culture.* New Brunswick, NJ: Rutgers University Press.

Selman, R. (1980). *The growth of interpersonal understanding.* New York: Academic Press.

Serpell, R. (1992). African dimensions of child care and nurturance. In M. Lamb, K. Sternberg, C. Hwang, & A. Broberg (Eds.), *Child care in context: Cross-cultural perspectives* (pp. 463–474). Hillsdale, NJ: Lawrence Erlbaum.

Sgritta, G. (1994). The generational division of welfare: Equity and conflict. In J. Qvortrup, M. Brady, G. Sgritta, & H. Wintersberger (Eds.), *Childhood matters: Social theory, practice and politics,* (pp. 335-362). Brookfield, VT: Avebury.

Shahar, S. (1990). *Childhood in the middle ages.* London: Routledge.

Shantz, C. (1987). Conflicts among children. *Child Development, 58,* 283–305.

Shelton, B. (1992). Women, men, and time: Gender differences in paid work, housework, and leisure. New York: Greenwood.

Shorter, E. (1977). *The making of the modern family.* New York: Basic Books.

Sidel, R. (1992). *Women and children last.* New York: Penguin.

Skocpol, T. & Wilson, W. (1994, February 9). Welfare as we need it. *The New York Times,* p. 16.

Skolnick, A. (1991). *Embattled paradise: The American family in an age of uncertainty.* New York: Basic Books.

Slaughter, D. & Dombrowski, J. (1989). Cultural continuities and discontinuities: Impact on social and pretend play. In M. Bloch and A. Pellegrini (Eds.), *The ecological context of children's play* (pp. 282–310). Norwood, NJ: Ablex.

Sluckin, A. (1981). *Growing up in the playground.* London: Routledge and Kegan Paul.

Smeeding, T. (1991). The war on poverty: What worked? Testimony to the Joint Economy Committee, The United States Congress, 25 September.

Smeeding, T., and Gottschalk, P. (1995). The international evidence on income distribution in modern economies: Where do we stand? Luxembourg Income Study Working Paper Number 137. Walferdange, Luxembourg.

Solberg, A. (1990). Negotiating childhood: Changing constructions of age for Norwegian children. In A. James and A. Prout (Eds), *Constructing and reconstructing childhood,* (pp. 118–137). New York: Falmer Press.

Stacey, J. (1991). *Brave new families: Stories of domestic upheaval in late twentieth century America.* New York: Basic Books.

Stack, C. (1974). *All our kin: Strategies for survival in a Black community.* New York: Harper & Row.

Stamback, M. & Verba, M. (1986). Organization of social play among toddlers: An ecological approach. In E. Mueller & C. Cooper (Eds.), *Process and outcome in peer relationships* (pp. 229-247). New York: Academic Press.

Statistical Office of the European Community (1990). *Demographic Statistics, 1988 and 1990.*

Stein, N. (1993). No laughing matter: Sexual harassment in K–12 schools. In E. Buchwald (Ed.), *Transforming a rape culture,* (pp. 313–314). Minneapolis, MN: Milkweed Editions.

Steinhauer, J. (1995, August 2). Study cites adult males for most teen-age births. *The New York Times,* p. 10.

Stephens, S. (1993). Children at risk: Constructing social problems and policies. *Childhood, 1,* 246–251.

Stone, L. (1977). *Family, sex and marriage in England, 1500–1800.* New York: Harper & Row.

Strandell, H. (1994). What are children doing?: Activity profiles in day care centres. Paper presented at the XIII World Congress of Sociology, Bielefeld, Germany.

Strayer, F. & Strayer, S. (1976). An ethological analysis of social agonism and dominance relations among preschool children. *Child Development, 47*: 980–989.

Survey: Family day care usually 'barely adequate.' (1994, April 8). *Bloomington, Indiana, Herald-Times*, p. A5.

Sutton-Smith, B. (1976). *The dialectics of play.* Schorndoff, Germany: Verlag Hoffman.

Sutton-Smith, B. (1986). *Toys as culture.* New York: Gardner Press.

Tannen, D. (1990). *You just don't understand: Women and men in conversation.* New York: Morrow.

Tatar, M. (1992). *Off with their heads! Fairy tales and the culture of childhood.* Princeton, N.J.: Princeton University Press.

Terry, D. (1994, February 3). 19 children found in squalid Chicago apartment. *The New York Times*, p. A1, A11.

Thorne, B. (1986). Girls and boys together . . . but mostly apart: Gender arrangements in elementary schools. In W. Hartup & Z. Rubin (Eds.), *Relationships and development* (pp. 167–84). Hillsdale, NJ: Lawrence Erlbaum.

Thorne, B. (1987). Re-visioning women and social change: Where are the children? *Gender & Society, 1*, 85–109.

Thorne, B. (1993). *Gender play: Girls and boys in school.* New Brunswick, NJ: Rutgers University Press.

Thorne, B. & Luria, Z. (1986). Sexuality and gender in children's daily worlds. *Social Problems, 33*, 176–190.

Time (1995). Cyberporn. 3 July, 38–45.

Time (1996). The young and the damned. 15 April, 36–39.

Tronick, E., Morelli, G., & Winn, S. (1987). Multiple caretaking of Efe (Pygmy) infants. *American Anthropologist, 89*: 96–106.

Twentieth Century Fund (1995). *Welfare reform: A twentieth century fund guide to the issues.* New York: Twentieth Century Fund Press.

Udry, J. & Billy, J. (1987). Initiation of coitus in early adolescence. *American Sociological Review, 52*, 841–855.

UNICEF (1995a). The state of the world's children. Oxford: Oxford University Press.

UNICEF (1995b). *The progress of nations 1995.* World Wide Web Version. Web Site: http://www.unicef.org/pon95/progtoc.htm.

U.S. Bureau of the Census. (1992). *Statistical Abstract of the United States, 1992.* Washington, DC: Government Printing Office.

U.S. Congress, House Committee on Ways and Means (1994). *Overview of entitlement programs, 1994 Greenbook.* Washington, DC: U. S. Government Printing Office.

U.S. Department of Health and Human Services. (1990). National Center for Statistics, *Monthly Vital Statistics Reports.*

Vandell, D. & Mueller, E. (1980). Peer play and friendships during the first two years. In H. Foot, A. Chapman, & J. Smith (Eds.), *Friendship and childhood relations,* (pp. 181–208). New York: Wiley.

Vygotsky, L. S. (1978). *Mind in society.* Cambridge, MA: Harvard University Press.

Walkerdine, V. (1986). Post-structuralist theory and everyday practices: The family and the school. In S. Wilkinson (Ed.), *Feminist social psychology* (pp. 57–76). Philadelphia: Open University Press.

Walkerdine, V. (1990). *Schoolgirl fictions.* New York: Verso Press.

Watson-Gegeo, K., & Gegeo, D. (1986). The social world of Kwara'ae children: Acquisition of language and values. In J. Cook-Gumperz, W. Corsaro, and J. Streeck (Eds.), *Children's worlds and children's language* (pp. 109–128). Berlin, Germany: Mouton.

Weisner, T. & Gallimore, R. (1977). My brother's keeper: Child and sibling caretaking. *Current Anthropology, 18*: 169–190.

Wentworth, W. M. (1980). *Context and understanding: An inquiry into socialization theory.* New York: Elsevier.

West, E. (1992). Children on the plains frontier. In E. West & P. Petrik (Eds.), *Small worlds* (pp. 26–41). Lawrence, KS: University Press of Kansas.

West, E. & Petrick, P. (1992). Introduction. In E. West & P. Petrik (Eds.), *Small worlds* (pp. 1- 8). Lawrence, KS: University Press of Kansas.

Westhoff, C. Calot, G., & Foster, A. (1983). Teenage fertility in developed countries. *Family Planning Perspectives, 15,* 105.

White, L., & Brinkerhoff, D. (1981). Children's work in the family: Its significance and meaning. *Journal of Marriage and the Family 43:* 789–798.

Whiting, B. & Edwards, C. P. (1988). *Children of different worlds: The formation of social behavior.* Cambridge, MA: Harvard University Press.

Wiggins, D. (1985). The play of slave children in the plantation communities of the old South, 1820–60. In N. Hiner & J. Hawes (Eds.), *Growing up in America: Children in historical perspective* (pp. 173–192). Urbana, IL: University of Illinois Press.

Wilkerson, I. (1993, April 4). First born, fast grown: The Manful life of Nicholas, 10. *The New York Times,* p. 16.

Willis, P. (1990). *Common culture.* Boulder, CO: Westview Press.

Winnicott, D. W. (1951). *Collected Papers.* New York: Basic Books.

Wober, M. (1975). *Psychology in Africa.* London: International African Institute.

Wolf, S., & Heath, S. (1992). *The braid of literature: Children's worlds of reading.* Cambridge, MA: Harvard University Press.

Wootton, A. (1986). Rules in action: Orderly features of actions that formulate rules. In J. Cook-Gumperz, W. Corsaro, & J. Streeck (Eds.), *Children's Language and Children's Worlds* (pp. 147–168). Berlin, Germany: Mouton.

Wulff, H. (1988). *Twenty girls: Growing up, ethnicity and excitement in a south London microculture.* Stockholm, Sweden: University of Stockholm.

Yates, M. (1995). *Community service and identity development in adolescence.* Ph.D. Dissertation, The Catholic University of America, Washington, DC.

Youniss, J. & Smollar, J. (1985). *Adolescent relations with mothers, fathers and friends.* Chicago: University of Chicago Press.

Youniss, J. & Yates, M. (in press). *Right place, right time: Community service and social responsibility in Black urban youth.* Chicago: University of Chicago Press.

Zelizer, V. (1985). *Pricing the priceless child: The changing social value of children.* New York: Basic Books.

Zukow, P. (Ed.) (1989). *Sibling interaction across cultures: Theoretical and methodological issues.* New York: Springer-Verlag.

Glossary / Index